White Backlash and the Politics of Multiculturalism

The murder of Stephen Lawrence led to the widest review of institutional racism seen in the UK. Sections of the white working-class communities in south London near to the scene of the murder, however, displayed deep hostility to the equalities and multiculturalist practice of the local state and other agencies. Drawing on extensive ethnographic research, this book relates these phenomena to the 'backlash' to multiculturalism evident during the 1990s in the USA, Australia, Canada, the UK and other European countries. It examines these within the unfolding social and political responses to race equalities in the UK and the USA from the 1960s to the present in the context of changes in social class and national political agendas. This book is unique in linking a detailed study of a community at a time of its critical importance to national debates over racism and multiculturalism to historically wider international economic and social trends.

ROGER HEWITT is Senior Research Associate at the Centre for Urban and Community Research, Goldsmiths College, University of London. He has published widely in the fields of racism, language and cultural processes and is the author of *White Talk Black Talk: Inter-Racial Friendship and Communication amongst Adolescents* (Cambridge, 1986).

White Backlash and the Politics of Multiculturalism

Roger Hewitt

*Goldsmiths College,
University Of London*

CAMBRIDGE
UNIVERSITY PRESS

CAMBRIDGE UNIVERSITY PRESS
Cambridge, New York, Melbourne, Madrid, Cape Town, Singapore, São Paulo

Cambridge University Press
The Edinburgh Building, Cambridge, CB2 2RU, UK

Published in the United States of America by Cambridge University Press,
New York

www.cambridge.org
Information on this title: *www.cambridge.org/9780521520898*

First published 2005

Printed in the United Kingdom at the University Press, Cambridge

A catalogue record for this book is available from the British Library

ISBN-13 978-0-521-81768-4 hardback
ISBN-10 0-521-81768-4 hardback
ISBN-13 978-0-521-52089-8 paperback
ISBN-10 0-521-52089-4 paperback

Cambridge University Press has no responsibility for the persistence or
accuracy of URLs for external or third-party internet websites referred to in
this book, and does not guarantee that any content on such websites is, or will
remain, accurate or appropriate.

For Ella and Oscar

Contents

Figures

Acknowledgements

The number of people who have helped in different ways during the research on which this book is based is very large. I extend my sincere thanks to them all despite the fact that only a few can be mentioned by name. I would like to thank in particular Professor Jagdish Gundara of the International Centre for Intercultural Studies, Institute of Education University of London, who supported and encouraged my work during its crucial period. Professor Michael Keith, Director of the Centre for Urban and Community Research (CUCR) at Goldsmiths, University of London, also provided me with the space and time to complete the book in its final stages. I had important support from Greenwich Council's Central Race Equality Unit, and from the staff of Greenwich Housing and Youth services, which I gratefully acknowledge. Those who helped me 'on the ground' when I was conducting field-work in south London were legion but I would particularly like to thank Dev Barrah, Linda Nash, Linda Corbell, Bernie Bristow, Loraine Webster, Paul Bailey, Arthur Blackman and Jeannette Cunningham. I also gratefully acknowledge generous grants from the Harry Frank Guggenheim Foundation, the Nuffield Foundation and the Economic and Social Research Council. I would like to thank Tony Skillen for his critical eye and helpful suggestions, also my friends and colleagues in the CUCR with whom I enjoy the intellectually stimulating and warm working environment that we have all been fortunate enough to inhabit. I thank Moira Inghilleri with whom I have shared so many conversations concerning the issues discussed in this book. She has been an unfailing support, critic and life-partner and contributed immeasurably to its completion. Finally, I would like to thank our children, Louis and Pablo, for the endless delight and distraction they have provided.

1   Introduction

During the 1990s, following three highly publicised racist murders, Greenwich in south London became known in the UK press as the 'racist murder capital of Europe'. Historically Greenwich was both a key site of British maritime and colonial history from the sixteenth century onwards and an important centre in the development of the labour movement in the nineteenth and twentieth centuries. These features alone might mark it out as the site of an unbroken elaboration of exclusive identities on at least two dimensions, both of which could arguably be related to its contemporary notoriety for racism. But the politics of race in the UK and particularly London reflect other developments at once more parochial and more global. The local features of Greenwich within London – its complex economy and political ambivalence – make its case more difficult. Furthermore, the unfolding of multiculturalist politics on the *international* stage from its point of origin in the USA is another factor that confronts attempts to determine why Greenwich in particular should have become the bearer of such a sorry record.

The murder of Stephen Lawrence in 1993 and the subsequent trials and inquiries brought the case against the criminal justice system to stark and undeniable prominence. It was said to be a 'watershed' in the nation's race and justice debate. Coming at the opening of the twenty-first century the Report of the Inquiry into the murder investigation[1] ushered in the most comprehensive review of 'institutional racism' ever seen in the UK. But while both black and white condemnation of police tardiness in the Lawrence case was widespread, beneath the complicated political alliances forming that public consensus, some local white discomfort at the attention it attracted, though unpublicised, was never far away. The Lawrence murder was the last and most notorious of three racist murders in Greenwich which became nationally prominent and

---

[1] Home Office, *The Stephen Lawrence Inquiry Report* (London, The Stationery Office, 1999).

generated their own local oral storybooks in the white working-class neighbourhoods where they occurred.[2] Racist and distorted as it may seem, rather than widespread sympathy with the black murder victims Rolan Adams (killed in 1991), Rohit Duggal (killed in 1992) and Stephen Lawrence, the white responses on a number of public housing estates in Greenwich were unrelentingly defensive and unsympathetic.

These locally told stories were not only versions of the 'real' truth behind the known events. They had their own messages about 'unfairness to whites' and the changing nature of justice. The mobilised responses to these murders had stirred up a cluster of resentments amongst some whites concerning the means by which black and minority ethnic causes get taken up in the public sphere through the agencies of the media and the state. These resentments were about the media's reporting of racial incidents, about equal opportunities in local government, about anti-racism and multiculturalism in schools and about police 'fears of being called racist'. They were complaints by the white have-nots about the impact on them of the black have-nots – or rather about the development of representation for minorities who seemed to them to outflank them in the everyday struggles for small advantage. The struggle to disarm the accusation of racism, either by inverting its meaning or by denying the validity of its application to particular instances, became part of the expression of resentment some whites felt about the prominence that black and other minority ethnic causes were receiving.

These phenomena were unique neither to Greenwich nor to the UK. During the 1990s increasing hostility to multiculturalism in its various forms was apparent both nationally and internationally. Thus, while repugnance at racial violence was widely expressed and a broad pro-forma consensus existed over the need to make multicultural societies work, there was also conflict over what multicultural*ism* meant and how or if it worked in practice. In the USA these issues were most evident in

---

[2] Following the first of these murders I was commissioned by Greenwich Council to conduct a study of racism amongst adolescents. This was followed by three further studies more broadly focussed on racist violence, community processes and communicative practices. These were funded by the Harry Frank Guggenheim Foundation, Nuffield Foundation and the Economic and Social Research Council and took place over the next six years, covering the period following the murder of Rohit Duggal in 1992 until 1997, four years after that of Stephen Lawrence. I gathered a great deal of information from interviews with young people and adults living on the estates in central and southern Greenwich and from community workers, council officials, youth workers, police and other professionals in the borough. This body of data forms a substantial part of the source material for this book.

academic circles and in a number of widely discussed publications appearing in the late 1980s and early 1990s that were critical of multiculturalism and of developments in race equalities politics.[3] In Canada the long taken-for-granted consensus aimed for in Canada's pioneering multicultural policy (1971) and its later articulation in the Multicultural Act (1988) also came under fire from several quarters.[4] In Australia hostility to immigration became expressed in the rise of Pauline Hanson's One Nation Party which attacked multiculturalism without ambiguity. Similar attacks on multiculturalism were evident from Scandinavian and other European populist parties.[5]

These were disparate but related phenomena. They included responses within specific local communities to policies regarding migration, community relations and racism, as well as the competition between political groups seeking to appeal to such constituencies of interest. In the USA the attacks on multiculturalism came out of a long-running contest over the nature and scope of institutional racism, the emergence of identity politics and the special role that the issue of racial equality had come to have in the wider political agendas of the Republican and Democratic Parties.[6] The opposition to multicultural-ism was evident in ideological argument, political activity and popular local issues, sometimes melding all of these. Each has been seen as part of a 'backlash' to the increasingly well-established profile of equal opportunities – and particularly racial equal opportunities – that had started to form during the 1960s, and to its contemporary re-articulation in multiculturalism. In the USA this 'backlash' was especially associated with the rolling back of equalities legislation during the Reagan and Bush administrations and with the response to the claims for recognition by the wide variety of identities uniquely included within the US version

---

[3] See below pp. 106–7.
[4] See for example Pan K. Datta, 'Multiculturalism: Has it actually Fed Racism?', *The Ottawa Citizen*, B3 (29 Apr. 1989); Vic Satzewich (ed.), *Deconstructing a Nation: Immigration, Multiculturalism and Racism in 90's Canada* (Halifax, Nova Scotia, Fernwood Publishing, 1992); Neil Bissoondath, *Selling Illusions: The Cult of Multiculturalism in Canada* (Toronto, Penguin Books, 1994).
[5] Bligh Grant (ed.), *Pauline Hanson: One Nation and Australian Politics* (Armidale, Australia, University of New England Press, 1997); Bill Cope and Mary Kalantzis, *A Place in the Sun: Re-creating the Australian Way of Life* (Sydney, Harper Collins, 2000); Katherine Betts, *The Great Divide: Immigration Politics in Australia* (Sydney, Duffy and Snellgrove, 1999); Paul Hainsworth(ed.), *The Politics of the Extreme Right: From Margins to Mainstream* (London, Pinter, 2000); Peter Fysh and Jim Wolfreys, *The Politics of Racism in France* (New York, Palgrave Macmillan, 2003).
[6] Edward Carmines and James Stimson, *Issue Evolution: Race and the Transformation of American Politics* (Princeton, N. J., Princeton University Press, 1989); Thomas Byrne Edsall and Mary D. Edsall, *Chain Reaction: The Impact of Race, Rights and Taxes on American Politics* (New York, Norton, 1992).

of multiculturalism.[7] Political developments regarding multiculturalism in the UK, Canada and Australia, and more recent ones on the European mainland were directly and indirectly influenced by developments in the USA.

The events in Greenwich during the 1990s, culminating in the Macpherson Inquiry Report of 1999, had both local and national significance. In being part of the wider pattern of political contests of the period, it is possible to examine them in coming to understand racial 'backlash' phenomena more generally in its continued relevance to issues of migration to increasingly plural societies. This book attempts to look closely at these relations through the prism of one part of south London made briefly infamous by racism and the Stephen Lawrence murder. Against a backdrop of high levels of racial harassment and the irony that in the heartland of a notorious case of injustice to a black family, the theme of 'unfairness to whites' should have gained such local prominence, it explores the narratives of daily life that show the larger historical dialogue at work. It also attempts to use parallels with the past and, although mainly focussing on the UK and the USA, with developments across the Western liberal democracies, to shed light on social and political processes that are key to contemporary social policy.

The 'white backlash'

What has been referred to as the 'white backlash' may more accurately be described as part of a socially disparate set of responses to equalities discourses as they unfolded from the 1960s to the present. The so-called 'white backlash' has not been unitary, nor has it had the finality which its name seems to suggest. It is part of an on-going dispute with an also socially and politically disparate equalities and multiculturalist agenda. It is an international phenomenon whose history, despite often deep national variations, continues to influence contemporary struggles over race and justice, migration and settlement and the national policies designed to address them.

[7] Dan T. Carter, *From George Wallace to Newt Gingrich: Race in the Conservative Counter-Revolution* (Baton Rouge, Louisiana State University Press, 1996), pp. 55–68; Stanley Greenberg, *Middle Class Dreams: The Politics and Power of the New American Majority* (New York, Times Books, 1996), pp. 39–49; Norman C. Amaker, *Civil Rights and the Reagan Administration* (Washington DC, Urban Institute Press, 1988); Stephen Steinberg, *Turning Back: The Retreat from Racial Justice in American Thought and Policy* (Boston, Beacon Press, 1995); Nathan Glazer, 'Multiculturalism and American Exceptionalism', in Christian Joppke and Steven Lukes (eds.), *Multicultural Questions* (Oxford, Oxford University Press, 1999), pp. 183–98; Todd Gitlin, *The Twilight of Common Dreams: Why America Is Wracked by Culture Wars* (New York, Henry Holt and Company, 1995).

Even in the USA, where it achieved its most strident forms, 'backlash' was by no means ubiquitous. When the impacts of the civil rights agenda began to move beyond the South, local responses to school segregation and bussing, for example, though fierce in many instances were far from uniform despite some familiar patterns.[8] The same was true with affirmative action in higher education and employment – the other major site of white protest in the USA. Much occurred smoothly and without overt opposition.[9] In the UK competition from black and foreign workers for jobs at certain periods had led to rioting and violence in the first half of the twentieth century.[10] However, the post-World War II immigration of black people from the Commonwealth and the recognition of black disadvantage and exposure to racist harassment prompted gradual accommodation alongside racist hostility and resentment at 'special treatment' in both countries. 'White backlash' to official policies aimed at providing equal rights, opportunities and protection under the law was by no means the only response from within white communities. It was, however, always susceptible to – if not always only expressive of – political interest and manipulation.

Negative reactions within white communities to (i) the proximity of black communities following migration, or (ii) the potential acquisition of new power and/or status by blacks, or (iii) the fashioning of policies or legislation to bring about greater equality between 'racial'/ethnic groups, or (iv) the enforcing of such policies or legislation, have all at different times and places led both to visible protest and the mobilisation of political pressure. (The initial Ku Klux Klan, immediately post-Emancipation, focussed on the possibility of blacks achieving positions within the judiciary and thus could be said to be amongst the earliest of 'white backlashes' to equalities legislation.[11]) Historically, each of these were spurs to reactions against the *possibility* of whites having to compete with blacks on legal, occupational, educational and/or residential grounds where white advantage would be diminished if not nullified.

---

[8] See Chapter 6.

[9] Erin and Frank Dobbin, 'How Affirmative Action Became Diversity Management: Employers' Response to Anti-discrimination Law, 1961–1996', in John David Skrentny (ed.), *Color Lines: Affirmative Action, Immigration and Civil Rights Options for America* (Chicago, University of Chicago Press, 2001), pp. 87–117; John Aubrey Douglas, 'Anatomy of Conflict: The Making and Unmaking of Affirmative Action at the University of California', in Skrentny (ed.), *Color Lines*; John Edwards, *When Race Counts: The Morality of Racial Preference in Britain and America* (London, Routledge, 1995), pp. 126–53.

[10] Peter Fryer, *Staying Power: The History of Black People in Britain* (London, Pluto Press, 1984), pp. 298-316; Ron Ramadin, *The Making of the Black Working Class in Britain* (Aldershot, Wildwood House Ltd, 1987) pp. 72–5.

[11] Tony Horwitz, *Confederates in the Attic: Dispatches from the Unfinished Civil War* (New York, Vintage Books, 1998), p. 153.

In the USA some of the earliest talk of a 'white backlash' came in the early to mid-1960s as the civil rights agenda of legislation began to be rolled out during the Johnson administration. It was apparent initially in George Wallace's impact during the 1963 presidential election campaign. Following the riots in American cities in the late 1960s there was even more pronounced negative reaction by whites and widespread talk of a 'white backlash'. Martin Luther King however, declared:

> There has never been a solid, unified and determined thrust to make justice a reality for Afro-Americans. The step backward has a new name today. It is called the 'white backlash'. But the white backlash is nothing new. It is the surfacing of old prejudices, hostilities and ambivalences that have always been there. It was caused neither by the cry of Black Power nor by the unfortunate wave of riots in our cities. The white backlash of today is rooted in the same problem that has characterised America ever since the black man landed in chains on the shores of this nation. The white backlash is an expression of the same vacillations, the same search for rationalisations, the same lack of commitment that has always characterised white America on the question of race.[12]

The case that all forms of white backlash were in essence examples of the same phenomena continued to be made by black activists as the stomach for further and more effective extension of civil rights began to diminish amongst whites and increasingly hostile and organised reactions became further articulated. This was a critical transition in which social class featured in both obvious and obscure ways. Early on a gulf had begun to grow between those sections of the middle class that had supported black progress and the white working-class groups who felt themselves to be materially threatened by the extension of racial equality in ways the middle classes were not. The case for taking seriously white working-class concerns over their hard-won but slender security in jobs and housing was drowned out by the welter of evidence of sustained oppression blacks had suffered and continued to suffer. Furthermore, not only did the case for urgent and effective remedies seem incontrovertible, but white working-class protests were sometimes expressed in language that was unambiguously racist. Thus the poorly articulated and morally flawed responses of white blue-collar workers became emblematic of northern red-neck-style bigotry, the South beyond the South, and of what stood in the way of social progress.

This was a new kind of class warfare in which, ostensibly at least, middle-class whites and the black working class made common cause

---

[12] Martin Luther King Jr, *Where Do We Go from Here: Chaos or Community?* (New York, Harper Row, 1967), p. 68.

against ingrained institutional racism and its popular supporters in the racist white working class. This particularly meant those 'white ethnics' – Irish, Italian, Slavs, Greeks, etc. – who had historically struggled most amongst the whites to maintain economic security and an acceptable social status.[13] It was not that these groups did not recognise the case being made against black's low wages, poor job promotion prospects, higher rents and institutional exclusion. Many of these things were well known, often more directly amongst blue-collar workers than by the middle classes supporting black protest. It was the fact that black progress appeared to be hitched specifically to greater economic struggle and less security for white workers – and with little or no consequences for the white middle class.[14] However, during the 1970s the gap in attitudes between these classes began to narrow as the domain of increasing and urgent interest to the middle classes – higher education – again became the target of equalities activists. SAT scores increasingly came to symbolise the frontier of black/white struggle and the sympathies of the middle classes seemed less certain.[15]

While there are often similarities in the content of anti-equalities talk in the late 1960s and the mid-1990s, there came to be stark changes in its meaning and significance, despite Martin Luther King's early characterisation of 'white backlash'. The working-class family had been exposed to several major transformations taking place over that period. The most important of these was de-industrialisation and the shrinking of the number of traditional blue-collar jobs, restructuring and the

[13] Thomas A. Guglielmo, *White on Arrival: Italians, Race, Colour and Power in Chicago 1890–1945* (New York, Oxford University Press, 2003); Thomas Sugrue, 'Crabgrass-Roots Politics: Race, Rights and Reaction against Liberalism in the Urban North, 1940–1964', *Journal of American History*, 82 (1995), pp. 551–77; Jonathan Rieder, *Canarsie: The Jews and Italians of Brooklyn against Liberalism* (Cambridge, Mass., Harvard University Press, 1985); Jonathan Rieder, 'The Rise of the "Silent Majority"', in Steve Fraser and Gary Gerstle (eds.), *The Rise and Fall of the New Deal Order 1930–1980* (Princeton, N. J., Princeton University Press, 1989), pp. 243–68.

[14] Richard Sennet and Jonathan Cobb, *The Hidden Injuries of Class* (Cambridge, Cambridge University Press, 1972); Jack Bloom, *Class, Race and the Civil Rights Movement* (Bloomington, Indiana University Press, 1987), pp. 155–213; Gary Orfield, 'Race and the Liberal Agenda: The Loss of the Integrationist Dream, 1965–1974', in Margaret Weir, Ann Shola Orloff and Theda Skocpol (eds.), *The Politics of Social Policy in the United States* (Princeton, N. J., Princeton University Press, 1988), pp. 313–55.

[15] Oldfield, 'Race and the Liberal Agenda'; George E. Curry (ed.), *The Affirmative Action Debates* (Reading, Mass., Addison-Wesley, 1996); Alan Matusow *The Unravelling of America: A History of Liberalism in the 1960s*, New York, Harper Row, 1984); Joel Dreyfuss and Charles Lawrence, *The Bakke Case: The politics of Inequality* (New York, Harcourt Brace Jovanovich, 1979); Stephan Thernstrom and Abigail Thernstrom, *America in Black and White, One Nation Indivisible* (New York, Touchstone, 1979), pp. 349–422.

growth in service and information-related work.[16] This had consequences for the voice of the 'little man' and for how it was incorporated
and manipulated by political forces. Secondly the political value of the
race issue changed enormously in kind between the 1960s and the
1990s. Race reconfigured the relationships between the Democratic
Party, the Republicans and the American people, and race also came to
have considerable political significance in the UK in the shifting fortunes
of the Conservative and Labour Parties. Thirdly the focus of
multiculturalist attention moved from the earlier issues of equality and
citizenship rights towards those of cultural recognition and identity.[17]
Finally, re-configuring this whole procession of change itself, the nature
of international migration and the variations within and between
migrant communities intensified greatly towards the end of the period,[18]
giving 'race' and 'racism' new, a-historical, 'post-modern' meaning
detached from reference and political aetiology.

The vulnerability to political manipulation that public opinion and
sectional interests were exposed to was evident in the kinds of politics
that arose. The newly emergent middle class in the USA had seemed
during the 1960s to display a left/liberal bias taken at the time and for a
while afterwards as definitional. However, in time its political allegiances
proved more malleable and more capable of responding to a range of
appeals. Furthermore, it was a class in the ascendant. Unlike the
industrial working class it had power and came to have a sense of its own
social leadership – particularly by the 1980s and 1990s.[19] Its destiny was

[16] Jefferson Cowie and Joseph Heathcott (eds.), *Beyond the Ruins: The Meaning of Deindus-
trialisation* (Ithaca, ILR Press, Cornell University Press, 2003); Barry Bluestone and
Bennett Harrison, *The Deindustrialisation of America: Plant Closings, Community Aban-
donment and the Dismantling of Basic Industry* (New York, Basic Books, 1982); Eileen
Appelbaum and Rosemary Batt, *The New American Workplace: Transforming Work
Systems in the United States* (Ithaca, Cornell University Press, 1994); Steven J. Davis,
John C. Haltiwanger and Scott Schuh, *Job Creation and Destruction* (Cambridge, Mass.,
MIT Press, 1997).

[17] Iris Marion Young, *Justice and the Politics of Difference* (Princeton, N. J., Princeton
University Press, 1990); Charles Taylor, 'The Politics of Multiculturalism', in Amy
Gutman (ed.), *Multiculturalism: Examining the Politics of Recognition* (Princeton, N. J.,
Princeton University Press, 1994); Nancy Fraser, 'Recognition or Redistribution? A
Critical Reading of Iris Young's *Justice and the Politics of Difference*', *Journal of Political
Philosophy*, 3, 2 (1995), pp. 166–80; Cynthia Willett (ed.), *Theorizing Multiculturalism: A
Guide to the Current Debate* (Oxford, Blackwell, 1998).

[18] Stephen Castles, 'The International Politics of Forced Migration', in Leo Panitch and
Colin Leys (eds.), *Fighting Identities: Race, Religion and Ethno-Nationalism, The Socialist
Register 2002* (London, Merlin Press, 2002), pp. 172–92.

[19] Manuel Castells, *The Rise of the Network Society* (Oxford, Blackwell, 2000); R. Reich,
The Work of Nations: Preparing Ourselves for Twenty-First Century Capitalism (New York,
Simon and Schuster, 1991); J. Rifkin, *The End of Work: The Decline of the Global Labour
Force and the Dawn of the Post-Market Era* (New York, Putnam and Sons, 1996); Krishan

one with the information age and politicians played to its gallery. In this context the 'backlash' to multiculturalism left the workshop and the street corner and located itself within the academy, journalism, foundations and their think-tanks and in government itself. The voice of the 'little man' was still rhetorically important but now as a token, not as a flesh and blood reality.

Second wave

The second wave of backlash in the USA was not articulated in popular, local arenas, like the earlier bussing and work-related white protests. It was conducted more in print and policy and claimed to be concerned less with specific instances of 'unfairness to whites' and more with general principles on which race-related social policy and legislation was based – individual versus group actions being the most prominent amongst them. It was partly the result of a convergence of features emerging from the late 1960s and early 1970s. These included liberal concerns over the direction of the equalities agenda; the articulation of a definition of racism amongst conservatives in both political parties that rejected the idea that it was politically and economically generated but insisted on its characterisation as a matter of individual prejudice or acquired bigotry. Most importantly it included the Republican Party strongly distancing itself from the Democrats' record with regard to race equality and successfully mounting political campaigns that simplified the issue of 'affirmative action' and portrayed itself as the party of common sense and the Democrats as the party of rash do-gooders.[20]

During the Reagan/Thatcher era government race policies in both the USA and the UK became primarily a matter of both denying the existence of any structural or institutional causes of racism and halting or reversing policies aimed at effecting equality of outcome. With the presidential election of 1980 the Republican Party cashed in on its long-evolving public image with respect to racial conservatism. Reagan's political record included opposition to the Civil Rights and Voting Rights Acts of 1964 and 1965. As president, Reagan's symbolic endorsement of white, small town 'home truths' struck a chord with

Kumar, *From Post-Industrial to Post-Modern Society: New Theories of the Contemporary World* (Oxford, Blackwell, 1995); Richard Sennett, *The Corrosion of Character: The Personal Consequences of Work in the New Capitalism* (New York, Norton and Company, 1998).

[20] Edsall and Edsall, *Chain Reaction*; John Higham (ed.), *Civil Rights and Social Wrongs: Black – White Relations since World War II* (University Park, Pa., Pennsylvania University Press, 1997).

disaffected white Democratic voters. By 1984, despite the political opportunity apparently offered to the Democrats by the recession of 1981–2, not only did the white Southern vote continue steadfastly Republican but white working-class voters in the *North* now also greatly contributed to the increased Republican base in returning Reagan. This was an important moment in the political mobilisation of the white backlash to the equalities movement in general, American multiculturalism and to race-based affirmative action.[21]

Key in Reagan's assault on equalities legislation was his infusion of 'racially conservative' appointments to the Department of Justice, and in particular in the Civil Rights Division which rapidly began challenging the existing bases of affirmative action in hiring practices from 1981 onwards.[22] In 1983–4 the Reagan Justice Department also filed suits declaring affirmative action agreements in Detroit, Boston and New Orleans to constitute illegal 'reverse discrimination'[23] – picking up on just those populist sentiments expressed by George Wallace a decade earlier.

In the UK the impact of three successive Thatcher administrations on equalities was less evident with regard to legislation. Indeed, although it generally did not advance equalities, 'positive action' in employment was actually endorsed by the Conservative government in the 1989 Fair Employment Act, which was aimed at the treatment of Catholics in Northern Ireland. Compared to the USA there was, of course, very little to dismantle. Although the Thatcher government was vocal in its opposition to anti-racism and multicultural education, local councils' rights to promote racial equality through business contracts were preserved in the Local Government Act 1988, despite pressure from the right wing of the party.[24] This Act, however, and the government's other legislation seeking to limit the power of local government did serve several purposes including the limitation of anti-racist and multiculturalist activity. However, the most evident assault on multiculturalism and on race-based public policy was in the realm of ideological and political rhetoric from quarters close to and sometimes directly part of

---

[21] Greenberg, *Middle Class Dreams*, pp. 39–49; Kevin Phillips, *The Politics of Rich and Poor: Wealth and the American Electorate in the Reagan Aftermath* (New York, Random House, 1990), p. 22; Amaker, *Civil Rights*; see also Norman C. Amaker, 'Reagan and the Civil Rights Legacy', in Eric J. Schmertz, Natalie Datlof and Alexej Ugninsky (eds.), *Ronald Reagan's America*, vol. I (Westport, Conn., Greenwood Press, 1997), pp. 163–74; Edsall and Edsall, *Chain Reaction*.

[22] Ronnie Dugger, *On Reagan: The Man and his Presidency* (New York, McGraw-Hill, 1983).

[23] John L. Palmer and Isabel V. Sawhill (eds.), *The Reagan Record: An Assessment of America's Changing Domestic Priorities* (Cambridge, Mass., Ballinger Publishing Company, 1984), pp. 207–8.

[24] 'Tory Right Urges Revolt on Race Contract Rule', *Independent*, 15 Dec., 1987.

government. In the early to mid-1980s a very vocal opposition to multiculturalism – primarily in education – was mounted in the Tory press and by right-wing think-tanks, predating by several years the major assaults by US critics of the American multiculturalist movement.[25]

As in the USA the period from the 1960s to the 1990s in the UK was marked by a dramatic decline in manufacturing and the growth of service industries. At the same time the failure of any political lobby to resist successfully the flood of propaganda against multiculturalism and anti-racism meant that within the working-class readership of the tabloid press, as within the readership of most of the broadsheets, a well-recognised, even *popular* opposition to anti-racist policies by local government made the erosion of institutional racism and racial harassment in the workplace and the street more difficult to achieve. By the early 1990s, caught in the shadow of this and of economic and social change, some of the least economically and electorally significant sections of the population began to register, *in purely local behaviours*, the dialogue being enacted on the bigger screen. Without any political force – even where its fringes became represented by parties of the extreme right – they reflected a clear after-image of the noise and political battles over multiculturalism. 'Backlash' it was of sorts, but a backlash of the weak, failing to make waves and succeeding only on the most local and limited of levels. It cannot be construed as a 'third wave' of backlash but rather, perhaps, 'collateral damage' from the second. The grassroots negativity in Greenwich surrounding the public outcry over the Stephen Lawrence murder was part of this damage, the steady decline in the number of traditional working-class jobs was its underlay.

The 'new class'

Much of the ideological groundwork for the Reagan/Thatcher and Bush periods and the second wave of backlash that it gave focus to was laid down in the earlier period when the *scale* of the social change, only then beginning to unfold, was as yet unknown.[26] The forebodings of the coming transformation surely hung over the white working classes in the late 1960s and 1970s. The signs of change of some kind seemed to

---

[25] See, for example, Frank Palmer (ed.), *Anti-Racism: An Assault on Education and Value* (London, Sherwood Press, 1986); N. Murray, 'Anti-Racists and Other Demons: The Press and Ideology in Thatcher's Britain', *Race and Class*, 27, 3 (1986), pp. 1–19; Paul Gordon and David Roseberg, *Daily Racism: The Press and Black People in Britain* (London, The Runnymede Trust, 1989).

[26] Daniel Bell, *The Coming of Post-Industrial Society: A Venture in Social Forecasting* (New York, Basic Books, 1973); Yoneji Masuda, *The Information Society as Post Industrial Society* (Tokyo, Institute for the Information Society, 1980).

suggest a 'black' future. Neo-conservative intellectuals also misidenti-
fied the exact nature of the emergent reality, seeing it only as a 'new
class' of leftist liberals burrowing into the academy and local
government bureaucracies.

It is worth taking a closer look at this 'new class' concept, how it first
appeared and how it worked within the American backlash – being
something of a forerunner of the attack on multiculturalism in the late
1980s and early 1990s and apparently ultimately exportable beyond
American and British shores.[27] From the beginning of the 1970s, Irving
Kristol unleashed a stream of attacks on and warnings against the 'New
Class', mainly in the *Wall Street Journal*.[28] Kristol's notion of the New
Class was derived from Lionel Trilling's concept of 'adversary culture'
in which the intellectuals' historical hostility to the bourgeoisie becomes
taken up by the newly educated middle class.[29] For Kristol, whose
approach combined an adopted aristocratic contempt for the 'newly
educated', with his long-lost Trotskyist penchant for seeing selfish
motives buried beneath apparently innocuous interests and activities,
the New Class was pursuing power in the name of equality. He wrote:
'The simple truth is that the professional classes of our modern
bureaucratized societies are engaged in a class struggle with the business
community for status and power.'[30] The 1960s student movement had
given a glimpse of the family life of this new class. Kristol also saw
campaigns against air and water pollution as part of an attempt to
transfer basic economic decisions from the market place, where they
belonged, to 'New Class operatives in the public sector'. Thus 'the New
Class's purported concern for the environment merely rationalised its
drive for power'.[31]

Although Kristol was the first to use the notion of the New Class as
part of a broader neo-conservative attack on left liberalism, the idea of a
class defined with left-liberal political objectives had first been put
forward as a *positive* opportunity by David Bazelon in his *Power in
America: The Politics of the New Class*.[32] Indeed Bazelon's book,
published in 1967 but with a copyright dating from 1963, appears to

---

[27] See below Chapter 7.
[28] Gary Dorrien, *The Neoconservative Mind: Politics, Culture and the War of Ideology* (Philadelphia, Temple University Press, 1993), p. 96.
[29] Lionel Trilling, *Beyond Culture* (New York, Scribner's, 1955) pp. 14–15.
[30] Irving Kristol, 'About Equality', *Commentary*, 54, 5 (1972), reprinted in Irving Kristol,
Two Cheers for Capitalism, (New York, Basic Books, 1978) cited in, Dorrien, *The Neo-
conservative Mind*, p. 97.
[31] Dorrien, *The Neoconservative Mind*, p. 98.
[32] David Bazelon, *Power in America: The Politics of the New Class* (New York, New American
Library, 1967).

be a very early attempt at stirring a form of cultural 'new class' consciousness. Michael Harrington also, in his *Towards a Democratic Left: A Radical Program for a New Majority*,[33] wrote of the potential for the new class to choose between using its education to work on behalf of less privileged groups or become their 'sophisticated enemy'.[34] Alvin Gouldner, much later, also wrote about the 'New Class' as a positive and unique political development in his *The Future of Intellectuals and the Rise of the New Class* (1979). Historically, however, it was the neo-conservative version that was most effectively put into service on the ideological battleground.[35]

Michael Novak's attacks on the new class were very much of the Irving Kristol kind. Like Kristol, Novak came to see the new class as concerned with its own self-interests, masked by a mawkish, self-flattering moralism. It was this dimension that he attacked in his controversial book *The Rise of the Unmeltable Ethnics*. The book was a timely warning about the need to take the responses and perceptions of America's white ethnic groups – the Poles, Italians, Slavs, Greeks, etc. – seriously when promoting values and policies that may be inimical to them. It was, however, not taken in that spirit by those Novak most wished to influence. He was much attacked for his honest, though heavy-handed, attempt to write about the issues of this neglected group.[36] He reported:

In my conversations with [white] ethnics in Chicago, Baltimore, and elsewhere, I have not found one who does not agree that blacks get the worst deal in American life, and that the number one injustice in America is the treatment of blacks. But their persistent question is why the gains of blacks should be solely at *their* expense. They themselves have so little and feel so terribly constricted.[37]

He also noted the trend towards a significant alliance:

The [white] ethnics believe that they chose one route to moderate success in America; namely, loyalty, hard work, family discipline, and gradual self-development. They tend to believe that some blacks, admittedly more deeply injured and penalised in America, want to jump, *via* revolutionary militance,

---

[33] Michael Harrington, *Towards a Democratic Left: A Radical Program for a New Majority* (New York, Macmillan, 1968).

[34] Ibid., p. 290.

[35] For an overview of the early history of the 'new class' idea set in the context of a recent re-theorisation of the notion of a new class *culture*, see Avrom Fleishman, *New Class Culture: How an Emergent Class Is Transforming America's Culture* (Westport, Conn., Praeger, 2002), pp. 53–74.

[36] Dorrien, *The Neoconservative Mind*, p. 218.

[37] Michael Novak, *The Rise of the Unmeltable Ethnics: Politics and Culture in the Seventies* (New York, Macmillan, 1972) p. 15.

from a largely rural base of skills and habits over the heads of lower-class whites. Instead of forming a coalition of the black and white lower classes, black militants seem to prefer coalition with white intellectual elites.[38]

These elites he identifies as the new class.

It is, in retrospect, clear that what both left and right observers were witnessing was an historically highly specific aspect of the emergence of the new middle class within the embryonic knowledge economy. *Whatever* ideological and stylistic currents of the 1960s and 1970s may have *seemed* fundamental to its nature, the switch towards services and away from centralised manufacturing industries began to generate both a much-expanded middle class *and* its educational support systems. The intimations on the left and right that a 'new class' was in the making were not far off the mark, but it was not the specific values and political standpoints of some of those early foot-soldiers of the information age that constituted its substance. The left should have felt less encouraged; the right less paranoid. The new strata of analysts and workers in symbol manipulation were far more politically and culturally varied and very soon shed what vestiges of any 'adversarial' essence they may have seemed in the early 1970s to possess.[39]

Multicultural discourse and its others

The intensity of the neo-conservative attack on the 'new class' straw man was but a forerunner of the assault on multiculturalism, which similarly threw truth-grains in with the yeast of party politics. Norman Podhoretz was to condemn multiculturalist educators on precisely the grounds that they were attempting 'to carry forward the work of destruction begun by their radical forebears of the 60s'.[40] In the late 1980s and early 1990s a full-scale attack on multiculturalism was mounted in a series of books and publications in right and centre/right-leaning journals and newspapers. These particularly focussed on educational issues and attempted to link it to other 'politically correct'

---

[38] Ibid., p. 35.
[39] See Hansfried Keller and Frank W. Heubergern (eds.), *Hidden Technocrats: The New Class and New Capitalism* (New Brunswick, N. J., and London, 1992) . This much was also recognised and forcefully argued in Daniel Bell's contribution to the 1979 book whose questioning title *The New Class?* found the most satisfactory answers to lie in the negative. In his chapter 'The New Class: A Muddled Concept', Bell's own conclusion was that the attributes described by most writers on the subject did not add up to the description of a class, only a certain mentality. See B. Bruce-Biggs, *The New Class?* (New Brunswick, N. J., Transaction Books, 1979), pp. 169–90.
[40] Norman Podhoretz, 'Hey, Hey, Ho, Ho, Western Culture's Got to Go', *New York Post*, 26 Jan. 1988, cited in Dorrien, *The Neoconservative Mind*, p. 356.

policies such as affirmative action, which was also continuing to come under heavy ideological fire in both the USA and the UK. Nevertheless multicultural discourse and the recognition of the multi-ethnic social reality continued to gain ground and the underlying terms and objectives – if not always their application – maintained steady broad acceptance. Thus a paradox arose: criticised so often and by such powerful enemies, multiculturalism went from strength to strength. By 1997 Nathan Glazer could declare that multiculturalism had 'won' and the following year Will Kymlicka, from a somewhat different perspective, also argued that liberal multiculturalism had won by default because there was 'no clear alternative position'.[41]

The solution to this partly lies in its divided nature. Although the language of multiculturalism is not settled or internally rigid, there are two distinct streams within it. Stream (1) is mainly used in specific domestic contexts. It has its roots in the moral and political vocabulary of the post World War II settlement, the aftermath of the holocaust and the American civil rights movement. Its intellectual origins lie in the European liberal tradition and the line of thought on ethnicity that goes from Herder and von Humboldt through Dilthey to Franz Boas and Ruth Benedict.[42] Stream (2) is arrived at and operates within an international framework, is less susceptible to sudden changes of circumstance and is closely tied to global issues concerning migration, settlement and rights. Key international treaties, agreements, laws and declarations also form an important part of the framework on which this stream of multicultural discourse draws. Its starting point is the Universal Declaration of Human Rights and the various later conventions on civil, political and economic rights including the United Nations Declaration on the Rights of Persons Belonging to National, Ethnic, Religious and Linguistic Minorities (1992) which declared that states should 'protect the existence of' these minority identities.

However effective these declarations might be, many of the terms in which they are couched form an important part of the over-arching conceptual apparatus of multicultural discourse. Furthermore, in being more lapidary and arrived at more slowly than those parts of multiculturalist discourse relating to group rights within a single nation,

---

[41] Nathan Glazer, *We Are All Multiculturalists Now* (Cambridge, Mass., Harvard University Press, 1997), p. 4; Will Kymlicka, 'Introduction: An Emerging Consensus?', *Ethical Theory and Moral Practice*, 1 (1998) p. 148, cited in Brian Barry, *Culture and Equality: An Egalitarian Critique of Multiculturalism* (Cambridge, Polity Press, 2001), p. 6.

[42] See George W. Stocking, Jr (ed.), *The Shaping of American Anthropology 1883–1911: A Franz Boas Reader* (New York, Basic Books, 1974); George W. Stocking, Jr, *Volkgeist as Method and Ethic: Essays on Boasian Ethnography and the German Anthropological Tradition* (Wisconsin, University of Wisconsin Press, 1996).

they appear to be more durable and have much to do with multi-culturalism's surprising resilience. They are, as it were, domestic multiculturalism's offshore resources. This has depended, in part at least, on the line between human rights and minority rights being blurred and/or being subjected to little scrutiny. However, under the strain of contemporary migration trends and the numbers of asylum seekers pressing into European countries, Canada, Australia and the USA, even these are being re-considered.

Events in Greenwich throughout the 1990s were partly the ricochet of these features. The rumblings of sub-political unrest on the estates were also part of the background to the Europe-wide murmur that in places coalesced into right-wing populist politics based on anti-immigrant feeling. The rise of European right-wing populist parties, directly linked to the rise in immigration, has not been based exclusively on far right *racist* organisations and segments of parties, but also on politically undramatic parts of electorates for whom change is unwelcome and who have reasoned if not selfless concerns. Even in Australia, the supporters of Pauline Hanson's One Nation Party were of this kind. Hence they were subsequently pulled back with relative ease towards John Howard's Liberal Party to rejoin the mainstream of Australian politics. It is also why Hanson distanced her party from the far right Australian groups such as Australia First and the Australian Reform Party. The Canadian Reform Party did the same, renaming itself the Alliance and merging with the Conservative Party. Similarly, Danish 'housewife' Pia Kiersgaard of the Danish Progress Party made her play for a popular anti-immigration electoral base beyond the ambit of the small racist far right and firmly within the realm of 'respectable' popular politics. Perhaps with larger parties, such as Jean-Marie Le Pen's *Front Nationale* (FN) in France, with its long history of fascist connections, the waters between the far right and the popular anti-immigration positions are more clouded. The FN's broad base is attested to by the fact that it consistently did better than any other far right party in Europe throughout the 1990s. In 2002, despite a split in the party, Le Pen himself was to come to prominence beating Socialist Prime Minister Lionel Jospin in the French presidential election race and leaving a shock wave across Europe.[43]

Like multiculturalism itself, the common ground between populist parties and far right racist factions appealing to mainstream voters with

[43] Tor Bjorklund, 'Radical Right-Wing Populism in Scandinavia: From Tax Revolt to Xenophobia', in Hainsworth (ed.), *The Politics of the Extreme Right*, pp. 193–223; Warren Kinsella, *Web of Hate: Inside Canada's Far Right Network* (Toronto, Harper Collins, 1994), p. 243; Fysh and Wolfreys, *Politics of Racism*, pp. 109-11, 236–9.

an 'anti-immigrant' politics appears to be a political figure with considerable durability. Indeed, at the start of the twenty-first century it already presents as a significant element in the structuring of politics in liberal democracies, influencing strategic choices by major parties in small and large ways. It is curiously both acknowledged and not acknowledged and continues to be that contradictory thing, a political pariah with a significant following.

The chapters that follow explore the fricative interface of backlash and multiculturalism as it was evident on the estates of Greenwich in the 1990s and internationally at other times and places. The borderline between the reasonable concerns of white non-powerful groups and the racialisation of those concerns is examined. These are placed in a social and political context to explore how multiculturalist and anti-racist ideas have performed when taking on the flesh of mundane reality. Macro political agendas and economic trends form an important part of this picture and the book concludes with a discussion of the relevance and adequacy of multiculturalist visions for the future.

2 Politics and 'backlash' on the large stage

Formative elements

The development of civil rights

The race-related 'backlash' during the 1980s to 1990s in the UK and the USA differed from that of the 1960s and 1970s in being in greater measure *political* in origin. While reflecting to some degree the perceptions and feelings within white communities in largely urban locations, it was more significantly the product of a political movement that was also to have a clear international dimension. The seeds of these changes lay in the reactions in the USA to the development of the civil rights agenda. This agenda has often been characterised as moving from the drive for guarantees of fundamental citizen *rights* for African Americans during its initial phase, to a post-mid-1960s phase focussing on the broader goals of equality of *outcomes* to set to right the wrongs of slavery and racism. It has also been seen as an attempt to move beyond the *de jure* equality established up until 1965 towards *de facto* equality, involving the main areas of racial exclusion – residence, education and employment – that would start to reverse the great discrepancies between the black and white populations. The reasons for the 'white backlash' to these developments were characterised as: (1) of the 1950s and 1960s – the civil rights movement was trying to go too far in imposing rapidly and by legal means what should have been developed more slowly and voluntarily; or (2) of the 1970s – that the urban riots in black communities in the mid- to late 1960s alienated whites who had previously been sympathetic; or (3) of the 1970s and 1980s – that, while agreeing with the principle of racial equality, few whites were willing to see that principle through where it involved sacrifices or setbacks to their own well-being.[1] Built on the back of whatever popular feelings these perceptions generated, there was also a distinct reaction to the

---

[1] Richard Hamilton, *Class and Politics in the United States* (New York, John Wiley and Sons, 1972) p. 551; Robert Cole and Jan Erikson, *The Middle Americans: Proud*

expansion of the civil rights agenda that was articulated over education. Education was key in the growth of the new middle classes and to the transformation of economies in Western democracies over this period. Its prominence in 'backlash' politics, particularly with regard to tertiary education during the 1980s, was importantly related to this fact.

In addition to these trends in popular reactions, the civil rights agenda was, quite early on, extrapolated to include a host of additional areas – rights for women, the disabled, mental patients, prisoners – many of which were to become, by various routes, well accepted by the end of the century. They constituted a determined transformation of the civil and economic rights of large numbers of previously excluded citizens, achieved within a relatively short period of time. Just as the movement for black equality was attempting to move towards implementing remedial measures, such as affirmative action, which were ultimately painful to some sections of white society, so some of these other rights that were being enacted also required difficult adjustments of values – if not immediately practices – by many communities, white and black. Rights for women and homosexuals, in particular, had implications for attitudes and values that had traditionally underpinned notions of family and community – values often supported by religious belief. This, to some extent, muddied the water of 'backlash', conflating race with a wide and varied range of legal, social and cultural changes that were taking place. These also formed the basis of what later came to be included in American 'multiculturalism' making it both distinct from other forms that became internationally established, and the target of much attack in the 1980s and 1990s.[2]

The neo-liberal agenda

Another movement important to establishing the shape of the backlash in the 1980s and 1990s was the coming to fruition of a long-germinating international neo-liberal economic agenda that was hostile to government interventions in social matters. In the UK the enthusiasm for this point of view reached a peak in the Thatcher years and included a spectrum of positions, some more morally defensible than others. Even Nigel Lawson, Margaret Thatcher's Chancellor of the Exchequer, was to write disapprovingly of the 'anarcho-capitalism . . . fashionable in

---

and Uncertain (Boston, Little Brown and Co., 1971); Orfield, 'Race and the Liberal Agenda'; Rieder, Canarsie, pp. 111, 118.
[2] Edsall and Edsall, Chain Reaction, p. 107.

some extreme free-market circles, especially in the United States, in the 1970s and 80s'.[3]

Following the Labour election landslide of 1945 Friedrich von Hayek, author of the neo-liberal foundational text *The Road to Serfdom* (1944), believed that it could take twenty years or more before economic liberalism could find successful political expression. However, the formation of the Mont Pèlerin Society, his forum for economics scholars from Europe and North America,[4] led directly to the establishment in 1955 of the more practically oriented Institute for Economic Affairs (IEA) by wealthy Conservative businessman Antony Fisher, whom Milton Friedman has described as the 'single most important person in the development of Thatcherism'.[5] These think-tanks had a profound impact on the political success of neo-liberal economic ideas in the late 1970s, 1980s and 1990s. This was particularly so in the UK with the IEA and its more applied offshoot, the Centre for Policy Studies, and in the USA with the Manhatten Institute and the Pacific Institute, but also in Canada, in the form of the Fraser Institute, and in Australia, with the establishment of the Centre for Independent Studies. By 1991 the number of institutes internationally created for the furthering of free-market ideas was nearing seventy, with many specifically targeted at countries with little previous history of neo-liberal economic thought.[6]

One *political* expression of this trend was to be found within the unfolding politics of the 1980s. In the UK during this period, earlier Conservative characterisations of Labour policy as Soviet-style planning became developed through a more theoretical profiling of interventionism *per se*. Now the Labour Party was portrayed as supporting a 'nanny state' of misguided bureaucracies giving exaggerated importance to marginal groups at the expense of the majority. This struck a chord with the electorate that was vigorously played upon by the press in a torrent of reports purporting to show the irrationality of the Labour Party, particularly as evident in the policies and practices of left-wing local authorities. Indeed, the struggle between central and local government was the recurrent theme of the Thatcher years, with the government passing some fifty separate acts affecting local government in its first decade, including the Local Government Finance Act and the

---

[3] Nigel Lawson, *The View from No 11: Memoirs of a Tory Radical* (London, Bantam Press, 1992), p. 6.
[4] Richard Cockett, *Thinking the Unthinkable: Think-Tanks and the Economic Counter-Revolution 1931–1983* (London, Harper-Collins, 1994), pp. 100–58.
[5] Ibid., p. 122.   [6] Ibid, pp. 306–7.

disastrous Poll Tax.[7] The greater the commitment to multicultural and anti-racist policies by local authorities, the more the argument for 'less government' could be made. This attack on equalities served several neo-liberal purposes. Because of their appeal to a section of traditional working-class Labour voters, anti-equalities arguments were capable of eroding the Labour Party's electoral base while at the same time appealing directly to working-class Tory voters. By the Conservative Party widening its support amongst the working class it was also possible to contribute to the weakening of the trade union movement. Finally it could attack the ideology of social interventionism itself at national and local government levels.

The Republican dawning

A third important formative feature of 'backlash' was, like Conservative policy in the UK, articulated at the level of political strategy in the USA. In the USA during the 1960s the Republican Party underwent a far-reaching re-appraisal of its position over race – despite the spectacular failure of Senator Barry Goldwater's challenge to Lyndon Johnson in the 1964 presidential elections. In particular it was the way in which Goldwater's hostility to any imposition of desegregation had for the first time *greatly increased the Republican vote in poor white neighbourhoods* in the South, that opened up new political possibilities. As Thomas and Mary Edsall put it: 'Goldwater demonstrated that the socioeconomic class structure of the New Deal alignment in the deep South could be fractured by the issue of race.'[8]

Within a year of the 1964 presidential election, negative white reactions to civil rights also began to appear outside of the South and Republican electoral strategists took note. It was, however, with the 1968 presidential campaign, in which Richard Nixon ran for the Republicans and George Wallace ran as an independent candidate against Democrat Hubert Humphrey, that the political depth of this state of affairs started to become apparent.[9] Wallace pursued a populist stance that conjured images of the elite Democratic establishment divorced from the lives of ordinary working men and women, and talked

---

[7] See G. Stoker, *The Politics of Local Government* (Basingstoke, Macmillan, 1988), ch. 9; Lawson, *The View from No 11*, pp. 104, 561–5.

[8] Edsall and Edsall, *Chain Reaction*, p. 41.

[9] In the event Humphrey took only 20 per cent of the Southern vote while Wallace and Nixon each took 34 per cent, massively eroding the Democratic command there. See Rieder, 'The Rise of the "Silent Majority"', pp. 249–50.

in barely coded language that played upon racist fears.[10] Nixon, on the other hand, discovered a delicate line that did not question the principle of racial equality still meaningful to large numbers of Republican voters. Like some Conservative politicians in the UK, Nixon asserted a belief in equality of the races while just as strongly opposing the use of federal intervention to bring it into reality.[11] It was this formula that began to weave the threads of electoral gold discovered in Goldwater's electoral defeat into the political fabric that adorned the Republican presidents who came later.

While the Democratic strategists persisted in believing that the electorate was the same familiar creature it had been since Roosevelt, the Republicans continued to lace their policies with the anti-interventionism that had been seen to work so well in combination with popular sentiments. The effects were ultimately devastating to the Democrats who were tarnished with the stigma of having promoted a wide variety of minority issues and with being in denial over the dramatic rise in black crime rates and black out-of-wedlock birth-rates. Un-historically, on the other hand, the Republicans emerged as the Party of 'the little man', fighting a rearguard battle against neighbourhood transformation and 'over-educated' elitist Democratic supporters.[12]

The synchronisation of the fate of the Democrats and the inability of the Labour Party to achieve national electoral success between James Callahan's premiership and the first New Labour victory is striking. Striking, too, is the role that equalities issues and the assault on social interventionism played in each. Indeed so much is this the case that it is hard to share Bernard Ingham's judgement of Thatcher and Reagan that: 'It was a happy co-incidence of history that two such soul mates came to work together in 1981.'[13] Co-incidence it was not. The convergence

---

[10] Seymour Martin Lipset and Earl Raab, *The Politics of Unreason: Right-Wing Extremism in America 1790–1977* (Chicago, University of Chicago Press, 1970), pp. 338–427.

[11] Interestingly, in stark contrast to Nixon, Wallace also represented the more traditional New Deal politics of the Southern Democrats. His American Independence Party called for increases in social security, supported government commitment to health and education provision and the right of collective bargaining. See Rieder, 'The Rise of the "Silent Majority"', p. 250. It was also the case, however, that Nixon's approach to race was, at that time, a tangle of differing strands. It was he who developed the Philadelphia Plan, and he was also given to pointing out to disgruntled whites the long-term predicament of America's black population. See, for example, Stephen Ambrose, *Nixon: The Triumph of a Politician 1962–1972* (London, Simon and Schuster, 1989), vol. II, p. 187.

[12] Spiro Agnew, Address, Delaware Public Dinner, 14 Oct. 1970, in Murray Friedman, *Overcoming Middle Class Rage* (Philadelphia, Westminster Press, 1971), pp. 317–18. That George Wallace recognised Agnew's attacks on the 'liberal elite' as an attempt to steal his political clothes is evident from his comments at that time. See Lipset and Raab, *Politics of Unreason*, p. 423.

[13] Bernard Ingham, *Kill the Messenger* (London, HarperCollins, 1991), p. 256.

reflected political and ideological activity both on the right and on the left during the preceding decade and earlier.[14] There had been active dialogue between American and British neo-liberals, both in academic and policy circles for several decades and Thatcher and Reagan were to some degree both recipients and reproducers of that political and economic culture. However, the political value of the race issue as an instrument for furthering many other ends was something that came to be clearly understood *in dialogue*. The friendship and 'special relationship' between Margaret Thatcher and Ronald Reagan was in large measure the product of this much longer process through which neo-liberal economic arguments and a younger but equally aggressive neo-conservatism came to find broad and explicit political expression at major government and international level during the 1980s.

Early working-class backlash in the UK and the USA and its political allies

In the USA the fall of the Democratic Party from its traditional bases of support, winning only in one presidential election between 1968 and 1984, was inseparable from the unfolding politics of race. However, the movement against 1960s 'liberalism' and the life-style politics of that period should not cloud the issue of race *per se* nor the relationship between the history of racism in the United States, the development of the various remedial approaches adopted towards it and the predicament of those white communities most closely tangled up in its unfolding. It was perhaps not that the Democratic Party's special attention to racial justice came to flaw its electoral chances, as has been argued by some.[15] It might with justification be equally argued that the way in which remedial race policy was pursued under the Democrats placed the goal of black equality in jeopardy by insensitivity to how policies and programmes especially affecting white working-class communities could best be implemented. In this process it was not only government that was implicated but a whole range of organisations and individuals active at local and community level.

As the cracks in Democratic blue-collar support that started in the South established themselves convincingly in the North, a strain of 'unfairness to whites' complaints emerged that were to set the tone for the future. As Jonathan Rieder points out:

[14] Early Conservative interest in Reagan when he was Governor of California, and several years before he met Thatcher, is described in Hugo Young, *One Of Us* (final edn, London, Pan Books, 1993), p. 250.
[15] Edsall and Edsall, *Chain Reaction*; Carmines and Stimson, *Issue Evolution*.

Such policies yielded a diffuse sense among many traditional democratic ethnic workers that they had become the victims of 'reverse discrimination'. This was more than a proxy for racist animosity. Unemployed carpenters might yell, 'Those quotas and Philadelphia plans made us angry. They should create plans to help both sides. Create jobs, but don't take from one to give to the other and create bitterness.' Former supporters of the early civil rights movement argued that blacks wanted to get ahead, 'they *should* get ahead. But not on my kid's back. Blacks are taking advantage.' As the lament suggests, 'reverse discrimination' also formed an ethical critique of the remedies advanced by liberals, the judiciary, and blacks. As well as a psychic economy and political economy of backlash, there was a moral economy of backlash.[16]

What was here perceived as a threat from newly empowered black workers, however, was an exaggeration. The real threat to blue-collar jobs was that far more significant but less immediately visible transformation of Western economies resulting in the shrinking of home-based manufacturing and related industries. White workers continued shadow-boxing with an opponent whose true identity was yet to be revealed.

Enoch Powell in the 1960s

In the UK the issue of race came out of a very different history, yet there is a striking synchronicity in the unfolding of backlash politics and white working-class resentments in the USA and the UK. Enoch Powell, Conservative Member of Parliament for the midlands industrial town of Wolverhampton, was, as it happens, amongst the few senior Conservatives at that time to have consistently argued for free-market economics from the 1950s onwards. He was also an occasional sojourner in the Mont Pèlerin Society and a frequent contributor to the work of the Institute for Economic Affairs. Nevertheless this fact had little relationship to how he conceived of, or politically handled, the issue of race. Just as 1968 was the high tide of George Wallace's political popularity within and beyond the South in the USA, so that year was the same for Powell in relation to the electorate who opposed Commonwealth immigration in the UK. Wallace's and Powell's relationship with their followers could hardly have been more different but they both gave voice to sentiments that had been rendered to some degree unspeakable. They uttered what their followers wished to hear expressed loud and clear in a national context and which other politicians had, with good reason, significantly failed to express. Powell recognised the political power of expressing what a community felt and he was to transform the face of British politics with that recognition by the end of the decade.

[16] Rieder, 'The Rise of the "Silent Majority"', p. 255.

The 1964 election campaign by Conservative candidate Peter Griffiths in Smethwick, another midlands industrial town, made it clear that the issue of black and brown immigration from the Commonwealth was capable of having exactly the same potent effect on the voting habits of a lifetime amongst working-class industrial communities in Britain as the Republicans came to see race having on the traditionally Democratic voters in the South. At a Conservative Immigration Policy Group meeting in the spring of 1965 Powell spoke of the way in which the issue of immigration could render the politician into a 'lightning conductor' of intense local feeling. He said: 'Those MPs who in any way supported local pressure against immigrants immediately become the focus of an anti-immigrant feeling, whether they like it or not.' This, he suggested, had happened to Griffiths.[17] It was, however, he himself who would set out to become, just three years later, exactly the kind of lightning conductor of popular feeling he had observed at Smethwick.[18]

Powell's 'Rivers of blood' speech was delivered against the background of the third reading of the Race Relations Bill. The Bill was the product of an a-typical 'liberal hour' of the Labour government during 1966–7 in which Home Secretary Roy Jenkins appointed as his special advisor lawyer and rights expert Anthony Lester, who had been closely involved with the American civil rights movement. During the same period, Jenkins set up the Race Relations Board, whose director, Mark Bonham Carter, produced a detailed report on American race relations simultaneously with the drawing-up of the Bill.[19] In the same year the worst race riot in American history occurred in Detroit, sparking further riots in other cities in the USA. These were covered widely on British TV and in the press. The spectre of these riots was a significant aspect of the imagery of Enoch Powell's 'Rivers of blood' speech. Thus both in the framing of the new race legislation *and* in the political articulation of the anti-immigrant racism that Powell represented, US race politics was a highly influential factor.

There were three main themes to Powell's speech. Two of these were concerned with the presence of Commonwealth immigrants – the need to end the right of settlement for the dependants of British citizens from the Commonwealth, and the need for the re-emigration of the latter. A third theme was directed at the anti-discrimination legislation proposed

[17] Robert Shepherd, *Enoch Powell* (London, Hutchinson, 1996), pp. 290–1.
[18] For a detailed background to Powell's relationship to events in Smethwick see, Paul Foot, *The Rise of Enoch Powell: An Examination of Enoch Powell's Attitude to Immigration and Race* (London, Cornmarket Press, 1969).
[19] Mark Bonham Carter, 'Measures against Discrimination: The North American Scene', *Race*, 9, 1 (1967), pp. 1–26.

by the new Bill. Arguing that the Bill would become a mechanism whereby the integrity of British democracy would be threatened from within, Powell suggested that if passed the legislation would enable 'outsiders' to 'pillory' white indigenous citizens for their behaviour.

For those he described as 'dangerous and divisive elements' in the immigrant population:

the legislation proposed in the Race Relations Bill is the very pabulum they need to flourish. Here is the means of showing that the immigrant communities can organise to consolidate their members, to agitate and campaign against their fellow citizens, and to overawe and dominate the rest with the legal weapons which the ignorant and ill-informed have provided.

With explicit reference to the rioting in the black urban ghettos of America at that time, Powell continued:

As I look ahead, I am filled with foreboding. Like the Roman, I seem to see 'the River Tiber foaming with much blood'. That tragic and intractable phenomenon which we watch with horror on the other side of the Atlantic but which there is interwoven with the history and existence of the States itself, is coming upon us here by our own volition and our own neglect.[20]

While his main popular appeal was to a broad range of fears and vindictive feelings towards the black migrant communities, one theme he touched on was to reappear articulated at grassroots level in later manifestations of 'backlash': the plight of the indigenous white worker:

For reasons which they could not comprehend and in the pursuance of a decision by default, on which they were never consulted, they found themselves made strangers in their own country. They found their wives unable to obtain hospital beds in childbirth, their children unable to obtain school places, their homes and neighbourhoods changed beyond recognition, their plans and prospects for the future defeated; at work they found that employers hesitated to apply to the immigrant worker the standards of discipline and competence required of the native-born worker; they began to hear, as time went by, more and more voices which told them that they were now unwanted. On top of this, they now learn that a one-way privilege is to be established by Act of Parliament: a law, which cannot, and is not intended, to operate to protect them or redress their grievances, is to be enacted to give the stranger, the disgruntled and the *agent provocateur* the power to pillory them for their private actions.[21]

This is an early formulation of the 'unfairness to whites' perspective, with its melding of the classic themes of those experiencing the community impact of migration, together with the new theme of the legal arming of those who already threaten by their very numbers.

[20] Enoch Powell, *Freedom and Reality* (Harmondsworth, Penguin Books, 1969), p. 289.
[21] Ibid., p. 286.

The latter, however, was far less developed, far less congruent with current popular concerns and far less capable of 'lightning conductor' transformation than the simple message of stronger immigration controls and repatriation where possible.[22]

If the speech was a disaster for Powell's political career, and produced widespread condemnation in the press – particularly in *The Times* – it was the start of a sometimes embarrassing but widespread popularity across the country. Opinion polls conducted following his sacking found that between 67 per cent and 82 per cent agreed with what he had said about immigrants and between 61 per cent and 73 per cent disagreed with Heath's sacking of him.[23] The massive volume of supportive mail he received also reflected the social vibrancy of the nerve he had struck.

For the left of British politics, perhaps the most perplexing aspect was the level of spontaneously organised trade union support for Powell.[24] These demonstrations have been perceived in different ways. Apologists for Powell have somewhat gleefully emphasised the fact that it was the largest public display of workers' concerns since the 1930s. Critics on the left drew attention to the fact that the dockers had recently been experiencing huge redundancies, due to the emergence of new arrangements at the docks which spelt the beginning of the end for dock workers and to the fact that the leader of the Smithfield strike had once been active in Oswald Mosely's British Union of Fascists.[25] There is, however, a clear connection between the very visible support from unionised labour for Powell's message and the long history of racially exclusionary practices in the trade union movement together with Labour's uneasy compromises with them. That history was also not unconnected with some of the forms of anti-black feeling that were later to follow into the Thatcher years and beyond.

After Powell

Race politics during the decade from the late 1950s to the late 1960s had focussed primarily on the regulation of the numbers of black and brown people entering the country to settle.[26] The counterpointing of immigration restrictions with 'race relations' and equalities legislation

---

[22] Frank Reeves, *Race and Borough Politics* (Aldershot, Averbury, 1989), pp. 8–60.

[23] Shepherd, *Enoch Powell*, p. 352.

[24] Ibid., pp. 354–5; Simon Heffer, *Like the Roman: The Life of Enoch Powell* (London, Weiderfeld and Nicolson, 1998), pp. 462–3.

[25] Shepherd, *Enoch Powell*, p. 355.

[26] Ira Katznelson, *Black Men White Cities: Race, Politics and Migration in the United States, 1900–30, and Britain 1948–68* (Chicago, University of Chicago Press, 1976), pp. 123–51.

provided an important political framework within which the predominant interest – the limitation of the size of the non-white population –
could be achieved without it becoming vulnerable to the charge of racism.
After Powell's 'Rivers of blood' speech and the public displays of support
it provoked, both Labour and Conservative governments wrestled with
this dilemma. It remained an emotionally resonant issue amongst a
significant section of the electorate but wider proposals than those
embodied in the Commonwealth Immigration Act of 1971 and the
British Nationality Act of 1981 were consigned to the domain of racist
political fantasy amongst all but a very few Conservative Party
strategists.[27] The 'immigration question' remained a string to be lightly
plucked by electoral hopefuls within the confines of avoiding the fate that
had awaited Powell in 'going too far'. Thatcher's own 1978 revisitation of
the scene of Powell's nemesis, when, as leader of the opposition, she
famously referred to the 'flood' of immigrants into the UK, ultimately
offended more than it pleased. That role for the issue of race remained
not only dangerous but also of little political purchase. Of far more
potential was the role it was later to have – in the form of the attack on
multiculturalism and anti-racism – within the wider Conservative
political and economic agenda. This move is reflective of the transition
from the industrial working-class reaction to equalities of the 1960s to the
new middle-class-targeted race politicking of the later period. It was only
then that it became re-synchronised with the USA. In the early 1970s
there was still some gap between US and UK race concerns.

In the USA, whatever the *positive* impact for black and white America,
it was particularly within white working-class communities that the
difficult and painful adjustments to the advance of equalities legislation
was most felt. Traditional white male preserves in jobs such as
carpentry, plumbing, sheet-metal working, that provided the economic
lifeblood of white working-class communities, came under threat.
Although the *scale* of that threat was not known, it was not just the
possibility of displaced entitlement that was felt to be at stake but, even
more directly, the ability to sustain the family income, feed children and
maintain a roof over their heads that was seen as threatened. Such
starkly economic consequences of change were rarely experienced by the
middle and upper middle classes. Furthermore, for middle-class groups
opportunities were in fact *expanding* not contracting during this same
period. In employment and in housing, it was consistently the working
and lower middle classes that were asked to absorb the impact of rapid

---

[27] Ian Spencer, *British Immigration Policy since 1939: The Making of Multi-Racial Britain*
(London, Routledge, 1997), pp. 129–51.

social transformation. There is little surprise therefore that racism and community conflict intensified during this period and that the architects of equalities policies, also identified with the expanding and ascendant group, came to be regarded as conspiratorially implicated.

It was these kinds of tension that had given the Republicans and George Wallace the opportunity, against the grain of traditional voting habits, to take advantage of the Democrat's commitment to equal rights. Wallace's and the Republicans' equating of the Democrats with aloof, middle-class intellectuals divorced from the realities of lower-income life-struggles went straight to the heart of the deeper class cross-currents that the economic changes wrought by the 1960s and early 1970s were partly responsible for generating. Even in the 1960s this equation was not new. Similar connections had been made in the 1940s and 1950s. In Chicago, conflicts over neighbourhood racial transformation in the vicinity of the University of Chicago had broken out that were as much the result of intra-white class differences over who was in charge of social change. 'Intellectuals and city planners' were soon identified by working-class whites as just as much their problem as the expansion of the black community into previously white districts of the city. As Arnold Hirsch notes: 'As a political problem, America's racial "dilemma" was . . . less a cause for individual self-scrutiny (although there was much of that) than it was for intra-white confrontation. The meaningful battles over racial issues in post-war America were not fought in the psyches of tortured individuals; they were waged between the engineers and the engineered.'[28] This was a fertile ground for those anti-interventionists who later helped to turn the political tide against the equalities revolution.

The main reason that the political right could make such an impact particularly on the northern white voters was that there *was*, indeed, a serious neglect of attention to the needs, legitimate wishes and feelings of white working-class communities. Because of the undeniable moral legitimacy of the black cause, it was widely accepted that, if bringing about a fairer society involved some pain and material losses for whites this should be regarded as inevitable. However, there was another, competing, truth. As radical activist Saul Alinski pointed out: 'unless we can develop a program which recognizes the legitimate self-interest of white communities, we have no right to condemn them morally because they refuse to commit hari-kiri'.[29] Neglect of such considerations was

[28] Arnold Hirsch, *Making the Second Ghetto: Race and Housing in Chicago, 1940–1960* (Cambridge, Cambridge University Press, 1983), p. 175.
[29] Quoted in Jim Sleeper, *The Closest of Strangers: Liberalism and the Politics of Race in New York*, (New York, W.W. Norton and Co., 1990), p. 122.

the principle flaw of equalities implementation in the USA and was to become an important electoral boon to Republicans in the USA. Conservatives in the UK were to become similar beneficiaries as the New Left failed to engage with the communities their political forebears had once regarded as their *raison d'être*.

The New Left in the UK

Traditional class politics in the UK meant that many Labour-controlled local authorities were slow to rise to the challenge presented by the establishment of black and Asian communities. However, with the appearance of the new urban left in the late 1970s local government became seized on as a potential arena for the expansion of the political agenda, and, after Margaret Thatcher's Conservative Party won the general election of 1979, a site of resistance to Tory policies. This new left sought an ostensibly more inclusive politics and was inevitably influenced by the black and feminist movements in the USA, but it developed these within a distinctly British context. Although most evident in London, the influence of the New Left in Labour councils was a national, if uneven, phenomenon.[30] Its development represented a locally based contrast to the cautious policies of the Callaghan government in the late 1970s, to the traditional class-oriented politics of the old party ideologues and to those coming to haemorrhage from the party into the Social Democratic Party (SDP) in the early 1980s.

The development of a structure of equalities-related posts within local government, together with the proliferation of anti-racist organisations partly in response to some local electoral successes by far right parties such as the National Front, made the issue of racism and anti-racist policies a highly visible matter. None of the formal policies adopted by even the most ambitious of New Left-dominated local authorities amounted to anything as radical as had been achieved by federal government in the USA. With respect to employment in particular, although several authorities tried to implement contract compliance, quotas were illegal in the UK and, unlike in the USA, no national government ever embraced contract compliance. Indeed, even the most modest recognition of the stark facts of racial disadvantage in the UK was strongly resisted in the right-dominated political climate of Thatcher's first two administrations.

---

[30] Gideon Ben-Tovim, John Gabriel, Ian Law and Kathleen Stredder, *The Local Politics of Race* (Basingstoke, Macmillan, 1986).

The politics of this resistance were complex, involving the convergence of two antithetical strands in Conservative thinking at that time. On the one hand resistance came from the Tory traditionalists and romantic nationalists whose concept of national identity allowed no space for the recognition that Britain had become significantly more multicultural than ever before in its history. On the other were the neo-liberals who primarily saw any unpopularity anti-racism might have as advantageous to the fight against local authority over-spending, the defeat of which they saw as the key to the development of a fully free-enterprise culture. The issue of race united the discordant strands into a theme of increasing popular and media interest. It was a gift to Conservative coherence of purpose.

The strategic inter-levering of these aspects of Conservatism around race was particularly evident in the activities of the various think-tanks flourishing and intimate with government policy formation in the early 1980s. While the Salisbury Group became unambiguously traditionalist under Roger Scruton's leadership, Digby Anderson's Social Affairs Unit, founded by the Institute for Economic Affairs to augment its work in the area of sociology and social policy, introduced clear neo-liberal themes to the right-wing theorisation of the race issue. In particular it drew heavily on the writings of black Chicago economist Thomas Sowell (once a student of Milton Friedman) as well as Walter Williams, another neo-liberal black American economist. These authors argued that federal programmes aimed at blacks led to dependence and thwarted the development of independent black leadership; affirmative action programmes stigmatise the majority of blacks, and government-enforced minimum wage standards increase black teenage unemployment.[31] Sowell had been fêted by the Manhattan Institute, offshoot of the IEA, at an event in 1981 linked to the publication of two of his books in that year.[32] Further links between the UK and American intellectuals of the right include Nathan Glazer's membership of the Social Affairs Unit's advisory council. In a Social Affairs Unit booklet *Reversing Racism: Lessons from America*[33] its authors argued for a similarly market-led approach to the issue of racial disadvantage in the UK. At the same time the Centre for Policy Studies published Antony Flew's *Education*,

---

[31] See especially, Thomas Sowell, *Markets and Minorities* (Oxford, Basil Blackwell, 1981); Thomas Sowell, *Ethnic America* (New York, Basic Books, 1981); Walter Williams, *The State against Blacks* (New York, McGraw-Hill, 1982).

[32] Manhattan Institute for Policy Research, Manhattan Report Special Edition, vol. I no. 8, Nov. 1981.

[33] K. Holland and G. Parkin, *Reversing Racism: Lessons from America* (London, Social Affairs Unit, 1984).

Race and Revolution, in which he argued that many remedial measures aimed at racism contributed to institutionalised racism against white people.[34]

Notoriously sections of the British press sympathetic to the Conservatives mounted a concerted attack on local government multiculturalism and anti-racist initiatives throughout the 1980s, with stories designed to demonstrate how basic common sense had evaporated in certain left-dominated London boroughs.[35] The press and the right-wing think-tanks were greatly assisted in their attack by the clumsy style of anti-racist policy implementation adopted by a number of left-dominated boroughs and by the ascendant new cohorts of race and equality advisors and co-ordinators across local authority departments. Racism awareness training courses for staff became common in local authorities as well as in some public services and often generated considerable resentment, deep hurt and confusion with little progress towards actually eroding racism. Furthermore, because of a heightened awareness of the issue of racism and its frequently 'invisible' nature, accusations of racism based on very flimsy evidence abounded, sometimes leading to disciplinary action resulting in unfair sackings.[36] As Lansley, Goss and Wolmar report:

> The tougher approach to racism also fuelled the tension created by the new policies within town halls. Supporters of the new stance felt it was justified in the promotion of greater equality, but the price was often an uncomfortable atmosphere in which accusations of racism could be made on the slightest pretext. Even committed officials began to talk of a 'climate of fear' and witch-hunts.[37]

It is not surprising that in such an atmosphere the already somewhat unfocussed objectives of 'town-hall anti-racism' should lose their way. These were serious own-goals that not only fed directly into the right-wing attack, but also became an embarrassment to the Labour Party and led to a subsequent distancing of Labour politics from anything bearing the name of anti-racism.[38]

---

[34] Antony Flew, *Education, Race and Revolution* (London, Centre for Policy Studies, 1984).
[35] Gordon and Rosenberg, *Daily Racism*.
[36] Stewart Lansley, Sue Goss and Christian Wolmar, *Councils in Conflict: The Rise and Fall of the Municipal Left* (Basingstoke, Macmillan, 1989), p. 129.
[37] Ibid. In some cases tribunals later reversed such decisions. On the case of Jackie Griffiths the white manager of a predominantly black nursery school in Brent compensated after three years for unfair dismissal see *Daily Express*, 28 Mar. 1996.
[38] See John Solomos, 'The Local Politics of Racial Equality', in Malcolm Cross and Michael Keith (eds.), *Racism, the City and the State* (London, Routledge, 1993), pp. 144–56; R. Jenkins and J. Solomos, *Racism and Equal Opportunity Policies in the 1980s*, (Cambridge, Cambridge University Press, 1987); Wendy Ball and John Solomos (eds.),

Partly the problem was with the insulation of the issue of racism from any wider set of political concerns. Although lip-service was often paid to class as a significant aspect of racism, in fact a tension existed between anti-racists and those who embraced strong class politics[39] focussing on the needs of white male workers to the exclusion of black, Asian and female labour – especially in the manufacturing sector.[40] At the same time by focussing exclusively on black and Asian discrimination and disadvantage, anti-racist activists often ignored the problems of the relationship between class-based disadvantage, race and racism and failed to face up to the complex problems of building alliances that would enable new anti-racist policies and practices to bed down successfully in white working-class communities. Indeed, the real concerns of whites in mixed or predominantly white areas – concerns that were capable of making some whites susceptible to the interpretations of racist political groups – frequently went unanswered or were dismissed as racist talk. Little attempt was made to engage with these as deep problems in social and economic relations or to drive a political wedge between legitimate, self-interested anxieties and the racist formulations of those anxieties. Such would have been a challenging but important task. In fact for the most part it proved not to be a concern of the anti-racist movement either within local government circles or without. This also made it far easier for the attacks from the right in the press and elsewhere additionally to capture the interest of the middle-class electorate, appealing to a 'common sense' that was free of ideological conundrums and strained reasoning.

Thus it was that throughout the 1980s the Labour Party found itself nationally in a comparable position to that of the Democrats in the USA and for related reasons. Just as the Democrats had become disconnected from their traditional blue-collar support even in the northern states, so the Labour Party had lost support nationally. Those of the New Left setting the political agenda had also become detached from the concerns of the white working class in the local constituencies. While the national party sought to chase the middle-class voters now attracted to the SDP, borough politics was engulfed in debates about equalities as feminists and anti-racists also explored the depths of their differences and sometimes animosities. Many working-class whites especially the

Race and Local Politics (London, Macmillan, 1990); Paul Gilroy, *There Ain't No Black in the Union Jack* (London, Hutchinson, 1987), pp. 114–52; Paul Gilroy 'The End of Anti-Racism' in Ball and Solomos (eds.), *Race and Local Politics*, pp. 191–206.

[39] Ben-Tovim, Gabriel, Law and Stredder, *Local Politics of Race*, p. 77.

[40] See the discussion of race and class in John Solomos and Les Back, *Racism and Society* (Basingstoke, Macmillan, 1996) pp. 92–3.

poorest and most excluded, felt abandoned in their predicament. At a time of a rapidly widening gulf between the rich and the poor in the UK, those benefiting least from the new economy were pitched into a sad and ultimately meaningless competition. Working-class whites, particularly in areas bordering on racially mixed communities, felt themselves to be unheard and neglected by the local politicians they would once have looked to for support.

By the 1990s in the UK at the level of community relationships an essentially disunited and politically powerless white working-class backlash to equalities policies and to the emergence of an increasingly confident multiculturalism began to take shape. It was also the least visible and the least articulated of the backlashes in any public arena. This sullen movement, unlike that reflected in the din of press headlines, was an inward-looking affair. Part 'underclass', part the political and economic forgotten, the homes where school failure was the norm and job expectations low were the site of grievances festering away in a political no-man's-land. The rise in the number of racist assaults and the level of local white indifference to it during the early 1990s was one manifestation of the mood tucked away on the predominantly white housing estates.

This new articulation of 'backlash' was not derived from the fear of competition in the workplace that had been an important element in Enoch Powell's popularity in the industrial midlands twenty years earlier. It was more abstract, partly the result of the ideological struggles of the late 1970s and early 1980s, partly the search for something to blame for the social and political detachment of a class fragment now numerically dominated by a middle-class whose concerns had come to constitute a taken-for-granted social reality that was an alien form of Britishness, with ASCII code as its sinister foreign language. Such was the condition on many of the public housing estates in Greenwich in the late 1980s and early 1990s, as the curtain rose on a series of tragedies that were to push racism once more on to the UK's national political agenda.

3 Greenwich and its racial murders

In Greenwich the proximity of far-right racist parties was not just a political one – it was also geographical. In the south of the borough some of the most expensive housing developments were interlaced with old and ageing, council-owned public housing estates. This itself was part of the balance of electoral forces that played out in local politics by returning the Conservative candidate for Eltham frequently to parliament and Labour majorities usually in the local council elections.[1] In the 1990s central and southern Greenwich were – as they largely remain – unambiguously white with very few non-white families and no non-white 'communities'. Just to the south of the more ethnically mixed areas of north and north-east Greenwich, these areas fray, on their northern and eastern flanks, into enclaves and spits of white territory that look for their identity southwards towards the county of Kent – 'the garden of England' – and the imaginary white hinterlands. And just into the next borough, Bexley – the last metropolitan borough before Kent – sat the 'headquarters' and bookshop of the British National Party (BNP) from 1989 until 1998. The direct electoral impact of the BNP was minuscule, but its symbolic significance was very relevant to the way racism and community were interpreted in Greenwich. It said things some wished to hear. It was not respectable. It was associated with violence. It was very far from being a populist or neo-populist party.[2] Nevertheless it was used as a reference point in emphasising the dangers that might be realised if certain policies continued to be followed by the council, or if minority ethnic groups continued to determine the local agenda, to have 'too loud a voice'. Thus there developed a local discursive economy in which the varied historically established political rhythms became syncopated by scary and oblique references to 'extremists on all sides'.

[1] The present borough of Greenwich is divided into three parliamentary constituencies: Greenwich, Woolwich and Eltham.
[2] Hainsworth (ed.), *The Politics of the Extreme Right*.

Industrial Greenwich and the turning tide

Lying in the south-east of the capital, the borough of Greenwich extends from the inner city districts on the south side of the Thames, southwards and eastwards to the more affluent suburbs. It contains almost all of 'Kentish London' – that part of south London which once marked the northernmost reaches of the county of Kent – with its northern towns of Woolwich, Greenwich and Deptford. There, from mid-Victorian times, the industries of engineering, metal-working and armaments, shipbuilding and construction provided the growth industries and skilled workforce on which the working-class organisations for which the area is famous – co-operatives and building societies, radical clubs and societies – were founded. Indeed, the area perfectly exemplifies the early co-ordination of trade union organisation and the movement for socialist political representation.[3]

The workforce at the Woolwich Arsenal was of critical importance in the national struggles for the eight-hour day, liveable wages for government workers and trade union recognition during the early years of the twentieth century. Arsenal workers were also key figures in establishing the highly successful co-operative for the purchase of affordable food for working-class families, the Royal Arsenal Co-operative Society. It lasted from 1868 until 1985. The locally published radical journal, *The Pioneer*, drew on the experiences of the Arsenal workforce to analyse the conditions of workers more widely. These accounts were in turn used by the first Woolwich Labour MP, Will Crooks, in his representations in the House of Commons concerning local and national labour issues. In the year of Crooks' election, 1903, the Labour Representative Association also gained a majority in the local council and returned two Labour representatives to the London County Council. Thus Woolwich was the first borough in the country to be represented by Labour at all levels of government.[4]

At this early stage, bridges were beginning to be built between skilled, semi-skilled and unskilled workers, the usefulness of parliamentary representation to the trade union movement was locally articulated and

---

[3] See Geoffrey Crossick, 'An Artisan Elite in Victorian England', *New Society*, 23/30 (1976), pp. 610–12; Geoffrey Crossick, *An Artisan Elite in Victorian Society: Kentish London 1840–1880* (London, Croom Helm, 1978).

[4] Paul Tyler, 'The Origins of Labour Representation in Woolwich', *Labour History Review*, 59, 1 (1994), pp. 26–33; William Pierce, 'Industrial Relations in the Royal Arsenal', in Beverley Burford and Julian Watson (eds.), *Aspects of the Arsenal: The Royal Arsenal Woolwich* (London, Greenwich Borough Museum, 1997), pp 111–25; Ron Roffey, 'The Arsenal and its Co-op Connection', in Burford and Watson (eds.), *Aspects of the Arsenal*, pp. 91–100. David Mitchell, *Women on the Warpath* (London, Jonathan Cape, 1966).

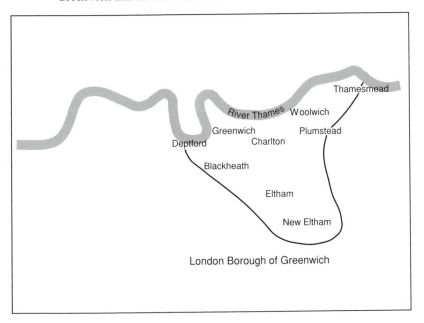

Figure 3.1. London borough of Greenwich.

acted on, and a strong culture of co-operation between the various trade unions was also established. The moderate stance of Will Crooks was what made him attractive to many local labour and socialist activists. His ability to unite a range of disparate interests contributed greatly to his political success and to the cementing of the relationship between organised labour and mainstream political organisations – especially the Labour Party. As one historian writes: 'Woolwich, instead of being the "Tory stronghold" of 1903, was transformed in a few years into one of the leading Labour strongholds in the kingdom, both industrially and politically.'[5]

At the same time, at the end of the nineteenth century, areas to the west of Woolwich such as Westcombe Park and Blackheath developed as 'prosperous residential localities', as had Kidbrooke and Charlton, inhabited by 'city gentlemen and others who generally occupied villa residences in good neighbourhoods'. Indeed, the political history of the area has been a protracted dialogue between its skilled 'artisan elite' and its solid professional and commercial middle classes, which some

[5] Paul Tyler, 'The Royal Arsenal and Independent Labour Representation: A Beacon in the Dark', in Burford and Watson (eds.), *Aspects of the Arsenal*, pp. 101–9.

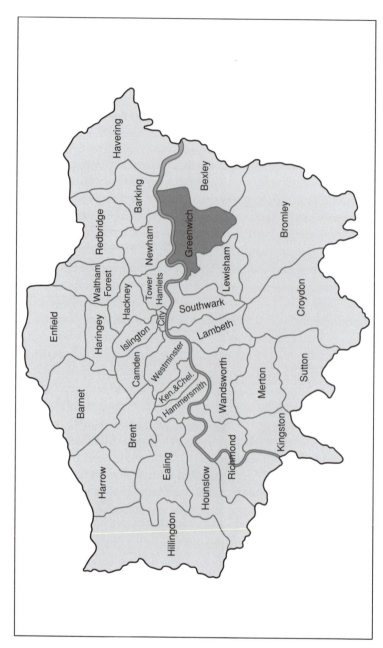

Figure 3.2. The borough of Greenwich within Greater London.

historians have characterised as a collaboration of a 'labour aristoc-racy' with middle-class values and aspirations, others as a process of struggle.[6]

Throughout the early and mid-twentieth century the area benefited from the presence of a number of major employers. The Arsenal consistently employed some 10,000 workers and above from the late nineteenth century, rising to 80,000 during World War I.[7] In the first decades of the twentieth century cable-making was another major employer. From before 1880 facilities originally used for rope-storage in Henry VIII's Thames-side ship-yards at Woolwich enabled submarine telegraph cables to be coiled directly into the holds of the ships from which they would be laid. A number of the largest cable firms had works in the Woolwich/Greenwich/Charlton area. With the eventual develop-ment of electricity for land purposes these firms had an initial superiority in the market for cables for lighting and power. The area consequently became – and for much of the twentieth century remained – the centre of this industry in London.[8] Companies such as the General Electricity Company (GEC), Associated Electrical Industries (AEI), Siemens and Western Electric were established as the cornerstone of the local economy, a feature which became especially significant once the pattern of re-location and merger started to transform the electrical industry in the 1960s.

Following the merger of GEC and AEI in 1967 the company announced that its Woolwich factory employing 5,500 men and women would close. The Woolwich Arsenal also finally closed in 1966 and in the south-east London employment area there were thirty-one closures resulting in major redundancies during 1968–9.[9] Furthermore, where such employers were replaced they tended to be by those of a quite different kind. As one commentator reported, 'While engineering and other manufacturing companies moved out, warehouses and offices moved in. Local people began to fear not only for their jobs but for their skills and occupational standing.'[10] With the change in borough boundaries to include Greenwich in 1963, the rebuilding of Woolwich

---

[6] Crossick, *An Artisan Elite*, see especially, pp. 13–23 and 251–4; J. Foster, 'Class Struggle and the Industrial Revolution: Early Industrial Capitalism in Three English Towns' (Ph.D. thesis, University of London, 1974).

[7] See Brigadier O. F. G. Hogg, *The Royal Arsenal* (2 vols., Oxford, Oxford University Press, 1963); also Burford and Watson (eds.), *Aspects of the Arsenal*, *passim*.

[8] London School of Economics and Political Science, *The New Survey of London Life and Labour*, vol. II (London, P. S. King and Sons), p. 188.

[9] W. W. Daniel, *Whatever Happened to the Workers in Woolwich? A Survey of Redundancy in South East London* (London, PEP, 1972), p. 1.

[10] Ibid., p. 2.

town centre from the mid-1950s[11] and the shift away from manufacturing and towards service industries in the late 1960s, the social composition and economic profile of the area began to change dramatically as the 1970s advanced. The polarising national budgets of the 1980s only served to emphasise the gulf between the economically stranded working class of the area and the new middle class.

During the 1990s, of the total borough population of 208,000, 117,000 inhabitants lived within the waterfront wards, some of which had male unemployment levels of above 30 per cent, reaching over 40 per cent in some months. Overall unemployment stood at nearly 15 per cent, and over the previous thirty years the area had seen a dramatic decline in manufacturing jobs available, from 33,000 in 1966 to just over 6,000 by 1995.[12] The local economy was severely depressed. Average earnings in the borough of Greenwich were low even for those in employment and average male earnings were far lower in Greenwich than in its neighbouring inner city boroughs to the west.[13] A 1994 study, *Breadline Greenwich*, showed that 26 per cent of Greenwich residents lived in households with an income of less than £5,000 a year.[14]

Despite the borough having a reputation for its historic buildings and nautical tourist attractions, parts of Greenwich exhibited many of the symptoms common to older inner city areas in decline. Beyond its historic core, the area as a whole suffered from industrial dereliction, run-down housing estates, unattractive shopping centres and a lack of open space and recreational facilities. The collapse in Greenwich's manufacturing base over the previous thirty years also accelerated and had a profound effect on the area, resulting in unemployment levels amongst the highest in London. Some 500 businesses and 10,000 jobs were lost between 1991 and 1993, by far the largest reduction of any London borough.[15] Within this, youth unemployment became particularly high, rising from a low of 6.8 per cent for the 16–19 age group in January 1990 to 22.1 per cent in January 1995, with levels of nearly 25 per cent amongst 16–19 year old males.[16] This is the broad context to

---

[11] E. F. E. Jefferson, *The Woolwich Story 1890–1965* (London, The R.A. Printing Press Ltd, 1970), pp. 402–3.
[12] Source: Department of Employment.
[13] Source: *New Earnings Survey 1990–1993*. See *Greenwich Poverty Profile*, Department of Planning and Regeneration, Directorate of Development, London Borough of Greenwich, November 1994, pp. 12–13.
[14] *Breadline Greenwich Report*, March 1994, prepared by BMRB International Limited for the London Borough of Greenwich, p. 34.
[15] By the late 1990s the borough had received more in Single Regeneration Budget government grants per head of population than any other area in the country.
[16] Source: Department of Planning and Regeneration, Directorate of Development, London Borough of Greenwich.

the period that was especially marked for the rise in both the number and seriousness of racial incidents and for the prevalence of male adolescents in the profile of perpetrators of racial assaults.

Immigrants from what was then called the British Commonwealth began to arrive in the borough in the early 1950s when people from south Asia – mainly Jat Sikh farmers – started to settle in small communities particularly in the Charlton and Plumstead Common areas. Gujerati Hindu small traders and Ramgarhia Sikh artisans from East Africa followed in the late 1960s, settling in Plumstead and Woolwich. According to the 1991 census, 4.2 per cent of the population (32.1 per cent of the ethnic minority population) described their ethnic origin as Indian, Pakistani or Bangladeshi. By the early 1980s people from the Caribbean constituted another distinct minority and came to comprise 2.5 per cent of the population (19.7 per cent of the ethnic minority population). Other groups, from Vietnam and Somalia and other parts of Africa, also made up the borough's 12.8 per cent ethnic minority population. The remaining 87.2 per cent were white. The ethnic minority population was most strongly represented in the wards to the north and north-east of the borough, where the percentage of minorities ranged from 20 per cent to above 30 per cent. These figures (drawn from 1991 census data) did not include many of the refugees living in Greenwich, since the number of refugees, especially those from Somalia, grew considerably throughout the 1990s. By 2000 it was estimated to have reached some 12,000. The wards in the south and in parts of the west are very predominantly white, with ethnic minority populations as small as 2.5 per cent to 5 per cent.

Eltham

These distinctly 'white' areas constitute a social mixture of red-brick, working-class homes and suburban mock-Tudor middle-class residences. Many of these neighbourhoods contain low-rent housing estates that were developed by the council during the 1920s, 1930s and 1950s. Those in the suburban area of Eltham provided accommodation for some 6,000 families who had been the beneficiaries of a housing policy, growing out of the local authority's historical bias towards traditional socialist values. From the 1930s onwards that policy sought to provide affordable homes in sufficient numbers for the local working-class population. It also importantly set out to guarantee the perpetuation of traditional community and kinship networks by allocating housing on the basis of kinship with those already settled on the estates – in particular, to those who were the children of established tenants. This 'sons and daughters' policy, as it is known, was an attempt to ensure a sense of community, safety and coherence and to replicate to some extent the 'village' ethos that was believed to characterise the large nineteenth-century/early twentieth-century classic working-class neighbourhoods.

This policy, benign in its intentions, had the consequence of creating institutionally maintained barriers to black and ethnic minority tenancies within these estates – once the demand from immigrants from the Commonwealth began to become established from the mid-1950s onwards. Despite the abandonment of the policy in the early 1990s, the estates remained very predominantly white. Black and ethnic minority families coming in experienced various levels of racial harassment from verbal abuse through to assault. Some families were driven off by perpetual harassment and had to be re-housed by the local authority. Even as late as July 2002 attacks were still occurring in the heart of Eltham.[17]

Eltham has a long history of returning Conservative MPs. From 1918 until 1943 the Conservatives held Woolwich West, as the constituency was then called. It fell to Labour in the landslide election of 1945 but by 1950 it was Conservative again, which it remained until 1964. For the following ten years it was Labour, with 50 per cent and above of the poll, and even when the seat fell to Peter Bottomley, the Conservative, in 1975, the Conservative vote continued to be some 2,000 under that of its combined opponents. Thus, despite its strong Tory record, Eltham was by no means a Tory safe seat. Bottomley was popular because he was perceived to be a diligent constituency politician. He was also concerned about social issues. His persistent popularity was partly a result of these attributes. The area's later reputation for racism was also not foreshadowed by votes cast for racist political parties or politicians. During the 1970s, when the National Front (NF) was making its strongest bid for electorability, the Eltham constituency showed no more interest in the NF than either of the other two Greenwich constituencies. Indeed of the three it was marginally the lowest with an NF share of 2.4 per cent in 1975 and 1.4 per cent in 1979. In the 1980s the BNP's support was even more derisory.[18] Thus, although the old council estates of Eltham have been targeted by racist parties during

---

[17] See *News Shopper*, 17 July 2002, p. 5, 'Our Streets Rocked by Race Hate'; *Mercury*, 17 July 2002, p. 10, 'Arrest of Fourth Man after Attack', and 'Two Hurt in Race Attack by Youths' by Mandy Little; also *Sun*, 4 July 2002, p. 23, 'Knifing has "Echoes of Lawrence"'.

[18] Patricia Arnold, *A History of Britain's Parliamentary Constituencies: The Constituencies of the London Borough of Greenwich* (West Malling, Patricia Arnold, 1992).

some national and local elections, there is no evidence of any politically significant pre-disposition in that direction.

Interestingly, in the adjacent constituency of Greenwich, a Labour 'safe seat' was famously upturned when its long-standing MP, Guy Barnet, died in 1986 and the seat was contested in a by-election. Social Democratic Party candidate Rosie Barnes took it with a campaign in which her virtues as a plain-speaking mother of three, set against Labour's Deirdre Wood, a 'hard left' candidate, fed a newspaper bonanza. Ivor Crewe and Anthony King described Wood as: 'a woman who might almost have been invented by the tabloid press to symbolise the London Labour party's "loony left"'.[19] In some cosmetic respects Barnes can be seen to share some of the features of those would-be Joan of Arc political housewife-mothers – Pia Kiersgaard, Pauline Hansen – who rose to popular appeal amongst working- and lower-middle-class voters who felt themselves to suffer from the effects of immigration and to have no political representative. Barnes, however, was no racist and she represented the interests of neither old Labour nor the disaffected working class. On the contrary, she was part of the new post-industrial Greenwich. For Crewe and King, Rosie Barnes 'might well have been chosen to exemplify the growing service class of highly qualified managers and specialists'.[20] It was her 'down to earth' approach to campaigning that set her in tabloid-narrative contrast to Dierdre Wood. This gave her some apparent affinity with the Hansens and Keirsgaards of politics who came to pitch themselves against political correctness. Race, however, was nowhere seen as an issue. Furthermore, in the Greenwich wards abutting those of Eltham – with the highest levels of unemployment and council tenancies (88 per cent in one case) – Barnes did worse than anywhere else in her constituency. She was no 'fish and chip lady' for fish and chip popularity. She worked in market research and her husband was a management consultant and SDP councillor. In a few years the couple would have been New Labour stalwarts. Then they were its precursors and she sought and found support from people like themselves.

In local elections to Greenwich council, racist politics was also hard to find. Racist party candidates were rare. In Sherrard, the Eltham ward that includes the Page estate, but nowhere else in the borough, the BNP took a surprising 12 per cent of the vote in 1994, the year following the Lawrence murder. This was the only electoral sign that anything might

[19] Ivor Crewe and Anthony King, *The Birth, Life and Death of the Social Democratic Party* (Oxford, Oxford University Press, 1995), p. 359.
[20] Ibid.; see also Pippa Norris, *British By-Elections: The Volatile Electorate* (Oxford, Clarendon Press, 1990), pp. 94–5.

be lurking beneath the surface. No racist boats were missed by would-be politicians in Eltham or in Greenwich as a whole. They were simply not to be had. The kinds of racism that flourished in Greenwich were not those that came articulated through conventional political means. They were registered and extrapolated primarily through talk, neighbourhood rumour, narrative and counter-narrative. It was this broad surface of quotidian communication that provided the support system for the high levels of racial harassment that were recorded in the crime figures of the 1990s and that continue to be recorded there. It required density rather than numbers *per se* and it clearly did not automatically translate into racist voting practices. As such it was politically invisible and, on the most public airways, mute.

The first murder – Rolan Adams

Of the three unambiguously racist murders to occur in the borough of Greenwich, the first, which did not take place in central/southern Greenwich but in Thamesmead at the extreme eastern end of the borough, brought to the fore many of the basic street-political elements that were to become important in the unfolding issue of racism in Greenwich during the immediately subsequent years. Thamesmead estate is predominantly white with a settlement of Vietnamese from the late 1970s, and a smaller number of Asian and Caribbean families. A network of streams and ponds divided the area into natural territories for the offensive and defensive adolescent gangs that flourished in the 1980s and 1990s, calling themselves after the locally abundant fish – the Ruds, the Carp, the Gudgeon. Some of these combined to form a large gang called the Goldfish which in time itself spawned a gang with several age-tiers of membership called the NTOs, standing for Natty Turn-Outs, later Nazi Turn-Outs.[21] This was famously the estate where Stanley Kubric's desolate film *Clockwork Orange* was shot – a claim to fame not lost on many of the older NTOs.

On Friday 21 February 1991 Rolan Adams, a black fifteen-year-old, and his brother Nathan, fourteen, were followed as they walked from Thamesmead's multicultural Hawksmoor Youth Centre towards the bus stop where they were to catch the bus home to the nearby Abbey Wood estate. At the bus stop they were surrounded by a large group of older white boys, members of the NTOs who had been drinking at the

---

[21] Centre for Multicultural Education, *Sagaland: Youth Culture, Racism and Education, a Report on Research Carried out in Thamesmead* (London, Centre for Multicultural Education, Institute of Education, University of London, 1992), pp. 23–30.

Wildfowler pub. Amidst the threats and menaces, one boy, nineteen-year-old Mark Thornborrow, stabbed Rolan in the neck with a knife. Rolan ran a short distance, pursued by the gang shouting 'niggers', before collapsing and dying. Thornborrow was jailed for life; the other members of the group were charged with lesser charges, some of which were plea-bargained away.

There were many problems with the prosecution of the case and there was also considerable disagreement over the extent to which racism played a part. The murder came at a time both of increased BNP activity in the area and unprovoked racist violence by NTO gang members starting in the summer of 1990. In September 1990 a black youth was stabbed by gang members near the Wildfowler and another was attacked in twenty separate incidents. There were no black gangs in the Thamesmead area and few black adolescents in general. In January 1991 a meeting of concerned parents outlined the attacks and warned police of a likely tragedy. In just over a month Rolan was dead.[22]

The arrest of five adults and four juveniles on charges relating to the murder followed within days, to which unknown locals responded with a firebomb attack on the Hawksmoor Youth Centre. There had been one earlier firebombing of the club during the previous year in apparent protest at the employment of a black female youth worker. This time it closed the Centre down. On 25 February six black families were moved by the council for their safety away from Thamesmead to temporary accommodation. A Rolan Adams Family Campaign was mounted by local groups attempting to halt racist attacks in Thamesmead and to expose the significance of the BNP. Although there was no suggestion that at the time of the murder any of the gang were involved with the BNP, the adoption of BNP insignia by NTO members became apparent on the estate in the months that followed and in response to the protest marches.[23]

There was also considerable local resistance to Rolan's murder being classified as 'racist' – although ultimately the judge sentencing Thornborrow was in no doubt. Amongst local white residents a backlash sought to re-define the murder by pointing to gang territorialism. The pattern of previous and subsequent attacks on black families, and the use of racist language during the attack on Rolan and Nathan, however, convinced the principal campaign co-ordinator, Dev

[22] Thamesmead: A Clockwork Nightmare, Greenwich Action Committee against Racial Attacks (GACARA) Annual Report, 1990–1, pp.27–40.
[23] Appendix A: *Thamesmead Incident Chronology of Main Events*, Race Equality Committee Agenda, London Borough of Greenwich, Item no. A1, Title: *Racial Terror in Thamesmead*, 30 Apr. 1991.

Barrah, of the need to make the campaign more nationally visible and to pressure the police and other authorities to take a tougher line. Knowing mainly of the press-worthiness of Reverend Al Sharpton of New York – though very little of Sharpton's style of operation – Barrah invited the community leader over to lead a march from Hawksmoor Youth Centre to the BNP headquarters just a few miles away. The tactic worked. Sharpton was nearly banned by the Home Secretary Michael Howard, then permitted to come. The national press fell over themselves to cover the story, while in the event the marches led by Sharpton were praised by the police as models of good order. Newspaper and television coverage of the murder raised its profile and began to turn the tide in favour of its interpretation as racist.

Sharpton had himself been similarly involved in leading another march over the murder of a black teenager, Yusuf Hawkins, in Bensonhurst, New York City, which shared some of the features of the Rolan Adams murder. At sixteen Hawkins was stabbed, 'holding a Snickers bar in one hand' by a gang of white youths on a Bensonhurst street where he had gone to look at a used car. As Jim Sleeper describes:

[Yusuf] had always been a good boy, with no police record and a dream of attending Transit Tech High School that fall. More than that he was a racial innocent. Watching a videotape of *Mississippi Burning* at a neighbor's house just before he met his death, he said, according to his friends, that he couldn't believe people could be so cruel to one another for no reason other than the color of skin. Growing up in black East New York, he hadn't yet begun to comprehend the weight of white hatred pressing in upon his community and everyone in it.[24]

The march of black teenagers Sharpton led into white and hostile Bensonhurst – not really a march, they were: 'stumbling along, huddled together . . . under the storm of hatred breaking over them, hanging onto one another and to Sharpton, scared out of their wits'[25] – was a political ploy to get racism taken seriously by exposing the extent of white aggression. Sharpton's tactics had been criticised previously by a local black activist when, following another Bensonhurst march in 1988 after a brutal assault on two black youths, an ugly counter-demonstration had alarmed black residents. 'He never contacted anyone here or spoke to white leaders in the community', the woman had said, adding that it was she and her neighbours who would be left to pick up the pieces.[26] Sleeper argues that Sharpton's deliberately polarising tactics served to intensify racial barriers and to reproduce the racism it claimed to confront. His cavalier attitude to local knowledge, forms of organisation

[24] Sleeper, *The Closest of Strangers*, p. 193.
[25] Ibid.   [26] Ibid., pp.193–5.

and attempts to build bridges between the communities, Sleeper argues, enshrined a 'politics of resentment' that could easily distract people from confronting the more prevalent and enduring causes of misery in black communities.

The march which Sharpton led from Thamesemead to the BNP headquarters in Welling six miles away primarily included black parents, anti-racist organisations and other local people from the Greenwich area. Some 1,200 people marched the six miles in protest about the levels of racial violence in Thamesmead, the inadequacy of the police response to it and the continued activity of the BNP in the area. Two weeks later, attempting to catch the tide of local resentment, the BNP circulated a leaflet advertising a 'Protest March' on 25 May under the heading 'Fair Play for Thamesmead' and 'Defend Rights For Whites'. It read:

The white community in Thamesmead is under attack. Do-gooders are coming in, blaming the white community for being 'racist'. We have even seen a black American troublemaker leading a mob against the white community. But what about *our* old folk who are scared to go out in case they are mugged. What about *our* children – what future have they got?

Despite being clearly provocative the BNP march was permitted to go ahead with modifications to its proposed route – from Hawksmoor Youth Centre and past the site of Rolan Adams' murder. It was an angry confrontation between 120 BNP supporters and some 1,500 anti-racist demonstrators.[27]

The murder and the subsequent marches received considerable coverage in the national press. ITV's London Programme also covered the events in detail and there was other television and radio coverage. Much of this exposure portrayed Thamesmead as a uniformly white racist area where hopeless, semi-employed parents reared their hopeless semi-literate children on a diet of racism and brutality. Actually, although certainly predominantly white, Thamesmead is a very large estate with a variety of kinds of housing and a range of economic groups. The residents of the area deeply resented the portrayal of them as all racists and much of this media coverage undoubtedly contributed to the confusion and tension in the area. Within this defensiveness in the face of media representation, there was also a coherent discourse articulated around the concept of 'unfairness to whites' which became locally narrativised in the months after the murder, particularly emanating from

[27] London Borough of Greenwich Council Meeting Agenda 2 July 1991, briefing paper from the Race Equality Committee, 'Tackling the Continuing Terror', Item A.11, Appendices A,B,C.; GACARA Annual Report, 1990–1.

an epicentre in the blocks of apartments in the 'Moorings' area – the vicinity of the Hawksmoor Youth Centre. Here and in the surrounding streets were the homes of many of the NTOs, their older siblings who had started families of their own, uncles, aunts and others forming a close social network of relatives and neighbours. These narratives, designed to counter the established public view of Thamesmead inhabitants, were largely concerned with claiming not that whites were unjustly accused but that the same forms of behaviour were not classified as 'racist' when performed by blacks. There was also a high level of transmission of this kind of talk from parents to children. The following quotations from twelve-year-old children echo adult attitudes at that time:

When a white person stabs a black person – like that Rolan Adams – it's all in the papers and on telly. But if a black person stabs a white you don't hear nothin' about it, the papers don't say a thing.

There was this white person who's with the NTOs . . . and he was waiting at the train station and he got stabbed. He wasn't doing anything. He was harmless. He was just standing up waiting for a train and these three black boys just came along and went stab, stab, stab all over his body and he didn't do anything to them. So I reckon the black people do it to whites.

The relationship of the younger adolescents and children to the NTOs was particularly telling. The playmates of younger siblings of NTO members and the brothers and sisters of girls who were girl-friends of NTOs became counted as part of the NTO 'family'. These fictive relatives regarded themselves as protected by the NTO and the NTO saw themselves as protectors – especially in potential conflicts with black youngsters. Hence the widely reported remark by NTO member Mark Thornborrow at the time of his arrest for Rolan Adams' murder – 'it's because they've troubled the little ones'.[28] This talk of protecting young children also became part of the NTO's self-legitimating narrative.[29]

In addition to the groundswell of defensive talk, the marches – by both anti-racist protesters and BNP supporters – were widely characterised in Thamesmead's white population as involving non-locals. There was much talk about the noise, mess and general disturbance to the neighbourhood that the marches caused. There was little or no distinction made between those protesting Rolan's murder and the BNP, and there was considerable local resentment of the media.

[28] *Guardian*, 9 Oct. 1991.
[29] Centre for Multicultural Education, *Sagaland*, pp. 26–7.

In Thamesmead denials of the relevance of racism continued. Accounts of racial assault in the borough – Greenwich Action Committee against Racial Attacks (GACARA) reported 119 racist attacks for the nine-month period August 1990 to May 1991[30] – were commonly dismissed as representing a smoke-screen for the putatively much greater number of attacks by blacks on whites; the police were accused of being negligent from fear of being called racist; racist verbal abuse, attacks on property were often regarded as adolescent pranks – though there were 23 cases of arson or attempted arson and 268 cases of racist criminal damage and graffiti in the borough[31] – and in one case a mob of over thirty youths laid siege to the house of one Thamesmead black family with bricks and other missiles for several hours.[32] The structure of relationships between the police and concerned community groups and between the council's anti-racist strategy and the white population's willingness to hear about racism became the frame on which further dramatic events were to unfold over the following few years.

All of these local relationships were in flux throughout the 1990s. This was partly influenced by the dominant voices within the ranks of the anti-racist protest and the ways in which local or national dimensions were foregrounded – whether it was effective local justice that was sought, or whether justice in the larger arena was at stake. In the case of the Rolan Adams murder, the name given to the lead campaigning group – the Rolan Adams Family Campaign – reflected both its local nature and the desire of its organisers to stay close to the concerns and perceptions of victims and their families. Furthermore, while highlighting the levels of racial assault in Thamesmead, it pointed the finger at the BNP headquarters in explaining the rise in these since the late 1980s. This reflected a desire to avoid a blanket accusation of racism directed at the white community and a genuine, if questionable, belief in the wider impact of the local presence of the BNP. What local protest organisers sought to avoid, however, the media provided in abundance. Through lurid generalisations about Thamesmead and its inhabitants, white locals came to feel that they were now widely regarded as a deeply racist community. The resentment of these portrayals in the press and on television was almost palpable. Those who drew attention to Thamesmead in the first place – not those responsible for Rolan's murder but the groups protesting it – were widely blamed, alongside the BNP with its turbulent march.

[30] GACARA Annual Report, 1990–1.
[31] Ibid.
[32] Author's interview with the victim family, 1991.

The second murder – Rohit Duggal

Less than a year after Rolan Adams' murder a second racist murder occurred, this time in Eltham, in the centre of the borough some three miles from Thamesmead. Again it featured a group of white youths and a knife attack, this time on a lone Indian boy of 16 outside a kebab house on a well-used parade of shops. Rohit Duggal died from a knife wound to the heart. Again only one member of the group of white adolescents was charged and found guilty of the murder.

The murder took place in June 1992 in the context of continuing high reported levels of racial harassment. The boy convicted was also found to be carrying leaflets produced by the BNP. It was never suggested that he was a BNP member but agitation against the continued presence of the BNP headquarters in Bexley was increased by local anti-racist campaigners. Again there was an intensely argued dispute over the designation of the assault as 'racist'. Black community and anti-racist groups now saw as even more urgent the need for strong action by the police and local councils (Greenwich and Bexley) to combat racism. The local white community, particularly on the ageing Page estate where Rohit's assailants lived, like their Thamesmead neighbours, came to resent the accusation of racism. An anti-knife campaign was initiated by the convicted boy's mother who felt that the problem of teenage conflict was turned into tragedy by the carrying of knives. Her campaign for parents and authorities to clamp down on knife possession was taken up by one local newspaper. Some anti-racist groups saw the campaign as a defensive distraction from the central issue of racism.

As the arguments about the nature of the murder intensified, the wider anti-racist movement began to take an interest in Greenwich, in the Rohit Duggal case and in the local presence of the BNP. Going over the head of the local campaigners, the newly emergent national campaigning group Anti-Racist Alliance (ARA) attempted to control the direction of the campaign. The Duggal family complained of the insensitivity of ARA and of its seeking to control all interviews with the media, and to exclude the local organisers. Such struggles between the ARA and the family supporters only muddied the anti-racist protest and its focus.

The third murder – Stephen Lawrence

If racist violence in Greenwich had come to national prominence by the end of 1992 it was but a shadow of what was to come. On 22 April 1993 a third racist murder was to occur in the borough that, for the next decade and beyond, would have far-reaching national repercussions. The murder of Stephen Lawrence and the series of police errors that resulted in his assailants escaping justice led to a major Home Office inquiry into the handling of the murder investigation and into racism in the criminal justice system more widely. The government-appointed inquiry team, reporting finally in 1999, not only found racism to be endemic within the Metropolitan Police Force, but raised the issue of institutional racism in a way that was to impact on *all* public bodies.[33] A wide-ranging review of police practice was conducted and innumerable reforms set in motion. However, while the national significance of the Stephen Lawrence murder was profound, it also inevitably came to impact on social relations and practices in Greenwich, both for the black communities who now felt acutely endangered but not adequately protected, and for the whites, many of whom were deeply shocked by what had occurred while others paradoxically had their resentments and hostilities re-kindled.

The circumstances of the Lawrence murder were similar in form to the previous racist murders in Greenwich. A gang of five or six white youths attacked two black teenagers who were changing buses at the route intersection when they were on their way home late one night. One of the assailants had called out 'What, nigger' as the group ran across the road towards the two boys. One of the boys, Duwayne Brookes, was already some distance from the gang. The other, Stephen Lawrence, was stabbed in the throat with a very long-bladed knife. The gang ran off. No evidence has ever been produced to suggest this was anything other than an unprovoked racially motivated attack.

What followed – the poor treatment of chief witness Duwayne Brookes by the investigating officer, the police neglect to follow up important lines of inquiry, submit potentially significant items to forensic testing, interview certain witnesses and so on – resulted in the Crown Prosecution Service deciding in July 1993 to discontinue the prosecution on the grounds of insufficient evidence. In June 1994 a new investigating team was appointed. The police now worked more closely with Stephen Lawrence's parents. Electronic surveillance devices were partially successfully employed to gain further evidence against the accused. However, in the absence of the case being supported by the Crown Prosecution Service, Neville and Doreen Lawrence brought a private prosecution of the five youths originally arrested. Three of these youths were sent for trial at the Old Bailey in April 1996. This time,

---

[33] This took effect through the Race Relations Amendment Act 2001 developed in the wake of the Stephen Lawrence inquiry.

however, important identification evidence by Duwayne Brookes was disallowed by the judge; the case consequently collapsed, the new evidence was never put before a jury, and the accused were acquitted.

Beyond the world of the criminal justice system, the Lawrence murder was also gaining significantly in *political* importance. This dimension had been displayed in the visit Nelson Mandela made to the Lawrence family in Greenwich during 1996 when Mandela was outspoken in condemning racism and racial violence in the borough. This wider dimension was also apparent in the importance placed on the Lawrence murder by the newly elected Labour government, in particular by Jack Straw the Home Secretary, who commissioned the Macpherson inquiry. The national press also took an unprecedented interest. Across the political spectrum the mishandling of the case and its implications for race relations were explored in a torrent of news-copy and commentary. The inquiry report was pronounced by Straw to be a 'watershed' for race in the UK, a sentiment repeated by Prime Minister Tony Blair on the day of its publication. Its findings were taken up into important new legislation – the Race Relations Amendment Act, 2001, and it ushered in a major review of policing practice and of the system more widely, paying particular attention to institutional racism in all public bodies.

The interplay between local and national issues evident throughout this period reflects well the transformation of the national inheritance of race politics since the late 1960s – the echo of the early postures of new left and new right, their transcendence in New Labour's initiation of the Macpherson inquiry and its incorporation of anti-racism within the less contentious 'social inclusion' framework. These processes are worthy of further comment.

New anti-racism

As racism in Greenwich became a national issue so elements of a local backlash became sensitive to the rehabilitation of anti-racism. This rehabilitation in the early New Labour period took two forms. One was an institutional form – the review of the criminal justice system and its later extrapolation in the Race Relations Amendment Act. The other was a popular, press-led condemnation of racist violence. The latter was less contentious than the first but both were class-inflected. They displayed a patina of middle-class suspicions about a working-class predisposition towards racism said to be evident in the routinely racist 'canteen culture' of the metropolitan police, and in the violence of working-class adolescent 'racist thugs'.

The release of a police surveillance video which showed several of the gang who had been accused of the Lawrence murder indulging in fantasies of racist violence outraged many people. A right-wing press usually silent on the issue of racism, became united in its condemnation of the accused, with one newspaper, itself regarded by some as frequently displaying racist attitudes in its reporting and editorials, going so far as to lead with the headline: '*Murderers* The Mail accuses these men of killing. If we are wrong, let them sue us', above photographs of the five accused. It was followed the next day with another front page headline reading: 'Lawrence Killers: The Video of Hate'.[34] The issue contained a series of stills from the surveillance video in which one of the group demonstrates how to stab someone with a long-bladed knife, using exactly the motion of the blow that killed Stephen Lawrence.

These kinds of journalistic expressions of hostility to 'racist thugs' evident across the political spectrum dovetailed well with *The Sunday Times'* return to the issue of the 'British underclass' – a concern the paper had developed over time with the help of academic Charles Murray. Indeed the lurid reporting of racism on predominantly white working-class housing estates became a favourite occupation of journalists in search of saleable copy in the late 1990s, and took place against a general demonisation of estate inhabitants and the culture of social decay. The message was that in looking for racism in the UK there was no need to look further.[35]

The new anti-racism was not of the 1980s Thatcher era variety. It was not 'anti-racism' in that sense. Its institutional forms were expected to influence national governance at all levels. As such it was apiece with New Labour's broader approach to social reform. It was also completely in keeping with the increasing hegemony of multicultural discourse in liberal democracies internationally. Furthermore the popular, press-led attack on racism was highly selective in its concerns. The press was not much driven by the desire to purge institutional racism but far more by a concern specifically with racist violence – probably racism's most blatantly unacceptable manifestation. The surge in public concern over racism should, to some degree, be seen in the light of other crime-related public outcries based on prominent individual cases.

The broader political intention behind New Labour's initiation of the Macpherson inquiry and the public revulsion against racist violence

[34] *Daily Mail*, 14 and 15 Feb. 1997.
[35] Brian Reade, 'Into Hell. On the day of the Lawrence report, Brian Reade visits the estate where Stephen's killers grew up . . . and finds racism seeping from every pore', *Daily Mirror*, 24 Feb. 1999, pp. 1, 11, 12, 13.

became synchronised in the hearings of the inquiry. These were deliberately made open to the public, conducted in the heart of south London and were widely covered by the press and broadcasting companies. They also did not lack drama, which included the inquiry team's Richard Stone pressing Chief Commissioner for Police, Sir Paul Condon, to agree that the police force as a whole was institutionally racist. 'Just say "yes"' pressed Stone. Sir Paul did not.

There was also no lack of spectacle when those originally arrested for the murder were forced to give evidence to the inquiry. Although, on the central Greenwich estates, the gang was widely hated and feared – its members were well known for a violence which extended beyond racially motivated attacks – there was, in some white adolescent circles, an element of local heroisation. This dimension became the beneficiary of the very public, even at times glitzy, nature of the inquiry. To a hostile crowd of demonstrators – including a phalanx of Nation of Islam be-suited and bow-tied – and a packed public gallery, the defendants delivered their predictably sullen and monosyllabic testimony through a Versace-style imagery of cool dark glasses and well-cut suits, emphatic-ally refusing to correspond to the popular image of the white-trash underclass portrayed in the press. Even in the performance of *their* role this political-legal spectacle was sustained as national drama.

In these ways numerous factors bore down on the particularities of Greenwich, just as its local contours – the nature of its community politics and leadership, and the historical character of its social relations – bore upwards, affecting the national race agenda. At that local level the impact of the Stephen Lawrence murder was an endlessly unfolding one, generating a constant flood of narrative and counter-narrative. Just as debates about what was and was not to be treated as 'racist' crime were originally part of a local struggle for racial justice – GACARA succeeded in getting nearly £1,000,000 in compensation from the local police for actions relating to police assaults on black people – so narrativised counter-claims became a fundamental aspect of the local backlash to the new national consensus over racism. At the same time there were also early rumblings of a nationally articulated backlash to Macpherson, both within the right-wing press – the *Daily Telegraph* was amongst the first to puncture the illusion of total consensus[36] – and within the rank and file of the metropolitan police itself.[37]

---

[36] See Polly Toynbee, 'The White Backlash: Macpherson is now a rallying cry for a vision of nation and race that is vile', *Guardian*, 3 Mar. 1999, p. 20.

[37] J. A. Hadley, 'Police Reform and Cultural Legitimacy: The Auratic Status of Nation-hood among Finnish and English Recruits in 2002' (Ph.D. thesis, Goldsmiths College, University of London, 2004).

Counter-narrative emerged in Greenwich as the cultural form that pre-eminently expressed resentments and grievances of whites that were, for the most part, not expressed in other forms. Electoral process, either by design of the system or by fatalistic choice, was not the arena in which these attitudes became voiced. Racism *per se* was something that was not *politically* endorsed. Many of the complaints about local authority emphasis on minority issues did not come from people who would ever have voted for racist political parties. Indeed, the backlash to equalities policies was articulated far more widely than was apparent from both electoral evidence and racial harassment figures. It was also found extensively amongst people who would never have condoned racism and for whom the ideas of the BNP were repugnant. This is why it was a shock for the people of Greenwich – and especially traditionally 'respectable' Eltham – to find themselves implicated in racist murders as social accessories.

Here was a divide that was not recognised by the press: a core of violent racist adolescents and their adult mentors, plus a small supporting cast of racial bigots, were located within a wider pool of people who were at odds with the local political order in which, to them, minority concerns were given precedence. The fact that there was an overlap in what this wider circle expressed about equalities policies and what the core of racists believed did not mean that they were both the same. This line between unambiguous racism and the rejection of equalities discourse constitutes significant uncharted territory in politics at the start of the twenty-first century.

4 Narrative, counter-narrative and the boundaries of legitimate discourse

Each of the Greenwich murder cases described in the previous chapter was reported in the media, two of them at great length. They were also discussed in the communities where they occurred. On the Thames-mead estate talk about the Rolan Adams murder circulated widely. In the Moorings ward, where the murder occurred, it was particularly intense. Stories about the firebombings, gangs and racial conflict, the marches and the protagonists in the murder were shared between generations within families, between adolescent peers and among mothers in the school playground. Amongst these stories of extraordinary events, the less dramatic issues over what racism was and was not, who was winning in the struggle to be heard and who were the 'real' disadvantaged also became voiced and relayed.[1]

Located some distance from the main shopping areas of the borough and cut off on the north side by the river Thames, Thamesmead was like an island. In this 85 per cent white area there were significant numbers of *young* white families, many related, so that although the community lacked the history of some communities in the borough, there was considerable extension through its dense social networks. In Eltham to the west, the estates abutting the scene of the Rohit Duggal and Stephen Lawrence's murders were similarly secluded worlds, although they had greater generational depth, some families going back to the 1920s when the estates were first occupied. These mainly local authority-owned estates were situated very near to larger, privately owned middle-class homes and, as a one-time destination for 'white flight' from multi-racial inner city areas like Deptford and New Cross, there were clear class distinctions according to which parts of the area people lived in. The most prosperous oriented towards the west and the south towards 'New Eltham' and, beyond the borough line, to the village charm of Chistlehurst with its ivy-clad cottages. From this perspective Eltham was seen as a similar, respectable, desirable area. It had a repertory

---

[1] Centre for Multicultural Education, *Sagaland* GACARA Annual Report, 1991–2.

theatre, the Bob Hope Theatre – the comedian was born in Eltham. Real estate in the area offered good investments.

In this vividly two-class town, the narratives concerning the racist murders had two distinct motors. One of these, with its social base in the largely working-class council estates, was concerned with legitimations and details relating to the gangs and individuals accused of being involved in the murders. It was incorporated into the talk of 'unfairness to whites' in which the press and police were seen as a primary cause. Related criticisms of the local council provided a parallel text in which over-attention to the concerns of black tenants and ignoring white grievances were themes with much currency. The other motor, with its roots in Etham's middle-class image and local property values, was also directed at the Labour-controlled local council, its anti-racist policies and its insistent multiculturalism, which many people claimed 'played into the hands of' the BNP and incited demonstrations that attracted unwanted attention. This division of labour created a vigorous local economy of narrativisation where the denial of the problem of racist violence was prominent and Eltham's well-known status as white and symbolically middle class was emphatically bought into by both parties.

Counter-narratives

The race-related oral narrative materials collected in Greenwich in the early to mid-1990s[2] were overwhelmingly, but not exclusively, counter-narratives – i.e. having the appearance of being proffered in response to a previous story or stories, and of anticipating further narrative moves by others. Not all narratives that seek to denigrate or complain about another group constitute counter-narrative. One story, for example, took up an ancient theme:

I had a mate who'd been waiting on the housing list – getting a house – for three years, and like a black family 'as come over, they were here for two weeks and they got a flat straight away.

While this story is concerned to illustrate 'unfairness to whites' it is not a counter-narrative. Similarly, the following, collected from an eleven-year-old girl, is clearly a classic racial bogeyman story:

[2] Narratives occurred in interviews and observational work conducted in community centres, schools, youth clubs, street and home settings. Over 200 hours of recorded data plus field notes were gathered over a five-year period for a variety of purposes and in relation to the research projects listed on p. 2. Publications based on this work and in part dealing with narrative include: Centre for Multicultural Education, *Sagaland*; R. Hewitt, *Routes of Racism: The Social Basis of Racist Action* (Stoke-on-Trent, Trentham Books, 1996).

I don't think Thamesmead's a nice place to live. A lot of people get murdered and raped around here. I know that white people kidnap little girls and rape them, but if you think about it, it's mostly blacks. Did you hear about that black man dressing up as an old woman? He kept grabbing little girls and taking them and killing them.

There are also stories about black muggings, about Asians 'throwing dirty baby's nappies out of the window' or about the origins of Aids as stemming from an act of bestiality by a black person who then spread the virus to whites – indeed a wide range of anti-black and Asian narrative.

By contrast a characteristic of oral *counter*-narratives is their being pitched against a putatively more powerful and influential pre-existing narrative or dominant discourse. The counter-narrative strives to tell a story that will capture succinctly a counter-vailing view. They have a very ambiguous relationship to material truth because their function is often to convey some known truth which their content merely exemplifies. The next example is typical of a certain kind of counter-narrative circulating amongst white adolescents following the Stephen Lawrence murder:

About a year ago there was a kid in our school and he was walking home, and he passed [another] school and loads of these black kids come up behind him with a big massive pole. Hit him over the head. Gave 'im about fifty stitches all round here, down to his neck.

Sometimes the already known truth is stated explicitly within the story, usually at the end:

When 'em Nigerians stabbed that kid on Plumstead Common all you heard about it was *once* on the news. Hardly anyone knew, but when Stephen Lawrence got killed, everyone knew.

There were many examples of stories of this kind, although not all were explicitly linked to the Lawrence case as is this one. They were simply recounted without the implication needing to be spelled out. Their force as counter-narrative was implicit and contextually understood.

A second feature of the counter-narratives collected is that they were aimed at demonstrating the 'misuse' of power or position by a public body or prominent agency. They were complaints about those with the most power or influence locally. This included the council, the police and the press. It also included the schools who were attempting to deal with the implications of the rising levels of racism amongst young people. Thus amongst school age youth there were numerous stories about the unfair practices within schools said to favour black school students. One young person who had recently left school recounted:

The teachers thought more of the blacks than they did of the whites. One day I had me feet on the table. Teacher told me to take 'em off. But a black kid had 'em on the table, and I went, 'Can you tell him to take his off', and he said 'No, he's alright.' So I just got up and walked out. I don't think that's right at all.

A young girl reported from the no-man's-land of interpretation:

My brother was in school and he hit one of 'em badly and got suspended. Then the other one stabbed him – like he got cut behind the ear and [the school] didn't do anything, and then my brother beat him up – went back and bashed him up, got his mates on him. Then [the school] said it was a racist attack, but he only done it 'cos he slashed his ear.

While another girl recounted:

In the first year I had a fight with a Turkish girl. She said to me first, 'You white ice-cream head' and I said, 'Shut up you Turkish delight.' I got done for racism, she didn't. My mum did a big complaint about it 'cos she said that's not fair, but the school believed [that I was racist] because I said that. That's the one thing I disagree with, that they're allowed to say 'you white this or white that', and we can't say anything back.

These explanatory codas – 'I disagree with that', etc. – that seek to make sure the listener has got the point, were common.

As was discussed in Chapter 3, the issue of what could and could not be classified as racist had a long history in Greenwich. It was a feature of the local debates following the murder of Rohit Duggal and, before that, the murder of Rolan Adams. It had initially been fought out between GACARA (the local racial incident monitoring group) and the police, and increasingly the dividing line between its local significance and its wider national significance became blurred. This ideological struggle over the definition of racism also became the motive of frequent narrativisation. There was a widespread unwillingness to acknowledge the seriousness of racist incidents which expressed itself through several strategies. One was to assert that there were equal numbers of incidents in which whites and blacks were victims and aggressors but that black people 'made more of it' – exaggerated or emphasised those which happened to them more than white people did. The protest marches that were organised following both the Rohit Duggal and Stephen Lawrence murders were cited as examples of black people making more of inter-racial murders than did white people – manipulating the media and making the headlines. A second strategy related to this was to deny that a particular incident – including each of the murders – was *racial* in nature at all. Counter-narratives suggested that *really* the murder of Rolan Adams was drugs-related and that Rolan had been dealing. Similarly, local slurs against Stephen Lawrence had him portrayed as a playground bully and as more generally 'not the angel he was made out to be'.

This kind of story, as well as 'blaming the victim', was an elaboration of the claim that the police treat any attack by a white on a black person as 'racial' when it is simply the kind of incident 'that might happen between any two people', even of the same colour. On the other hand, it was asserted, attacks by blacks on whites were ignored. The following two stories exemplify this kind of counter-narrative circulating amongst teenagers and school children:

My dad saw a black man stab a white man. The police questioned the man who said, 'You've got something against my race and my colour', so they let him go [white girl aged 12].

I was down in Greenwich, right and we see this kid all stabbed up. We went up to this kid and he said – I'll use the exact what he said – 'Some niggers beat me up', right. And they stabbed him in the head and all that, so we took him over to the police, right . . . and they said, 'Oh we don't need you no more', and they took him away. It weren't in the newspaper or nuffing, but if it was, like, a black man getting killed it would be in the newspapers straight away. That's what I don't agree wiv [white boy aged 17].

The police, on the other hand, denied the truth of these stories. In interview, an officer from a Racial Incident Unit reported:

The Home Office definition is actually very, very wide. If either the victim or the officer investigating or any third party feel that it's been a racial crime or incident then it has to be investigated as such. We have had a number of white people come forward and make reports, allegations of incidents that they consider to be racially motivated and they've been investigated in exactly the same way. In fairness, a vast proportion of our work involves ethnic minorities being the victims, so these kinds of allegations really are in a minority, but, yes, it happens.[3]

The police, however, were not regarded as impartial in this issue – particularly where sentencing and plea-bargaining practices came into the equation. The question of racism as a motive for violence became particularly important to some white young men because of the additional sentencing magistrates and judges could impose where racism was established as a contributing factor. Here it intersects with some of the more 'innocent' discourses of 'unfairness to whites'. Some young white men complained that *any* fight with a black person that ended in injury could be treated falsely by the police as 'racist' to increase the penalty.

---

[3] Roger Hewitt, *Routes of Racism: The Manual: A Handbook for Youth Workers and Other Professionals Working with Young People, to Accompany the Video Routes of Racism* (London, Central Race Equality Unit and Greenwich Education Service, Greenwich Council, 1997), pp. 21–2, abridged.

This concern amongst young whites who were frequently in trouble with the police may have affected accounts of an attack on a sixty-five-year-old black man by a group of white youths. The versions of this event circulating in the area threaded a careful course through the local narrative order, for the road in which the attack took place was the same as that in which both Rohit Duggal and Steven Lawrence were murdered. Much remedial work was needed if this, too, was not to be seen as a racist incident. How the accused constructed their version for the purposes of the trial *may* have had an impact on local belief and narrative concerning this case. It is only possible to speculate about whatever truth lay behind the 'official' narrative produced in their defence. That the account of motivation served very clear local needs is, however, unmistakable. Amongst the numerous accounts, a version by a youth worker is particularly interesting for its absorption of the perspective of the counter-narrators:

I remember one discussion I earwigged with young people – no, I think it was part of some youth work – and it was, em, some young people went out, got a bit drunk, they had knives and so on and one of their friends got bashed by somebody, and eh he was slapped in the face, punched in the eye, that type of thing. Afterwards he says 'anyone that turns that corner, I'm gonna do 'em. I don't care, I've just been bashed, I'll do anyone who turns the corner.' So happened that it was a sixty-year-old black man who turned the corner. They went, he started to assault this guy, obviously using appropriate language to this person. It was not necessarily a, a . . . a racist attack, it was an attack of someone . . . just . . . it was . . . The black man pulled out a knife to defend himself and the friends joined in. After that they beat the guy, you know, threw the bin on him and that type of thing, and the guy went down and it was being treated as a racist . . . Em, that was an, an example of how things can go when it's not necessarily seen to be, . . . it's not necessarily, is, *in essence it is not a racist attack, it's just an attack* . . . but with the trimmings.

Perhaps this 'message' had been emphasised in the overheard version because the youth worker (who was black) was visible to the speakers. But it was clear, at least, that of all the things that might have been said about the incident, the racial/ethnic arbitrariness of the assault was chosen as the 'moral of the story'.

We may draw a little closer to the process of social narrative construction as we get closer to the events 'themselves' – that is in the earliest stage in the process of narrativisation. An interview with one of the assailants contained the following, more detailed account:

INFORMANT: We went to some park here and had a fight with these kids and like my mates – well, *he* ain't my mate – were all here. Some kid – he was with us, Dave, – he got beat up in the fight. He never got beat up but he come off worse, you know what I mean. We walked down the road and he was going, 'Watch, watch. Next person I see I'm going to beat up', and all. I'm thinking, like, he's like just, like, [thinking he was] well hard and all that you know what I mean, big stud, walkin' down the fuckin' [road]. . . Then, like, we see this geezer and he just started like getting lairy [menacing] to the geezer and he pulled out a knife and that was it, you know what I mean.

INTERVIEWER: You mean he pulled out a knife?

INFORMANT: Yeah.

INTERVIEWER: The geezer? How old was he then? . . . About thirty or something?

INFORMANT: Oh forty, fifty . . . He had a knife . . .

INTERVIEWER: So you lot steamed in?

INFORMANT: No, er, all them jumped in and like I went in like. They're all sixteen, seventeen, but they're well small like, for their age . . . So I was like just watching them really you know what I mean, I weren't . . . I never got involved in the fight at all . . . I was keeping an eye on them making sure they never got hurt and then like Dave took out a middle of a dustbin – like the metal casing thing – hit the geezer over the head. So I was, like, 'No', 'cos I felt a bit sorry for him, you know what I mean. I've got my back to him, pushing Dave away, saying 'No leave him alone, leave him alone', and then he gets up behind me and stabs me in the arm, you know what I mean? After that I was like, 'I don't give a fuck, kill him. I don't care' [I] run across the road, like, 'Go on, kill him', you know what I mean? Then like the Old Bill come . . . We all run off like.

INTERVIEWER: Nobody was trying to mug him? It was just an exchange of words and he pulled a knife?

INFORMANT: Yeah. Well it weren't . . . like I . . . like I felt sorry for him really 'cos . . . he was walking down the street, pretty old, y'know, well . . . not *well* old but he's pretty old. Someone walked up to him and the first thing he says is, 'I'm going to kick your face in', and all that. And he's like, 'what? what?' And there was five of us, so like I thought and that's why he probably pulled the knife, you know what I mean.

INTERVIEWER: Because somebody actually said 'I'm going to kick your face in'?

INFORMANT: Yeah. That's the first thing he said to him, you know what I mean, they were going to beat him and all that.

INTERVIEWER: Do you think he was frightened because there were two murders in exactly that area?

INFORMANT: Yeah, in that same road.

INTERVIEWER: He probably thought this is another racist attack.

INFORMANT: Yeah probably, yeah.

INTERVIEWER: Would those blokes have said those things to him if he hadn't been black?

INFORMANT Yeah.

INTERVIEWER: Yes?

INFORMANT: 'Cos when we were walking down, er, Dave was saying – because we had a fight up the pub and he had like a big cut on his eye, he already had a cut on his hand but he's like sort of leaked, left lip split back open, so

like there's blood coming from his head and his hand, he's going like –
'What's next? Next person we see.' Y'know what I mean? Could have been
black, white, could have been anyone, he would 'av still, like, you know
what I mean?

For this informant one of the most important features of his account was
personal: he was innocent; the others were younger and a bit wild. (He
was twenty.) He 'felt sorry for the man' and tried to protect him, till he
himself got stabbed by the old man. Then from that moment he could
not care less and said, 'kill him'.

As far as the randomisation of the victim goes, the part of the story in
which the attackers words are quoted – 'Next person I see I'm going to
beat up' – actually emphasises the juvenile bravado of this. It is not at
this point linked to the issue of race. That does not happen until the
exchange beginning with the question: 'Do you think he was
frightened?' And here what he says as one of the perpetrators seems
to support the version circulating in the community that the victim *could*
have been of any colour. The fact is, however, that this gang were all
from the same area where the emergent counter-narratives concerning
the Steven Lawrence murder and other similar narratives were
generated. So well does their story fit into the corpus of 'denial'
material that the influence of that corpus on the formulation of the
defence narrative cannot be ruled out. If the assault was deemed by the
court *not* to be a racist attack, it could attract no additional penalty. Such
a consideration might lend particular inventiveness to any subject's
powers of recall, particularly about an event that occurred in the same
street as two recent notorious racist murders. Whether the local
narrative corpus aided the production of the defendants' accounts or
not it is clear that the prevailing moral circumstances through which
racist violence was locally perceived were enacted in narrative forms and
were able to be part of the retrospective construction of the events, and
possibly even of their contemporaneous construal.

It is possible to see, through these accounts, how some events may
occur already saturated in narrative. In cases such as this any *gap*
between 'actual events' and their being taken up into narrative form may
be impossible to establish. The narrative process is part of the event in
being part of the contemporaneous perception and/or construction of
the event – as when someone is attacked in revenge. Social action and
the local narrative order, which lay so closely together in this instance,
may well be merged far more often than can usually be demonstrated.
Its possibility has certainly been frequently asserted by social theorists,
though usually from a position of epistemological principle.

'Three black boys at the scene of Stephen Lawrence's murder'

The following narrative, collected in the heart of Eltham, typifies many of the social uses of narrative. Community-located narratives frequently achieve a special significance in wearing their 'community' on their arm. Like racist jokes, race-related stories, by their repetition, demonstrate their previous acceptance as relevant to the lives of those they circulate among. Though relatively freshly minted, this narrative is already hung-about with its social warrants. It occurred within a discussion between three teenage girls and the author. Prior to this stretch of talk, two of the girls had been describing their distress at the murder of Stephen Lawrence exactly a year before. A third girl, reacting to what had gone before, then led into the following narrative, which falls into two parts. The first part describes a conversation the speaker had had with her mother; the second recounts how her mother's friend witnessed three black boys approaching Stephen on the night of his murder. Interactively – in the context of the unfolding conversation – it was unambiguously a counter-narrative.[4] It also drew on two or three pre-existing narratives, one of which – the evidence of her mother's friend – strove to contradict the evidence that a gang of *white* boys had killed Steven.

My mum showed me something in the paper the other day and it was, I think, three Indian boys stabbed a white boy to death and my mum said like 'Was there any mention of racism there?' It was just like an attack, no reason for an attack, but I mean there weren't really no question about it and sometimes there is a bit of like . . . you know what I mean . . . not looking into it, *or* looking into it too much because my friend's mum, when Stephen Lawrence was murdered, she said that er . . . straight away it was er . . . because her husband his mate works in the place, and they said straight away they was looking into it as a racist attack. And then like . . . mum's cousin – I don't know, a good friend of my mum's – she was down there that day and she saw a group of three boys. She saw them, three black boys going up to him. She said three times she had to phone the police and bring it to their attention before they even . . . before they actually sent someone round to . . . She said . . . they kept taking her number and they kept saying they'd get back in contact but she said they didn't seem to be interested. She said they wanted to . . . it was as if they wanted . . . they wanted it to be a racist attack . . . You know what I mean? It's just like . . . she says she don't really know what

---

[4] It is this interactive sense of 'counter-narrative' that first gave it its name in the methodology known as Conversational Analysis. See David Silverman, *Harvey Sacks, Social Science and Conversation Analysis* (Cambridge, Polity Press, 1998); Gail Jefferson, 'Sequential Aspects of Storytelling in Conversation', in J. Schinkein (ed.), *Studies in the Organisation of Conversational Interaction* (New York, Academic Press, 1979), pp. 219–48.

was going on, whether they would have got back to her or not she don't know, but she kept phoning and they sent someone round.

This text is interesting for a number of reasons. The first part reports an interaction between a mother and a daughter in which the mother shares her understanding of the *significance* of the event reported on in the local newspaper. She moves from the newspaper article she is reading directly to what she finds most relevant: the murder of the white boy was not reported as a 'racist' murder. The *content* of the newspaper account is side-stepped. Instead its significance within the local community's interpretative framework is focussed on and it becomes symbolic of a wider 'truth'. This she conveys as a rhetorical question which the daughter cites in direct speech: 'Was there any mention of racism there?' The daughter then explicates this with the comment that there was no apparent motive for the Asian boys' attack. By adding 'but I mean there weren't really no question about it', the girl seems to be asserting that it *could* have been a 'racially motivated' attack on the white victim. She then moves to broaden the discussion with the generalisation that the police are differentially inclined to categorise events as racial: 'And sometimes there's a bit of not looking into it' – i.e. when there is an assault by a black person on a white – 'or looking into it too much' – i.e. when there is an assault by a white on a black. Then comes the putatively hard evidence confirming the truth of this last point: someone who works in the police station dealing with the Stephen Lawrence murder came to learn that immediately after the murder occurred the police said that they were looking into it as a racial attack.

In the above passage the two murders are juxtaposed and the institutional – press and police – responses are analysed through the lens of an intimate domestic moment set within a broader community of talkers. This last aspect – the implicit white community context of the story – displays how speakers invoke and see themselves as embedded in a community of like-minded people whose presence ratifies the truth of what the narrative asserts. This narrative is *thick with the voices of the community through which it is said to have passed.* At this midway point we already find the following people present:

speaker—speaker's friend—speaker's friend's mother—speaker's friend's mother's husband—speaker's friend's mother's husband's mate—'they'(1) (particular policeman/men) who reported on how 'they'(2) (the police as an institution) were treating the murder of Stephen Lawrence.

The issue of this 'communicative community' is of special significance both as the actual social basis for the relay of ideas, opinions, narratives, gossip, jokes, etc. – all of which can contain race-relevant material – and as an imagined warrant of densely social knowledge behind any individual utterance.[5] It is the final court of appeal and legitimator of social opinion and action and it is often invoked within passages of narrative where some evaluation of the story is being offered as commentary by the teller.[6]

In the second part, with the introduction of the apparent eye-witness report of her mother's friend, the narrative lifts to a quite different level. This evidence, were it to be true, would be serious stuff. The claim being made in this part of the story is that a female witness, close friend or cousin of the narrator's mother, saw three black male adolescents going up to Stephen at the time and place of his murder. Set against the testimony of the other eye-witness accounts, this constitutes an extraordinary claim. Its implication is that Stephen's murder was not committed by the five or six white assailants reported by the other eye-witnesses. The police records of information received from the public between 22 April and 7 May 1993 – the 'calendar list' – show nothing that resembles this witness's report.[7] Neither does any other record of such a witness exist. This section of the text re-iterates the argument made in the first part, that the police wilfully sought to racialise the Lawrence murder. It is also recognisable as part of the local corpus of narratives which generally deny the truths of accounts of white on black racial assaults and murders and is suggestive of the kinds of racialised 'legal hoaxes' discussed by Katheryn K. Russell in her *The Color of Crime*[8] where, from a variety of motives – often financial – whites accuse blacks, and less frequently blacks accuse whites, of criminal offences. (The most famous of the latter being the Tawana Brawley case.) It is thus a counter-narrative serving two apparent purposes: (1) to shift the blame from the white murder suspects; (2) to reassert the argument made in the first part that the police deliberately sought to racialise the

---

[5] Dell Hymes, 'Models of the Interaction of Language and Social Life', in John J. Gumperz and Dell Hymes (eds.), *Directions in Sociolinguistics: The Ethnography of Communication* (Oxford, Basil Blackwell, 1986), pp. 35–71.

[6] Despite the availability of many narrative grammars, Labov's structural analysis of narratives of personal experience has been over-applied by writers in many fields, perhaps because of its simplicity. However, it draws particular attention to the 'evaluation' segment in this kind of narrative which the Greenwich corpus clearly displays. The earliest statement of Labov's model was W. Labov and J. Waletzky, 'Narrative Analysis: Oral Versions of Personal Experience', in J. Helm (ed.), *Essays on the Verbal and Visual Arts: Proceedings of the 1966 Annual Meeting of the American Ethnological Society* (Washington, University Press, 1967) pp. 12–44.

[7] Home Office, *The Stephen Lawrence Inquiry Report*, Appendix 11, pp. 57–61.

[8] Katheryn K. Russell, *The Color of Crime: Racial Hoaxes, White Fear, Black Protectionism, Police Harassment, and Other Macroagressions* (New York and London, New York University Press, 1997).

Lawrence murder. It concentrates on the two main powerful agencies – the press and the police – and it does so through the distinctive narrative genre of complaint and challenge typical in counter-narrative.

Having 'a voice' and having a politics

The fact that so many of the stories collected and arising in interviews in Greenwich during the 1990s were counter-narratives, embedded in on-going debate with other narratives and positions, is very striking. Indeed, it would appear that counter-narrative has a special place within at least some types of 'backlash' and may be its quintessential popular expression. The reasons for its prevalence seems to have lain in the common perception on the estates in Greenwich that other, more powerful voices dominated the airways. Alongside counter-narratives of these kinds, where apparent motivation could stem from a range of causes including some of pure self-interest, a widespread belief in the local white community's *discursive exclusion* from mainstream public media and the national and local state was evident. In this it echoed similar complaints in other places in earlier times. It was reminiscent of the residents of South Boston during the anti-bussing campaigns in the 1970s who had complained: 'How come when Negroes have a civil rights march people pay attention . . . but when we do nobody stirs. Don't we have civil rights?'[9] It also echoed the Italians and Jews of Canarsie, New York, in the same period, who, in Jonathan Rieder's words, 'used the metaphor of noise to represent the resourcefulness of blacks and their own relegation to the status of a class without influence'. According to a Canarsie rabbi:

The blackman is the low man on the totem pole and he is screaming loud because he figures he has nothing to lose so he might as well scream his head off. I think the government favours the group which makes the most amount of noise. The high echelons of society make a lot of noise because they have big clout, and the middle income people make the least noise. The little man in Carnasie gets caught in the middle.[10]

Despite such similarities, however, there were considerable differences between the Greenwich working-class 'silent minority' of the 1990s and the working-class and lower-middle-class communities during the 1960s and 1970s in both the USA and the UK. The economy, class relations and the politics of race were very different from previous decades and in

[9] R. Formisano, *Boston against Busing: Race, Class and Ethnicity in the 1960s and 1970s* (Chapel Hill, University of North Carolina Press, 1991), p. 152.
[10] Rieder, *Canarsie*, p. 204.

the UK a dislocation of cohesive practices within some large social housing estates had eroded any positive sense of collective identity.[11]

To see how the perception of discursive exclusion may be related to counter-narrativisation, it is illuminating to look at instances where counter-narrative has been self-consciously used for political purposes. This was true of the narrative strategy suggested by some Critical Race theorists – writers in the Critical Race Theory movement that grew out of Critical Legal Studies in the USA. Writers such as Derrick Bell Jr, Kimberle Williams Crenshaw and Richard Delgado have attacked the American legal system, citing the ways, for example, that the First Amendment – the right to free speech – has been used to tolerate racist abuse and to avoid redress for those who have suffered from it.[12] As Richard Delgado puts it:

An outgroup creates its own stories, which circulate within the group as a kind of counter-reality . . . The dominant group creates its own stories as well. [These] provide it with a form of shared reality in which its own superior position is seen as natural. The stories of outgroups aim to subvert that reality.[13]

Critical Race theorists point to a black 'storytelling movement', founded on the work of Derick Bell Jr[14] that is said to generate 'Black' counter-narratives as ideological/cultural interventions designed to challenge racist myths. Such counter-narratives are stories which capture an underlying political truth and may go on to serve as templates in the social interpretation of incidents, facts and cases disputed in and out of the courtroom.[15] The black storytelling movement perhaps brings to consciousness something that is usually more *embodied* than articulated in narrativising practices in daily life.

Regina Austin, another Critical Race theorist, has argued for the value of popular conspiracy stories. She believes that although the conspiracy

---

[11] R. Burrows, *Unpopular Places? Area Disadvantage and the Geography of Misery in England* (Bristol, The Policy Press/Joseph Rowntree Foundation, 1998); A. Power and R. Tunstall, *Dangerous Disorder: Riots and Violent Distrurbances in 13 Areas of Britain, 1991–92* (York, Joseph Rowntree Foundation, 1997).

[12] Richard Delgado, *The Coming Race War? And Other Apocalyptic Tales of America after Affirmative Action and Welfare* (New York and London, New York University Press, 1996), pp. 21–3.

[13] Richard Delgado, 'Legal Storytelling: Storytelling for Oppositionists and Others: A Plea for Narrative', in Richard Delgado (ed.), *Critical Race Theory: The Cutting Edge* (Philadelphia, Temple University Press, 1995), p. 64.

[14] Derrick Bell, *Faces at the Bottom of the Well: The Permanence of Racism* (New York, Basic Books, 1992).

[15] These issues are also more broadly treated in Peter Brooks and Paul Gewirtz, *Law's Stories: Narrative and Rhetoric in the Law* (New Haven and London, Yale University Press, 1996).

stories concerning black oppression circulating in African-American communities may not be literally true, as popular accounts they provide black people with part of the armour they need to resist the racism of American society. She argues:

Even though conspiracy theorizing is far from an ideal form of discourse and leaves much to be desired as a manifestation of black critical judgement, it has its usefulness . . . The theories represent critiques of major institutions and social systems by a people who are and have been foreclosed from full participation in them. Antiblack conspiracy theorizing generates a counter-response to exclusions and discrimination by mobilizing collective black self-interest in a way that contributes to the growth and the strength of the black public sphere.[16]

It is sometimes also added to this set of arguments that as narrative is the natural articulation of 'black thought', in contrast to Western logic and rationality, counter-narrativisation is a particularly appropriate form of black political practice.[17] But while counter-narrative has had a role to play in resisting racism, it cannot be claimed to be peculiarly or even characteristically a 'black' form of resistance. It is arguably an expressive instrument of any individual or group experiencing discursive exclusion and perceived injustice. And while this has been true of many black communities, it has also been true of some white groups and especially of white working-class communities that perceive themselves to be economically under threat and/or without adequate mainstream representation from political and cultural agencies and organisations.[18] This is evident in the white working-class groups who see themselves as being invisible in the ideological market place and see instead a multicultural discourse that validates the very groups that appear to threaten them. However, why counter-narrative came to be such a prominent aspect of the Greenwich material is not entirely explained by this account. To see better the processes involved it is necessary to take a step back and remind ourselves of the already well-established relationship between racialisation and narrative in general.

---

[16] Regina Austin, 'Beyond Black Demons and White Devils: Antiblack Conspiracy Theorizing and the Black Public Sphere', *Florida State Law Review*, 22, pp. 1021ff (1995).

[17] See Andrew Hacker, Foreward to Delgado, *The Coming Race War?*, p. xiv.

[18] This is also true of feminist narrative interventions. See, for example, Trinh T. Minh-Ha, *When the Moon Waxes Red: Representation, Gender and Cultural Politics* (London, Routledge, 1991); The Personal Narratives Group, *Interpreting Women's Lives: Feminist Theory and Personal Narratives* (Bloomington and Indianapolis, Indiana University Press, 1989). Indeed, counter-narrativisation may even be produced by elite groups perceiving themselves to be under pressure.

Narrative and race

Issues of race and ethnicity have been amongst the most narrativised topics in urban settlement and community relations. Indeed, narrative and 'race' have maintained an almost inseparable closeness – the kinds of explanatory work that 'race' performs rendering it uniquely suited to community processes of transmission and sense-making through narrative reproduction. Beyond outright racial slander there is a range of narratives that goes from the incorporation of racial and ethnic stereotyping to the recounting of personal experiences that implicitly or explicitly confirm negative views of minority groups, and/or account for someone's success or failure to get a home, job, school place for their child or early doctor's appointment, with reference to race. Such narratives make sense of individual or shared misfortunes and provide an explanatory structure that irons-out specific circumstances and personal responsibilities, placing them within a framework supported by familiarity and narrative coherence. In the UK during the 1920s a young worker's fortunes and misfortunes would have been conversationally explained and narrativised by peers and 'organic intellectuals' – through a set of community-based, political and social beliefs about labour and capital far more than today. By the 1930s the corpus of such accounts of the social origins of personal mis/fortunes also included anti-Semitic and anti-immigrant motifs recycled from the late nineteenth century and re-enforced by contemporary fears brought on by the Depression.[19] This social life of narrative is critical to the status of explanations, influencing the narrativising 'spin' that turns personal biographies into social fabula, 'experience' into collective 'wisdom'.

Race-related oral narrative circulating within white communities has had a significant role to play during periods of demographic, economic and political change. The same was true in the backlash to early advances by equalities lobbies. Prior to the civil rights period, the role of race-rumour in weaving resentments and hostilities into narrative can be seen almost everywhere non-white communities made their appearance in the USA and Europe. Tales of opium dens and the lechery of Chinese men for white women in London's first 'Chinatown' in Limehouse during the early years of the twentieth century became fully blown into 'common knowledge' by the 1920s.[20] During the 1950s in the midlands

---

[19] George Orwell, 'Anti-Semitism in Britain, in *George Orwell: The Collected Essays, Journalism and Letters, Vol III* (Harmondsworth, Penguin Books, 1970), pp. 378–88; Tony Kushner and Katharine Knox, *Refugees in an Age of Genocide: Global, National, and Local Perspectives during the Twentieth Century* (London, Frank Cass, 1999).

[20] Although there was more substance to the former than the latter both combined to conjure an image of obscure menace. See H. V. Morton's classic vignettes 'White and

stories about race and community relations constituted a major form of social expression about race at the local level.[21]

In the USA rumour also lay behind the hysteria of white crowd attacks on black individuals and communities in New York in August 1900 when 'Negroes were set upon whenever they could be found and brutally beaten' and white Street gangs mobbed the street cars on Eighth Street where 'every car . . . was stopped by the crowd and every negro on board dragged out'.[22] Rumour inflamed events in Chicago in the summer of 1919 when, on a single day twenty-three blacks and fifteen whites were killed and 500 Chicagoans of both communities sustained injuries, following the killing of a black child by a white man.[23] Its capacity to inflame fears and anxieties was exploited by real-estate agents in Detroit in the early 1950s intent on profiting from white-panic property sales by deliberately starting rumours of black home-purchases in certain white areas. These activities contributed to the creation of one of the most active and widely supported white grassroots neighbourhood political movements for 'defended communities' in American history.[24] These pre- and immediately post-World War II phenomena represent older forms of social response to apparent and real threats to white livelihoods and fragile residential striving, stirred up by political and economic beneficiaries and underwritten by racist ideologies. Despite a period of some overlap in the 1950s, this was distinct from the increasingly media-driven and politically resourced post-equalities era.

The rise of the counter-narrative and the boundaries of legitimate discourse

Contemporary narrative theory pays surprisingly little attention to the issues of transmission and circulation that once occupied late nineteenth-century and early twentieth-century narrative 'diffusionists' and formal analysts like Aarne, Propp, Parry and Lord.[25] Yet these

Yellow' and 'Chinese New Year' in *London* (London, Methuen, 1941), pp. 354–6 and 389–91; J. P. May, 'The Chinese in Britain: 1860–1914', in C. Holmes (ed.), *Immigrants and Minorities in British Society* (London, Allen and Unwin, 1978); also Douglas Jones, 'The Chinese in Britain: Origins and Development of a Community', *New Community Journal of the Commission for Racial Equality*, 7, 3 (1979), pp. 397–402.

21 See Introduction in Foot, *The Rise of Enoch Powell.*

22 Gilbert Osofsky, *Harlem: The Making of a Ghetto: Negro New York 1890–1930* (2nd edn, New York, Harper Torchbooks, 1971), pp. 46–9.

23 William M. Tuttle Jr, *Race Riot: The Red Summer of 1919* (New York, Atheneum, 1970) pp. 8–10.

24 See Thomas Sugrue, *The Origins of the Urban Crisis: Race and Inequality in Postwar Detroit* (Princeton, N.J., Princeton University Press, 1996), pp. 209–57.

25 See, for example, Martin Cortazzi, *Narrative Analysis* (London, Washington, Falmer Press, 1993); Elizabeth Tonkin, *Narrating our Pasts: The Social Construction of Oral*

issues, in their focus on the *interactive social contexts* of production and reproduction, are essential to any *social* theory of racialisation as well as to the theorisation of oral narration in everyday settings.

As a contemporary social practice bound up with processes of transmission, narrativisation also exists within a discursive context composed not only of other oral narratives and narrative fragments. It is also composed of all related text within the public sphere – including that found in newspapers and on television – and the gamut of local and national state communications published through specialised agencies. Lyotard's analytical binary of discourse *or* narrative[26] seems to deny the possibility of narrative itself having a role within discourses, yet in the area of race, as with many other contested domains, it clearly does. What specifically characterised race-related discursive production during the second half of the twentieth century was that it was increasingly *dialogic*, in being not only inter-textual (having reference, meaning and resonance within a *corpus* of discursive material) but in being fundamentally demonstrative of its own relation to that corpus. Race-related utterances increasingly *addressed* their discursive 'others' and not uncommonly in agonistic forms. This Bakhtinian dimension[27] was increasingly evident as multiculturalist discourse gradually established its legitimacy and prominence. Race-related discourse of all political hues from the 1960s onwards was redolent with alternate and pre-existing voices as it strove to counter the process of unwelcome attribution. Race-related *narrative* was also frequently party to this kind of conversation.

The blossoming of counter-narrative at the level of national politics can be seen tied to the steady – if always contested – growth of multicultural discourse outlined in Chapter 1. The USA re-opened its doors to immigration in 1965 after forty years; Australia had relinquished it's 'whites only' policy in the early 1970s. New Zealand and Canada had turned to embrace ethnic diversity and multicultural policy in the interests of greater economic flexibility, with Canada

History (Cambridge, Cambridge University Press, 1992); Richard Bauman, *Story, Performance and Event: Contextual Studies of Oral Narrative* (Cambridge, Cambridge University Press, 1986); Albert Lord, *The Singer of Tales* (Cambridge, Mass., Harvard University Press, 1958); Vladimir Propp, *Theory and History of Folklore* (Manchester, Manchester University Press, 1984); Antti Aarne and Stith Thompson, *The Types of the Folktale: A Classification and Bibliography, Translated and Enlarged by Stith Thompson* (Helsinki, Folklore Fellows Communications (second revision), no. 184, 1961).

[26] J.-F. Lyotard, *The Postmodern Condition: A Report on Knowledge* (Manchester, Manchester University Press, 1984).

[27] M. M. Bakhtin, *The Dialogic Imagination: Four Essays*, ed. Michael Holq (Austin, Tex., University of Texas Press, 1981); M. M. Bakhtin, *Speech Genres and Other Late Essays* (Austin, Tex., University of Texas Press, 1986).

initiating its multicultural policy in 1971. At the same time some European powers also struggled with the social implications of the shifting world economy. This included recognising the underlying imperative to erode traditional community closure against migrant workers and to develop broad-based, diverse and 'tolerant' societies ideally capable of social change without conflict or disturbance. While the ways in which this issue played out differed both *between* national boundaries and *within* – often depending on party political fortunes, leadership and short-term political objectives – the underlying trend was towards embracing the idea of diversity and the rhetoric of universal social justice, at the same time as keeping a weather-eye on the response of indigenous labour and the white electorate.

Partly as a consequence of the post-war settlement and in the aftermath of both the holocaust and the American civil rights movement, the new discourse, if not a new practice, began to be established across the liberal democracies internationally. It was affirmative of multicultural objectives and conspicuously opposed to racism and racist ideologies. Furthermore, the ground rules of acceptable and unacceptable discourse shifted in favour of pluralist frameworks. This discourse has been described as a fundamental feature of liberal democratic states, which, it has also been argued, tend to be more liberal than public opinion. According to this view, throughout the 1970s and 1980s and into the 1990s the liberal democratic states developed an approach to migration in which the boundaries of legitimate discussion were narrowed and critiques that reflected the (less 'liberal') popular sentiments were excluded.[28] William Rogers Brubaker has argued that while it is evident that a constrained discourse which stigmatises a certain range of anti-immigration arguments as illegitimate or racist was apparent, this is 'not a [defining] feature of liberal democratic politics as such' but rather 'a historically specific and contingent feature of public discussion at certain times and places'.[29] Brubaker writes:

I would argue that in immigration policy debates, as in other policy domains, the boundaries of legitimate discussion are one of the crucial stakes of the debates, and that these boundaries change over time in response to broader developments in the environing culture and polity. Shifts in the boundaries of legitimate discourse in liberal democracies occur in both directions. Previously acceptable

[28] Gary P. Freeman, 'Modes of Immigration Politics in Liberal Democratic States', *International Migration Review*, 29, 4 (1995), pp. 881–903 at pp. 883–4.
[29] William Rogers Brubaker, comments on 'Modes of Immigration Politics in Liberal Democratic States', *International Migration Review*, 29, 4 (1995), 904–5.

modes of discourse may become stigmatized and excluded; but on the other hand previously illegitimate and effectively marginalized themes may gain a legitimate foothold in public debate.[30]

Whether defining or contingent, the signs of the emergent discourse were clearly visible in the change towards more ethnicity-blind immigration criteria in the admissions policies adopted by the USA, Canada, Australia and New Zealand variously between 1965 and 1974 and ultimately became an important part of multiculturalist argument. Asserting the illegitimacy of identifying welcome or unwelcome migrants in terms of national origins, race or ethnicity and affirming criteria derived from universal principles became the discursive standard – though not an across-the-board *practice* – for liberal democracies during the last quarter of the twentieth century. Into these universal terms even the far more restrictive northern European countries were also drawn to varying degrees. It was politically supported both by ideologically liberal lobbies concerned with human rights, and by employers and neo-liberal strategists keen for the removal of any constraints on the movement of labour.

It was against the grain of this influential trend, however, that the alternative story of responses emerged. In the first instance there was the direct political assault mounted during the Reagan/Thatcher years and the 'culture wars' in educational and other fields in the USA and the UK.[31] At the national level in the UK during the 1980s and 1990s the dialogues included the right-wing popular press in *its* distinctive counter-narratives which served to invert or deride the products of the anti-racist movement. Examples of these kinds of journalism enjoyed a long life and still appear from time to time. Even well into the 1990s the *Daily Express* front page story – WHITE RACE VICTIM AGED FOUR – about a white girl in the otherwise all-black nursery school who alone was excluded from receiving a Christmas present, and the subsequent tribunal that found the Nigerian-born school head guilty of racism – is a good example of counter-narrative by inversion. The *Sun's* classic *reductio* front page headline from the same period: 'DOG ON RACISM CHARGE – Jail's drug hound "picked on Asian"', was pure counter-narrative mischief-making. This media-based counter-narrativisation had been part of a struggle that embraced the agitation for and retreat from affirmative action in the USA, and the elaboration of and

---

[30] Ibid.

[31] P. Berman (ed.), *The Controversy over Political Correctness on College Campuses* (New York, Laurel, 1992); S. Dunant (ed.), *The War of the Words: The Political Correctness Debate* (London, Virago, 1994).

opposition to anti-racism and multiculturalism in the UK and USA in the 1970s and 1980s. It also related to the political struggles over multiculturalism elsewhere in the world. Australian press accounts of protests over the building of a bridge to Hindmarsh Island, South Australia, because it was alleged that Agarrindjeri women had certain spiritual beliefs that this would damage their fertility, allowed anti-multiculturalists to have a field day.[32] Pauline Hanson's One Nation Party also used official reports that 'almost 90% of Aboriginal organisations were guilty of financial "irregularities"' within their own complexly racist argument against state support for 'the Aboriginal industry'.[33]

Beyond this, there grew up the localised reflex of which 'grassroots' counter-narrativisation was a part. Like the counter-narrativisation that had taken place in the press, it was a response not necessarily against *actual* local incursions by migrant and minority communities – though that was sometimes part of it. Rather it was based on how their perceptions of 'diversity' were stigmatised or ignored and not recognised in the wider public sphere where, despite the clatter of press headlines, multicultural discourse appeared to be hegemonic. It was as though they observed a battle of the sound-bites, watching in dismay as, despite valiant assaults, multiculturalism always emerged strong and unscathed.

About 'truth'

If such are the wider political conditions within which counter-narrative flourished and which seemed to mould and focus popular beliefs and perceptions, what is it possible to say about the 'truth' of any particular narrative? Is all 'community-approved' narrative merely a reflex of super-ordinate forces and is all social perception necessarily invalidated by the narrative frames by which it is circulated? From the point of view of reflexive ethnography which this research has broadly embraced, the realities of informants and other subjects within communities studied are characteristically treated as parts of social reality whatever the *content* of those realities. The ethnographic task is to describe its contours and changes through attention to texts both social and linguistic. Truth

[32] J. Kerin and K. Towers, 'Aborigines Claim Bridge Racism', *The Weekend Australian*, 9–10 Dec. 1995, p. 4; M. Weidenhofer, 'Photos like Swastika to the Jew', *The Advertiser*, 9 Sept, 1995, p. 5; C. Pearson, 'Time to Embrace a Few Home Truths', *The Australian*, 19 Sept. 1996, p. 9.
[33] K. Sweetman, 'Aboriginal Groups Misuse Funding', *The Advertiser*, 15 Oct. 1996, p. 3; 'Hansonism: We Are All Australians', http//www.gwb.com.au//onenation/truths/conclus. html (10-21-97).

claims made by informants may be set beside other potential sources of information, even in the spirit in which multiple versions of 'the same' narrative might be assembled – with either a reasonable scepticism about the veracity of all of the texts, or with no expectation of or interest in their truth status.

In the latter case what is being investigated is the anatomy of a social practice or set of social practices. In the former, part of the analytical practice is to act 'as though' a reality approximating to or in some way having bearing on the produced text exists, not *beyond discourse*, but beyond the discourse at hand. There is also the possibility that the analyst/ethnographer may hold the belief that the fact that similar phenomena may be represented within other texts may be more than accidental and that each representation is built on a subsisting reality.

Beside the epistemological strengths and weaknesses of this realist position,[34] however, there is more to recommend it to ethnographic method in its refusal to assert a radical disjuncture between the hermeneutic processes of the individuals and groups who the ethnographer hopes to understand and the development and analysis of that understanding. In dealing with texts such as the one above headed 'Three black boys at the scene of Stephen Lawrence's murder', it is scarcely irrelevant to examine the police records of volunteered witness evidence or other materials to see what light, if any, it might shed on the narrative. With the narrative about the black man attacked by the gang of white youths, it is similarly relevant to explore the relationship of the variously constructed narratives both to the needs of the narrators and their audiences and to the legal issues that may influence the direction which narrative construction might take. For these reasons the position taken here has been, as it is elsewhere in this book, a realist one which takes into account constructive processes insofar as they are apparent, relevant and usefully analysable. For while, as Judith Butler argues in her analysis of the impact of the video evidence in the trial of the LA police officers in the Rodney King case:

what the [King] trial and its horrific conclusions teach us is that there is no simple recourse to the visible, to visual evidence . . . that it is already a reading and that in order to establish the injury on the basis of the visual evidence an aggressive [counter] reading of the evidence is necessary.[35]

---

[34] See Tony Skillen, 'Post-Marxist Modes of Production, or Discourse Fever', *Radical Philosophy*, 20 (1978), pp. 3–8.

[35] Judith Butler, 'Endangered/Endangering: Schematic Racism and White Paranoia', in Robert Gooding-Williams (ed.), *Reading Rodney King: Reading Urban Uprising* (New York and London, Routledge, 1993), p. 17.

It is not necessary also to assert an all-pervasive 'white racist episteme' that is monolithically creative. Indeed, Butler is at pains to distance herself from this implication.[36]

Despite the realist stance, it is also not the view taken here that all stories of 'unfairness to whites' are 'untrue' or 'racist distortions'. Many of them are, as has been discussed above, clearly confections generated within a specific local climate under particular historical conditions and some of these are unambiguously racist. Others, adopted into the same genre as these, can, on the basis of forms of evidence beyond the narrative, make reasonable claims to correspond to reality and to arise from contact with reality. The fact that they are generated within an oral genre of 'unfairness to whites' counter-narratives tells us something about what has been locally selected for narrativisation, but not whether a story is true, half-true or false. Neither can it tell us whether a particular narrative is in itself 'racist', despite claims to the contrary by some discourse analysts.[37] A faithful witness could give an account that then becomes part of ignorantly circulated racist gossip. In the course of the field-work for the research reported on in this chapter, a number of narratives of personal experience by white adolescents and adults were collected whose testimony was elsewhere corroborated and which supported the claim of unfairness *in that instance*. It was not necessary to embrace what has been called 'standpoint epistemology' – allowing each reality-account its own incommensurable integrity – to achieve that understanding.[38] Amongst some white adolescents a deep sense of grievance had been engendered by youth workers and teachers disbelieving their accounts of occasions on which they had been treated unfairly by the education system on the basis of race. Often these young people became subsequently lost to any beneficial influence the adult professionals might have had. Taking stories of unfairness as at least 'true for the teller' would have done nothing to counter the currency of the genre. It would not have altered the social and political conditions surrounding the selection, elaboration and use of such narratives. It may, however, have done something for the value of the professional's relationship to the young person and for the 'shared sense of justice' on

---

[36] Ibid. p22.

[37] Teun van Dijk, *Elite Discourse and Racism* (London, Sage, 1993); Teun van Dijk, *Communicating Racism* (Newbury Park, Calif., Sage, 1987).

[38] Donna Haraway, 'Situated Knowledge: The Science Question in Feminism and the Privilege of Partial Perspective', *Feminist Studies*, 14 (1988), pp. 575–99; P. T. Clough, *The End(s) of Ethnography* (Newbury Park, Calif., Sage, 1992); Norman Denzin, *Interpretive Ethnography: Ethnographic Practices for the 21st Century* (Thousand Oaks, Sage, 1997), pp. 53–89.

which anti-racist youth work and education is predicated and which was encouraged by the council's youth and education services.

Thus while important sociological dimensions emerge through a deeper historical and political account of counter-narrativisation in which the 'truth content' of particular narratives is not relevant, these dimensions remain not the only aspects significant to the complex business of framing policy and practice responses to address racism. In that endeavour the achievement of mutual understanding may be of greater value and of immeasurably greater difficulty.

5 Residence and resistance: the case of the Eltham Tenants Forum

The salience of racism to explanations of the disadvantages experienced by black communities was key in the articulation of white backlashes against racial equalities policies in several countries. The endorsement by national and local governments of the view that racism had contributed to inequalities caused some to see local politicians, officials and bureaucrats as implicated in the proximity of minority groups to their neighbourhoods and the frustration of their own economic hopes. The struggle in Greenwich over what was and was not a 'racial' matter was no isolated instance. The sites where those arguments became internationally articulated were also not arbitrary but often concentrated in key areas of employment, education and residence, although an ecumenical range of cultural skirmishes over this issue has also existed.

Residence had always been in the forefront of issues where large-scale migrations occurred both *within* countries, as in the USA or *between* countries. Furthermore, the ways in which patterns of residence took shape in the wake of migration to Western democracies – not just of racial and ethnic minorities but of all those groups attracted to areas of economic vitality – itself helped to forge how social minority status and 'race' itself was constructed.[1] Thus while the facts of inequalities and injustices in the housing and rental markets represent one dimension, the *imagery* of socially segregated urban communities in economic contrast and the social positioning that involved, served to construct the ways of thinking 'race' itself and minority/majority relations.[2]

---

[1] Joe William Trotter, Jr, *The Great Migration in Historical Perspective: New Dimensions of Race, Class and Gender* (Bloomington and Indianapolis, Indiana University Press, 1991).

[2] Susan J. Smith, *The Politics of Race and Residence* (Cambridge, Polity Press, 1989); Susan J. Smith, 'Residential Segregation and the Politics of Racialisation', in Malcolm Cross and Michael Keith (eds.), *Racism, the City and the State* (London, Routledge, 1993) pp. 128–43; Anne Power, *Estates on the Edge: Social Consequences of Mass Housing in Northern Europe* (Basingstoke, MacMillan, 1997) p. 347; Douglas Massey and Nancy Denton, *American Apartheid: Segregation and the Making of the Underclass* (Cambridge, Mass., Harvard University Press, 1993); N. Ginsburg, 'Institutional Racism and Local

In the UK during the 1980s the domain of public housing was prominent in the struggles between central government and local authorities. The Conservative agenda of dramatically cutting the spending power of local government and limiting its capacity for social programmes was expressed in a number of pieces of legislation including giving council tenants a 'right to buy' the homes in which they lived and taking the exclusive responsibility for social housing out of the hands of the local authorities. By the early 1990s the collapse in the housing market, which left many home-owners in negative equity, dampened the demand for council house purchase whilst leaving a sense of foreboding. At the same time plans to move the housing stock from local authority control aroused anxiety amongst many tenants already watchful over the impact of the government's privatisation programme. Amidst these anxieties, the politics of race again became articulated within the discourses of residence and the imagery of belonging. It brought into play a number of contested issues including (1) the legitimate role of the local authority; and (2) the identification of a 'racial' dimension in local community concerns touching on personal safety and the inclusiveness of local democracy.[3] Set in their wider political frame, these already had the potential for community conflict and a backlash politics to emerge.

In Greenwich, while the murder of Rolan Adams initiated a borough-wide concern with racism, that of Rohit Duggal shifted the spotlight from Thamesmead to Eltham. The local authority's response to these and other developments was a series of 'Equality Action Plans' with targets and time scales required from all service departments. Despite powerful constraints on local authority spending imposed by three successive Thatcher administrations, and particularly by the 1989 Local Government Housing Act, Greenwich council's Directorate of Housing Services chose to swim against the tide of central legislation and defend equal opportunities/race equalities interventions within its area of activity. Thus from within its 1993/4 budget it secured funding for five Race Equality Advisor (REA) posts. Its Equalities Action Plan for that year also included work with the various refugee organisations in the borough; addressing the plight of asylum seekers; a move to facilitate the establishment of a borough-wide tenants association (TA) for Vietnamese and Chinese tenants; the development of translation

Authority Housing', *Critical Social Policy*, 24 (1988), pp. 4–19; Commission for Racial Equality, *Race and Council Housing in London: Report of a Formal Investigation* (London, Commission for Racial Equality, 1984).
[3] B. Campbell, *Goliath: Britain's Dangerous Places* (London, Methuen, 1993); P. Sarre, D. Philllips and R. Skellington, *Ethnic Minority Housing: Explanations and Policies* (Aldershot, Averbury, 1989).

services; and a set of policies aimed at its responsibilities as a major employer in the borough. There was a council stock of 35,865 homes, the administration and maintenance of which involved a long payroll and impacted greatly on local people.[4] Amongst the Plan's many stated objectives were the stepping up of legal action against perpetrators of racial harassment, increasing black and ethnic minority representation on tenants/residents associations, seeking to employ more black women and black middle managers, and employing more black caretakers.[5]

Each of the five REA posts was assigned a different area of the borough within which to work. By the time Eltham's REA was appointed Eltham's second racist murder, that of Stephen Lawrence, had just occurred. Thus when newly appointed Beekay Oyelowo came to introduce himself and his role to Eltham Area Tenants Forum (a meeting of representatives from all of the TAs from each of Eltham's council estates) the issue of racism was already clearly to the fore. His audience of twenty-two late middle-age to elderly whites was notoriously hostile to the council's housing department and suspicious of anything that came with its blessing. Nine council officers, several of very high rank, also unusually swelled the numbers that night to just over thirty. The fifth item on the agenda, and following a long discussion on the government's new requirement of competitive tendering for the provision of services in local housing, Mr Oyelowo opened by describing his work. It was to respond, he said, to all forms of racial harassment and provide appropriate support for victims. He was setting up a Victim Support Group and was also a member of the Racial Harassment Panel which dealt with complaints of racial harassment as they came to the Directorate of Housing. He and his fellow REAs needed the support of the whole community and he sought to work in close co-operation with various agencies, including tenants groups. He was also trying to raise black tenants' awareness of the tenant movement in Eltham and encourage them to participate.

His first question from the floor was: Did his brief apply equally to black against white and white against black harassment? It did, he answered. Two further statements from the floor expressed less provocatively the apparent feelings of some: 'Many people in the local

---

[4] London Borough of Greenwich, *Housing Report* (1991).
[5] This last item had been carried forward from the plan of the previous year which had aimed 'to address under-representation of Black and Minority Workers in the caretaker service' and had set itself a target of 10 per cent black caretakers by April 1994. Directorate of Housing Services, *Equalities Action Plan 1993/4* (Director of Housing Services, Greenwich Council, 1993); Directorate of Housing Services, *Plan 1992/3* (Director of Housing Services, Greenwich Council, 1992).

community are annoyed at reports in the press that Eltham is a racist area. Inca Drive Tenants and Homeowners Association undertook to work with [housing] officers but bad feelings generated by press reports mean that Beekay and [the other] officers might have a tough time in Eltham.' Trouble was being caused by the emphasis on the issue of racism in Eltham, it was said. Mr Oyelowo responded that equality was part of quality. Equal service should be given to everybody irrespective of race. Perpetration of racist attacks has to be dealt with. His duty was to the tenants of Eltham. The chair of the Forum then made her own contribution, complaining about 'misleading and deplorable media coverage' concerning supposed racism in Greenwich borough.[6]

The final contributor was from the council's regular housing team who responded to a request from the floor about the scale of racial harassment in the area. During 1992/3 there were thirteen or fourteen reported incidents. 'This year so far [between April and June] there have already been eleven reports. Three of these have been so serious as to justify moving the tenants. A recent survey indicated that there were only about sixty black or ethnic minority tenants in Eltham.'[7] Mr Oyelowo sat down and the meeting moved on to other items.

The Eltham Forum's response to Mr Oyelowo's presentation was no surprise – part of the explanation for the strengthening presence of senior council officers. At an earlier meeting a BNP leaflet that had been circulated on the Page estate was discussed and the Forum decided to take no action because its content was thought to be 'basically true'.

Quite independently of the work of Beekay Oyelowo, a related objective was being pursued by a small project based in Greenwich council's Housing Rights office. Funded directly by the Department of the Environment[8] its aim was to create a black and ethnic minority tenants association similar to the one proposed by the Directorate of Housing for Vietnamese and Chinese tenants. Having been unsuccessful in finding black tenants who were interested in being involved elsewhere in the borough, one of the project's two workers canvassed identified families on the Eltham estates. There she encountered a black twenty-three-year-old graduate, Donna Carr, who was living with her aunt, a long-time resident.

Arriving in the period immediately following the murder of Stephen Lawrence, the project worker found Donna and her aunt very receptive. In interview Donna subsequently explained:

[6] Eltham Area Tenants Forum, *Minutes of a Meeting Held on Wednesday 16th June 1993*, pp.7–8.
[7] Ibid., p. 9.
[8] Funds provided under Section 11 of the 1966 Local Government Act.

It was after the death of Stephen Lawrence so there was still a lot of feeling in the air about racial harassment in Eltham. I suppose we were ripe for this sort of group at the time. What [the project worker] was saying was absolutely true. If you're talking about something that's making sense to us and its relevant to us then we'll get involved and if it isn't we won't. But we could see how much we didn't know about housing issues. I mean everyone should know what a TA is and we just did not even know basic things like that.

They did have personal experience of harassment on the estate, however. When her aunt had moved into the area with her parents and brothers and sisters some twenty-five years earlier, local residents including her next door neighbour had started a petition to get the family removed. There had been very few such breaches of the 'sons and daughters' housing policy but those black families that were allowed in experienced hostility and name-calling from locals. At the age of eight Donna had lived for a while with her aunt's family and remembered that kind of treatment. However, over the years those few early black families gained a kind of acceptance. For more recent arrivals the level of harassment was far higher. There were several recent cases that she had personal knowledge of, one on her aunt's estate, where a black woman had suffered many problems from neighbours including people urinating in her milk bottles, dog's excrement placed on her door-step, her car being broken into and later burned, and she was threatened with a gun. A court injunction was eventually enforced protecting her. Another woman on the Page estate was harassed by several related families. 'These were not youngsters at all. These were older people, over forty, maybe fifty. It finally came to the point she just had to run away like a refugee from her own house.' Such physical forms of harassment represented a substantial change from the older patterns.

Donna identified how different age groups of those involved in racial harassment applied different kinds of pressure:

I think most of the smashing windows, the trashing cars and stuff like that is mainly done by the younger group and the psychological stuff, the constant gnawing at you kind of racism – basically mental cruelty racism – is done by the older people. Like this woman down Middle Park. People telling her why do you keep having your grandchild in the flat. He's making too much noise. Don't walk in the flats with your high heels, they're making too much noise. Don't wheel your grandchild in the wheelchair through the flats 'cos it's making too much noise. Don't do this, don't do that, don't do this, don't do that – constantly trying to restrict her movements so that she'll feel so trapped she'll just leave. And that's the way the older people work. It's very much that type of mental harassment, which people don't see as harassment at the time. They want a great big dirty brick through your window before they want to do anything. That mental sort of harassment the council tends to see and tends to call nuisance harassment . . . and unless someone sort of burns out your flat or puts a swastika on the door then its not racism somehow. They call it nuisance. That isn't nuisance, that's hounding you out of your home.

While the issue of racial harassment was a major part of the impetus behind her initial engagement with the move to create a black and ethnic minority tenants association, it was not the only one. There was also the notion that a black perspective could contribute a different dimension to civic process – a matter of inclusion in local democratic activity. In recent years Eltham Area Tenants Forum had had a black member, an Asian man who was no longer active in this group. He discussed with Donna the idea that many small but significant sums of council money were at the disposal of TAs and it was important for black tenants to be part of discussions of how these monies were spent. This kind of concern with participation was also very much in alignment with the broader objectives of fuller black and ethnic minority involvement being tentatively promoted by the council. However, the extension of the strategy from initiating and supporting a *presence* within the TAs to the creation of a separate black organisation had both practical and symbolic ramifications. In both regards, however, there was some overlap between the objectives of the black tenants' participation project and Beekay Oyelowo's concern with 'victim support' in the Eltham area. Logically, therefore, a single group was formed to encompass all of these interests. It was to be called the Black and Ethnic Minority Tenants Association (BEMTA).

For such a group to be meaningful it needed council recognition, a membership and, preferably, the recognition of the other local TAs. Neither of the last two needs were to prove easy to satisfy. The minority ethnic presence in central and southern Greenwich was very small, vulnerable and scattered.[9] While some black families knew each other personally, others were only noticed in the shopping areas or other public settings. While some of these people may have had personal experience of harassment there was no context in which this knowledge was shared or discussed. Black people who had been the recipients of low-level hostility or none knew nothing of the experiences of those who had had the worst treatment from neighbours.

As far as support from the local TAs was concerned, that too was problematic. The members of Coldharbour TA – one of the groups on the Eltham Area Forum – were from an estate that was on the western edge of the borough. One man – the ex-chair of the TA – and his wife

[9] Keith Jacobs, 'Institutional Housing Practices and Racism: the Brooke Estate, Eltham', *History Workshop Journal*, 48 (1999), pp. 198–201.

were in their mid-seventies. They had come to the estate in the late 1940s from Woolwich and Plumstead. They and most of their friends brought up their children in the 1950s and 1960s. The TA was established at that time. 'Now the TA is one of the best – if not the best – in London. Financially self-supporting with a rep in every street, monthly meetings attended by about thirty people in the local hall', the man said in interview. This TA now had a strong sense of its local muscle, claiming to have 'got the local off-licence shut down' because it encouraged young people to congregate there. The core members were of the view that the council's anti-racist policies 'cause racism' – an opinion, they believed, not confined to white residents. 'Local blacks also think its wrong', they said. In any case, they argued, 'nearly all the ethnics on the estate are home-owners. They wouldn't have bought there if it was a racist area.' An example of the council's 'crazy' anti-racist policies, he said, was evident in the current case of a council-employed childminder who had been reported by a black council officer for racism because she had a 'gollywog' among the toys available for the children she looked after. The national press and local radio had made much of this classic 1980s-style 'loony left' story. Cases like these, the Coldharbour members believed, lead to people turning to the BNP and NF: 'The NF cause violence. We don't want them on the estates and the council's actions encourage them, specially with elections coming up soon.'

Another member of the Coldharbour group explained that one other reason why the older couple were hostile to the council was that they had learned of its 10 per cent target for black caretakers. Several of the members interpreted this as a 'quota'. 'Having a forty-year-old unemployed son living at home with them makes them resentful about this' it was said. This couple reported that they had been accused to their face of being racists by Beekay Oyelowo. But they lived next door to a black family with whom they got on well they said. They were not opposed to black people being members of the TAs. 'If blacks who attended TA meetings experienced fear, as Beekay Oleyowo claimed, they are bound to – just as everyone does at first.'

At the same time as laying out their criticisms of council anti-racism, the members of the group were very aware that some vocal participants in the Forum were explicit racists and that this caused their own views to be misconstrued or lumped together with these racist ones. Indeed a previous chair of the Forum had recently been narrowly voted out of his position partly because of his frequent expression of unguarded opinions. 'He is a bit of a racist', they explained. 'He wants to keep his mouth shut.' There was, however, an implicit pact of solidarity over race in the interests of presenting a unified front against the council. Thus the suspected BNP sympathisers were tolerated within the Forum because of some overlap of concerns with those of more temperate opinions, provided they did not expose the rest to accusations of racism that undermined the legitimacy of their views.

The Coldharbour estate is physically the closest of the Eltham estates to up-market Chistlehurst and its older inhabitants wore its flinty gentility with pride. Somewhat different was the Page estate which was first built in the 1920s, part of it incorporating the Progress estate – initially built and run as cheap housing for poor families. Its 2,500 properties were and seemed old.[10] There was an underlying sense of grinding failure and the impossibility of 'progress', of thwarted attempts to succeed and move out, of a trapped population that also lacked community. The BNP enjoyed some patchy popularity there amongst some tenants and the estate was targeted for leafleting by BNP activists on several occasions. Some young people and adults from the Page were in evidence on a BNP counter-demonstration to a protest march over the murder of Rohit Duggal. One Page estate resident reported:

'My neighbour was out in the street and she said like – the BNP were coming from Eltham down the back streets and she said – there's a woman that lives opposite her that was actually saying, "Go on my son, do it for the rest of us."'

The Page Estate Tenants and Residents Association (PETRA) had been organised and run for a very long time by a salt-of-the-earth couple in their fifties who were well known within the dense social networks existing in the area. With few helpers they maintained a small group in active engagement over issues concerning council and tenant relations, even though their impact on most of the Page residents was sporadic and at a low level. More comfortably working class than the activists in some of the other Eltham TAs, they lived out the contradictions and paradoxes of residential politics and the interference of BNP noise on the airways of community talk. They complained that it was rare for anyone on the estate to volunteer to do anything for the TA, let alone put themselves forward to be on the committee. They dealt with mundane bread and butter issues like goading the council into renovating the 700 'Laings Easiform' houses that had reached a critical state of structural dilapidation; arguing for better street lighting, and reporting the harassment of elderly tenants – which included fireworks and excrement through front-door letterboxes – to the police and the

---

[10] Greenwich Community College, *The Five Estates Survey: Brooke, Horn Park, Kidbrooke Park Middle Park, Page* (London, Housing Services, London Borough of Greenwich, 2000).

housing office. This issue had been one of long-running concern and was related to the council's building of a number of small, one-bedroom bungalows for elderly tenants on narrow islands of land close to other houses within the estate. The idea behind this policy had been to avoid isolating the elderly in segregated areas by placing them close to young families and other non-elderly tenants and thereby including them in the social life of the neighbourhood. The construction of these bungalows had been resisted by PETRA because some foresaw a far less peaceful existence for the elderly involved. Now, several years on, elderly people in the bungalows were suffering from frequent harassment and even violence from adolescents, children and others. The tenants characterised this as feeling like prisoners in their own homes, not knowing what would come through their window or letterbox next. Other concerns of PETRA included the threatened privatisation of social housing by the Conservatives keen on pushing local government to abandon its role in housing.

The wife in this dedicated PETRA couple had over the past two years become wheel-chair bound but had assumed the greater responsibility for the work of the TA, since her husband also had serious health problems – including lead poisoning after years of working directing traffic on the Woolwich Ferry that carried cars and trucks across the Thames. Like the elderly couple at Coldharbour, they had been accused by Beekay Oyelowo of being racists because they were opposed to the idea of a separate black TA. Mr Oyelowo had also accused his colleagues in the local housing office of racism, and was beginning to get a reputation for making this accusation. She, in particular, was troubled by the changing face of race and, unlike many of the other leading TA activists in Eltham, was far from settled in her views and attitudes. One of her daughters was happily married to a black man whom she was very fond of and she had grandchildren from that marriage. One of her grandchildren had suffered racial bullying in his junior school and had been approaching the move to secondary school with trepidation. She reported, 'He said, "I'm a bit worried, Nan . . . They might pick on me cause I'm a half-caste." I was dumbstruck.' Apparently uncomfortable with the implications of this she added, 'It seems now your face has to fit. If your face fits you get in anywhere. If your face doesn't fit, it doesn't matter what colour you are, then that's it.' This could be construed as simple denial or playing down of the race factor. Like almost everything else she said that related to race, this also bore the signs of work in progress. The lateral pressure from other Forum members to become part of the opposition to a separate black organisation, together with the intense Page estate talk about 'unfairness to whites', was clearly taking its toll on her. She was conflicted and frequently compromised, even, she reported, in the eyes of her daughter and black son-in-law.

A BNP leaflet that had come through her door seemed to pick up on local sentiments. She reported:

[It said] if a white person gets killed, you never get it in the paper that it's a black youth. You always get it told that it was 'youths', 'killed by youths'. They don't say 'black', they don't say 'ethnic', it's 'youths'. If a black person is killed then its always 'white people' are named and its blown up. It's put in the newspapers.

A small boy sitting within earshot of this interview added, 'It's always called racist. A lot of black people kill white people. It's not called racist.' She continued:

Yeah, that's it . . . I mean I can see both points. Even my son-in-law turned round and said, 'Mum what they wrote is true.' And funny enough that week in the paper a caretaker at Plumstead had been attacked and it's put 'attacked by youths'. It wasn't until three days later it was 'attacked by Asian youths'. It seemed like they had to wait to get the OK before they put 'Asian' in.

One consistent feature of her accounts was the role of the council in forging racial conflict by insisting on fore-grounding racial identities. Her knowledge of the formation of the BEMTA fitted exactly with her image of council activity. She said:

I says to her down the estate office 'You're making the harassment. You are causing the problems.' I mean I'm fighting a case now. We've got erm . . . we've got to call 'em 'ethnic' [people] . . . They reckon they are scared to join in with our TA because we are white. They feel that if they come to our TA it would be wrong. So, we have got a new harassment officer down at the estate office, he came up with this bright idea of having a meeting but he now calls it the Black and Ethnic TA. Well, as I pointed out, you cannot have two TAs on one estate. You can have sub-committees, you can have action groups but you cannot have two TAs. That is council ruling. And he done his nut. I'm a racist [he told me]. I'm a racist. Erm, I've got problems. So I said 'Yeah and you're my biggest one.' I said 'We're all tenants on this estate, or else we're owners.' I said 'We're not black, we're not green, we're not orange, we're not yellow, we're tenants.' He's done his nut. He's done his nut.

BEMTA at the Eltham Tenants Forum

A presentation of the case for the BEMTA was to be made by Donna Carr and her aunt at one of the Forum's forthcoming meetings. As the date grew nearer knowledge and anticipation of BEMTA's purposes spread throughout Eltham's TA network. Opposition to the proposal was widespread. As well as Coldharbour and Page estate TAs, those of

Middle Park, Tattersall Close, Horn Park and others also bridled at the idea, and, as the months following Stephen Lawrence's murder passed and national interest in Greenwich increased, Eltham's name came to appear frequently in unflattering profiles. This media coverage intensified local resentment that racism had been forced into prominence by outsiders.

The chair of the Forum, Josie Barber, was a fluent and forceful woman from the Coldharbour estate. During the run up to the Forum meeting she was in the process of writing a letter to the local newspaper complaining about the Equality Plan's 10 per cent 'quota' for black caretakers in the council's employ. On her shoulders would rest the responsibility for dealing with the BEMTA item and steering it without upset through the meeting. Her approach would be to give the BEMTA speakers a polite hearing, allow the voices of support and opposition to comment and then move smoothly into the next item. Problems might arise from two sides. BEMTA speakers with the support of senior council officers might articulate their case too disturbingly, causing upset and affront to the Forum members. On the other hand, the most racist members of the Forum might say offensive and explicitly racist things that would bring shame on the proceedings and rule out the preferred outcome of hearing the proposal with neutrality whilst recommending the *status quo*. Neither of these potentials did Josie Barber have much control over, although the ex–chair who had spoken favourably of the BNP in the past was open to some pressure. 'Tell him to keep his mouth shut tonight' an ally was requested on the afternoon before the meeting.

On the evening of the Forum meeting[11] the presentation by BEMTA was the third item on a full agenda. The hall was packed with TA representatives from all of the Eltham groups and a small number of council officials from the local estates office were also present. When the item was introduced Donna Carr and her aunt were welcomed by the chair with the words: 'Welcome to the Eltham Forum. We are delighted to have you here and we hope you will have long and successful dealings with this Forum. Can I ask you exactly how you set yourself up? Are you canvassing on all the estates with the local TAs?' Donna Carr explained, a little falteringly at first, that they were knocking on the doors of all black and ethnic tenants, getting them aware of housing issues and encouraging them to get involved. They were doing this because in the past black tenants had maybe been too frightened to come or thought

[11] See Eltham Area Tenants Forum, *Minutes of a Meeting Held at Eltham Local Housing Office*, Wednesday 17 Nov. 1993.

they would not be welcomed. 'I hope you reassured them and tell them we are a tenants forum and the people here are all from tenants associations . . . so you will find no prejudice here and hopefully none at your local TAs' replied the chair, who then made her key point: 'Could I suggest that perhaps you work with your local TAs. If you are on Page why not work with PETRA, if you're on Middle Park work with Middle Park TA.'

After a number of brief, polite exchanges Donna Carr attempted to make her case for a separate TA without actually spelling it out. She said:

Can I just say one other thing. We're encouraging black and ethnic tenants to become involved because it's very important, what with CCT and things like that coming in. . . Well, there's not many of us around, I think there's about 100, 120 black and ethnic tenants actually in the whole Eltham area. So if you do come across any, can you make them as welcome as possible because it is a very hard thing, for someone who's been a victim of racial harassment from people in their area to come into a predominantly white setting.

This led to a request from the chair for Donna to expand on the reasons why black tenants were 'reluctant to join their local TAs'. Donna began by saying that people had told her that they thought the TAs were 'made up of people that didn't want them there'. This was interrupted with a great deal of noise from the audience in the form of loud laughter and shouts of 'No! No!' Josie Barber tried to quieten the audience and Donna continued bravely with, 'You may laugh, you may laugh. I haven't finished yet. You may laugh but for one reason or another, this is the way a lot of black people in Eltham think and feel and we can't ignore that.' Josie then reiterated her main point: 'Can I suggest that you actually do get in touch with the local TAs . . . [You] will find them more than pleased to welcome tenants on board because we are tenants associations, we are not white tenants associations, or Scotch tenants associations. We are all council tenants associations and everyone, I'm quite sure, would be made very welcome indeed.' One benign male voice from the audience made the point that it would help, also, if TAs themselves made contacts with black and ethnic minority tenants. Donna agreed. The ex-chair wanted it minuted that the Eltham Forum had had the first black tenant's representative in the borough, and added that Donna should be referred to Beekay Oyelowo who dealt with these matters. Josie herself said, not without a sceptical edge, that she was 'very distressed' if it really was the case that tenants were going along to local TAs and not being made welcome. 'We are all so desperate now to get as many tenants as possible.'

Another of the TA representatives in the audience then returned to the fundamental point: 'Just a quick word on this "them and us" business again. We're trying to integrate these ethnics. The last thing we want is either the whites or the blacks to get together to form separate units. You waste time integrating otherwise.' Donna's answer was less than circumspect.

The question of racial harassment, by and large, only affects black and ethnic tenants. We have to have groups like us to address these problems within ourselves. There's a lot of people in this area who have undergone serious and severe harassment and they want to talk to people who can empathise and sympathise and understand where they are coming from because they are feeling very frightened, very isolated and very alone.

This was a strong reply to a difficult question. From the point of view of the others, however, Donna's response was heard as a refusal to ratify their genuine concerns about adopting a 'separatist' approach within the TA. Furthermore, as Josie's response indicates, in highlighting racial harassment Donna was seen to be denying the reality of what they took to be the equally 'serious and severe harassment' directed at the elderly people living on the estate:

There are lots of those incidents that happen to a lot of people on a lot of estates. We have elderly people who for a period of a couple of years on Coldharbour were absolutely terrified by a gang of about six or seven kids – young kids – and they terrorised these old people. So you know it's not all one way. It's not all being directed to your black and ethnic.

But Donna did not sense the need for, or believe in, a change of tactic. She continued: 'Well I have to disagree with that because a lot of it is. A lot of the violence has been proved to stem from the fact that people are of a different colour and people don't like that.' With much shouting and interruption at this last remark, Donna called above the noise, 'You cannot ignore the fact that racism exists in Eltham. You cannot ignore it, I'm sorry.'

At this point there were many clamouring to speak. Some were saying that too much time had been wasted on this issue, while others were pressing to get their counter-examples heard. A woman at the front described how her daughter had been harassed for about seven months by black girls from her estate. 'My daughter couldn't walk the estate without being pushed off her bike, kicked in the head, and it was by two black girls.' Another talked about the current week's local newspaper that had carried a story on the front page about her daughter who had been attacked by two black men in the area. Donna had little chance to comment on the torrent of remarks being made. The audience had the floor and so did a potentially ugly agenda. Josie had few strategies for calming things down other than asking people to be brief and reminding everyone that minutes were being taken and only one person should speak at a time.

Arriving like the cavalry, the Housing Area Director then rose to speak at Josie's nod:

Donna has said we're a new group trying to find our feet . . . encouraging our members to get involved, but black people do have issues that are of singular importance to them . . . She said treat us with a bit of sensitivity. And the discussion goes along for another five or ten minutes and it turns into a bloody argument. That's hardly showing sensitivity.

He then made a long appeal for the Forum members to be more accommodating before going into his main points which attempted to be even-handed with regard to black on white violence while insisting that white attacks on black victims were often on the basis of race alone. He went on to describe an estate in the north of the borough in which he had once worked and where the TA met with him monthly to discuss matters such as day-to-day repairs, the caretaker service and environmental improvements.

But there was a separate group of tenants on the estate who formed a separate group and they were black tenants . . . [who] didn't give a fig about day-to-day repairs or what the caretaker service was like. Their agenda was why do people racially harass us on the estate and what are you going to do about it. They would have looked on it as sheer luxury to get down to talking about the caretaking service but their focus was always on things that were of immediate importance – was it safe to go out tonight, what would happen when they got home from work tonight.

He described how there was friction between the two groups at first but over time they came to work together and eventually merged. He then made the general point that TAs often divide, groups of tenants set up new associations and many estates have more than one TA. Council policy was to work with any group of tenants who want to form an association. 'That's the way it's always been and that's the way it's going to carry on being, and just because one of those groups happens to be black . . . great.'

It was a long speech, faultless in its logic and reasonableness – a fine example of enlightened and inclusive local government. But the last word fell to Josie:

No. I disagree Martin, because in today's climate we have got those nasty NF people wandering around. They pick up on that sort of issue and with elections coming up the last thing in the world we want, especially in this borough and certainly in Eltham, is to have those people crawling out of the woodwork and putting themselves up for election and if you do have black groups this is the sort of thing they are going to point to because they play one [group of people] off against the other.

Turning to Donna she added: 'I am extremely happy to see you here tonight and I hope that you will come and ever more. But I would ask that you do work with the local tenants associations as well.' A few more calls from the floor, another snatched re-statement from Donna and it was over.

The presentation had achieved very little other than announcing BEMTA's presence. There were also many unresolved issues. There were two difficulties that vitiated the case Donna was trying to make. First, Donna never had actually attempted to make contact with her local TA or attend any of their meetings. Until the project worker from Housing Rights approached her she did not know what a TA was and claimed not to have consciously seen any of the newsletters put out by her local TA. There was also little beyond plausibility to the claims being made about the anxieties of black tenants approaching the TAs. Secondly, given the average age of Forum members and their inevitable interests, it was a strategic error for Donna and those more experienced individuals who had been advising her not to have addressed and embraced as a legitimate concern *non-racial* forms of harassment also occurring on the estates. This worked against the possible emergence of a more constructive dialogue around shared concerns. Proportionately, given the very small number of black and minority ethnic tenants, racial harassment was at a high level relative to the harassment of the elderly who were numerous. None the less despite the clear and humane reasons laid out in the Area Director's justification of BEMTA, it is not difficult to see how these would have been negatively construed by Forum members and ultimately regarded as irrelevant. Furthermore, his example of the grassroots black tenants group that had flourished in the north of the borough was far from an exact parallel with BEMTA as it stood at this stage. BEMTA's membership was very small and not yet stabilised. It had come into existence by direct council stimulation – certainly at a time of widespread black anxiety but it did not emerge spontaneously. Ostensibly this was not an unwarranted intervention by the council, but its execution in that context was clumsy and its results, in the end, were more destructive than positive. It was too easy for some to fall into the trap of seeing local resistance to BEMTA as 'racist' and be blind to the legitimacy of those who saw the move to form a separate group as divisive and who regarded harassment of elderly tenants as a common and serious problem. Both sides were seeing similar features but some read them as a duck, others as a rabbit.

There was, additionally, the issue of the place of actual racist attitudes in relation to the TA activists' critique of BEMTA. Anti-racist strategies during that period in the UK were not good at separating the legitimate concerns of white social groups from the racism which sometimes came attached. While the better strategy was to drive a wedge between legitimate concerns and racist articulations of those concerns, more commonly a confrontationalism was practised in the name of honesty and moral/political righteousness. BEMTA's ultimate demise, within six months of this meeting, also came about from a legitimately argued but confrontational politics that took no cognisance of how grassroots backlash phenomena worked.

So it was that, as the May local government elections approached, the TAs of Eltham were beginning to discuss how best to spend their Community Safety Budget of some £30,000, and proposing projects such as improvement to street lighting and the fencing on certain estates. BEMTA also became interested in the issue of community safety, interpreted in the light of the BNP's determination to put up a candidate for the Eltham area in the forthcoming elections. They now came to the Eltham Forum with a proposal for the safety of black residents that would not cost a penny. BEMTA asked the Forum to endorse a statement explicitly saying that they were opposed to the BNP and to any co-operation with the BNP during the coming council elections. The meeting[12] almost became a riot with speaker after speaker expressing anger and opposition to BEMTA's request. Josie Barber said that the BNP was a *bone fide* political group, 'even if I disagree with its politics' and that the Forum could not endorse the statement. A policeman and local estate resident who had been invited to the meeting as an observer felt moved to say that the BNP was a terrorist organisation and not just another political group. At this remark the meeting exploded with everyone talking at once. 'Everyone was angry with him for saying this', said one participant. 'I thought one man was actually going to hit him.' This was, it seems, the last straw for the meeting. Josie Barber left the chair and stormed out and everyone poured from the room. BEMTA decided never to return to the Eltham Area Forum and planned to expose it as a racist organisation.

Effectively this was the end for BEMTA. The Forum's rejection of the proposal was predictable. Formally treating the BNP as just another political party was not only widely practised at the national level, it was an approach that many had defended on the grounds of free speech. Even if the proposal had been a ploy to get the Forum to expose its 'real'

[12] Eltham Area Tenants Forum, 15 Mar. 1994.

nature, it was in the realm of confrontational politics, and carried major risks. The leading figures in BEMTA came to feel soon after that they had been used by the council advisors who had encouraged them to form and they disbanded with a bitter taste in their mouths. Meanwhile, in the May local elections, the BNP got its highest share of the vote in Sherard ward, where the Page estate was located, achieving 12 per cent. Elsewhere in the borough they were far less fortunate.

Reflections

How valid is the argument, evident in a number of interviews, that what occurred in the case of BEMTA and the Tenants Forum was largely the result of the artificial introduction of racial difference by local authority action in a context where it was not seen by local people as salient? It is unambiguous that high levels of racial harassment were experienced by black residents on the predominantly white estates of Eltham, relative to their numbers. Even by 2004 intimidation of black people, including death threats, although not routine, continued to occur there.[13] Thus one very stark racialisation of residency was already present – even where it did not directly affect every local black resident. The question remains, however, how far the local authority did engage in a further process of racialisation in responding to racial harassment in the way it did in this case? And is all 'racialisation' harmful?

The earliest usage of 'racialisation' in British sociology was simply as the word for a *categorisation* in which racial terms were being used to describe segments of a population – seeing social phenomena through the grid of race.[14] A second usage, developed by Robert Miles in his critique of the 'race-relations' problematic, used the term to denote where 'social relations have been structured by the signification of human biological characteristics in such a way as to define and construct differentiated social collectives'.[15] It can be argued that any appropriate response to quotidian racism in Eltham at this time required broad recognition that serious harassment was taking place aimed specifically at black people. This recognition in itself did not involve any extension of the racialisation process that was occurring, it merely articulated and made explicit what was covert and not widely acknowledged. Protective measures introduced for black families could not be construed as 'racialisation'. However, where responses include treating any individual

[13] See, for example, *Sun*, 4 July 2002; *Metro*, 11 July 2002; *Woolwich and Plumstead News Shopper*, 17 July, 2002, pp. 1 and 5; *South London News*, 17 July 2002, p. 10.
[14] Michael Banton, *The Idea of Race* (London, Tavistock Press, 1977), p. 18.
[15] Robert Miles, *Racism* (London, Routledge, 1989), pp. 74–5.

instance of harassment as more deserving of sympathy and collective action than another on the grounds of race or age, gender, sexual orientation and so on, this constitutes a subdivision setting up the conditions for collective action by those forming the subdivision. This thereby *institutionalises* the category and ratifies its 'difference' from the rest of the population. The racialisation process evident in this dimension resides in the institutionalisation of the social form generated from a racial categorisation.

In this sense it may be true that in going beyond protective measures the instigation of BEMTA *was* a form of racialisation but one which may be regarded by some as *benign*: one which (like 'strategic essentialism') is performed to combat racism and racial violence, and can also form the basis of a political identity. The question arises then as to how far the *benign racialisation* in some particular context functions positively to counter racism and how far it becomes the basis for more racism than it combats. The issue of conflicting kinds of racialisation may be responsible for the *intensity* of many of the disputes characteristic of the local backlashes to racial equalities policies. Just as segregation – including mass public housing involving the 'sons and daughters' policy in a white majority context – can be seen as one form of racialisation, so, it may be argued, other related forms may also include *patterns* of racial harassment generated by such segregation *together with* some equalities-based responses and interventions.

There are two aspects to this possibility. One lies on the pragmatic surface. If a form of 'benign' racialisation employed without taking into account the context in which it is employed produces a surge of backlash at least some part of which – and maybe all – is expressed through racist forms, then it is arguably a matter of strategic and longer-term decision as to whether or not to repeat the process. It was this kind of intervention – but performed *knowingly* – that formed the basis of Martin Luther King's early strategy in the march in Selma, Alabama, in 1963. In this case it was to become an important political instrument, used sparingly and with calculated risks. Without that strategic calculation, however, it can be merely a poorly thought out tactic that backfires. The other aspect concerns a deeper issue of social and political identity. The conflict of racialisations in Eltham could be seen as the subversion by the black tenants group, of the attempt by the TA activists group to impose its definitions of either the *invisibility* of the black tenants group – 'they should have been "tenants" not "black tenants"' – or of the intrusion of the group as 'threatening outsiders', 'trouble makers', etc. That subversion or resistance to being positioned through the various enactments evident in, say, the Eltham Tenants Forum meetings can be viewed in one of two ways. It can be viewed as an unavoidable *political imperative* for members of the black group, and/or as part of a reflective struggle against the internalisation of a forced identity. The conclusion of such a struggle might be the production of either the useful resistance or the excessive reaction alluded to above in the description of the pragmatic response. This is the territory of 'performativity' and 'interpellation' discussed by Judith Butler,[16] where pragmatic options based on objective assessments of situations are rationalist fantasies, where all social situations come already loaded with their positional baggage and where 'sites of resistance' are primarily semiotic and discursive in nature.

There seem reasonable grounds for believing that in some form or another this kind of pragmatic calculation *was* active in the formation of BEMTA at that point in the development of Greenwich Council's approach to racism and that it took a path that led directly to a stand-off and a stalemate. It is worth noting that in 2002, following advice from a firm of consultants for establishing a plan for community involvement in social housing, the consultant's recommendation that a dedicated black and minority ethnic forum be established was comprehensively rejected by all groups of local people consulted – both black and white. An inclusive 'Diversity Revue Panel' serving elected area panels was proposed instead and this was soon initiated and came to be regarded as a success. What this meant at the level of pragmatic choice is therefore clear. What it meant about the political identities at play is less clear.

The question remains, however, as to how far the views and actions of the TA activists can be analytically approached as 'racist' or, if they are so approached, what purchase this gives on their broader political significance. Many of the interviews with council tenants shed light on how 'racial' difference and the claims about the situation of black tenants were regarded at that time. One female tenant activist posed the rhetorical question: 'Who gives you the right to say 'cause you're black you're hard done by, you've got to have more laws for you, no-one is to say a wrong thing to you because you can take them to court? But if you're white you can't, and this is what causes problems on the estates.' Another told how:

I was shocked, actually, when they said about this racial harassment. To me I don't care what colour they are – blue, green, yellow, orange – you're all supposed

---

[16] Judith Butler, 'Performativity's Social Magic', in Richard Shusterman (ed.), *Bourdieu: A Critical Reader* (Oxford, Blackwell, 1999), p. 125; Judith Butler, *Excitable Speech: a Politics of the Performative* (New York and London, Routledge, 1997), pp. 153–4.

to be tenants. If you're all tenants you should all be treated the same. I feel this council has made one of the biggest cockups in history. They've made people feel just because they're a different colour, a different race, they're something special. Now they can't back down. They can't treat them all like tenants.

The conviction of reasonableness is apparent in the incredulity at the mention of racial harassment. Even if this informant did not care 'what colour [people] are', her conclusion – 'If you're all tenants you should all be treated the same' did not lead her into a reappraisal of her local understanding but rather to a renewed criticism of the council's support for black tenants. There is a deep confusion here over the processes of ways of redressing wrongs, with few footholds for climbing out.

An elderly white male tenant who had suffered a vicious attack by two local white young men was more analytical in his reflections and denied the salience of race in local attacks on black people in the following way:

I have a great belief that this racial business, quite frankly, it doesn't matter. It's a load of bullshit. Because really, what it is, is if they're not having a go and saying 'You Paki bastard' or 'You black bastard', right, they're saying, 'You *old* bastard', right, or they're saying 'You *crippled* bastard.' It just so happens that when they say 'racial harassment', that is the one they are having a go at. The actual people that are doing it are the same people, no matter whether they're having a go at the aged, whether it's the Pakistanis, the Vietnamese . . . it's the same people that are doing it. It's nothing to do with a particular race or anything . . . I think it's a symptom, not a cause . . . One of the problems of saying it's racial, one of the problems that you've got with actually singling people out, making them racial, saying that this is a *racial* attack is that you immediately single them out from the crowd and make them different, right? It becomes a 'them and us' situation. The classic example nowadays is if a white fellow goes and mugs a black fellow it's racial, if the black fellow goes and mugs the white fellow it's a mugging, and that is where we've gone wrong, quite frankly. We've now got 'all men are equal but some men are more equal than others'. You can't have that. That's like having one rule for the rich and one rule for the poor.

The interview continued:

INTERVIEWER: Up here, where there have been two racial murders, do you think there's a reason to be more alarmed?
TENANT: There's been two racial murders?
INTERVIEWER: Yes.
TENANT: How the hell do you know they're racial? There's been some old people been murdered as well. What were they? There was a woman quite recently who was murdered in Plumstead. They can't figure out the reason. What are we going to put that down to? There's no such thing as a racial murder, right. It is an excuse. A murder is a murder, is a murder.

INTERVIEWER: But with the Stephen Lawrence case it is said they were actually calling out 'nigger' before they killed him.
TENANT: Round here they call me you *old* bastard, so what is that?

He then took his account a little deeper:

But 'racial' is something that has been played up and played up and played up till it's actually been *brought into existence* in effect, quite honestly . . . The council has took it on from the press, the press originally started to play it up. But then you've got what they call do-gooders, but in actual fact they're not. You've got certain – how can I put it – people with a vested interest who want to lay in a particular line . . . and put something forward which for them would be a good thing. And that is it, I mean for a number of reasons. One, they intend to get a job out of it. That's one. Two, it's a belief in their mind, right. *I mean they actually do believe it exists. I think personally it's something which has been taught into people, quite frankly.* If you have one law for one and one law for another, then you will have a difference and that difference will stand out. If you have one law for everyone, no matter who they are, how they are or what they are, then that is the law of England and that is the law you abide by.

This is, of course, the liberal position on justice that is argued against communitarian claims within the multicultural debate. It is also the 'national solidarity vs diversity' critique of the tensions within multiculturalism that is often voiced. It is obvious from these passages that the denial of 'racial harassment' is not *simply* a protection of 'white' interests, although such denials may contribute to racial harassment not being taken seriously. What we find, rather, is a clear and coherent view that 'difference' is almost created by council policy and by the press. It is, in the usual sociological sense, a 'construction' – and in this 'creation of difference', communities are set against each other or, in a new third sense, 'racialised' through an act of conceptual engineering. Furthermore, there is also here a social account of the generation of this construction in the allusion to the material *self-interest* also evident in those 'people with a vested interest who want to lay in a particular line' – even though they 'actually do believe [racism]exists', i.e. an account of the institutional and economic concerns of those involved in the promotion of the term 'race'. We have here a 'folk version' of the theory of the 'new class' of self-interested public policy workers and academics discussed in Chapter 1.

Of course this viewpoint's 'coherence' ignores a great deal, but it has to be perceived not as 'irrational racism' but as holding together as a truth for significant numbers of people. They believe it and they deeply *feel* it to be true. It is a position held by many whose politics are regarded as very far from racism. It is also profoundly connected to the wider discursive struggles internationally evident across the period over the rival claims of multiculturalist notions of justice, and the classical liberal notions of 'blind justice'.[17]

This passage in particular opens on to an important issue in the politics of race. Such sentiments as those expressed by these informants are often dismissed by some multiculturalists as hypocritical, as ignoring the oppressive racialisation that has been fundamental to Western ideologies for years. But the argument clearly cuts both ways and lies at the heart of the paradox of the 'unreality of race' argument in anti-racism.

There also appears to be a possible additional and circumstantial *social* contest of competing voices/'identities' going on here. The informant categorically refuses the relevance of *race* or *ethnicity* in this context, just as he draws a parallel in rejecting the potential use of *age* as a relevant category – despite himself and others he knows having suffered from attacks possibly related to age. He sees age as a form of vulnerability on his estate and regards race in the same way. His argument is that harassers harass the vulnerable – of any kind. But behind this point lays the wider community of elderly people who make up the core of the TA activists and Eltham Forum members. As Christian Joppke and Stephen Lukes point out, for the most part, a sociology of multicultural debate would suggest that within these political contests (but obviously not more widely in other political arenas) minorities rarely speak for themselves.[18] Their causes tend to be championed by intellectuals and bureaucrats. In this instance the black minority group was championed through a local bureaucratic attempt to stimulate a grassroots organisation – though the BEMTA did 'speak for itself' albeit with council encouragement and protection. It is possible for the responses of the largely elderly TA activists to be seen as an unchampioned 'elderly' minority group in conflict with the black minority, each seeking recognition. The black group was institutionally sponsored while the elderly group was not. This kind of conflict is a strand of the multicultural in local contexts that is rarely examined, yet

---

[17] William Rogers Brubaker (ed.), *Immigration and the Politics of Citizenship in Europe and North America* (Lanham, Md., German Marshall Fund and University Press of America, 1989); David Miller and Michael Malzer (eds.), *Pluralism, Justice and Equality* (Oxford, Oxford University Press, 1995); Will Kymlicka, *Multicultural Citizenship: A Liberal Theory of Minority Rights* (Oxford, Oxford University Press, 1995); Joseph H. Carens, *Culture, Citizenship and Community: A Contextual Exploration of Justice as Evenhandedness* (Oxford, Oxford University Press, 2000); Paul Kelly (ed.), *Multiculturalism Reconsidered* (Cambridge, Polity Press, 2000); Barry, *Culture and Equality.*
[18] Christian Joppke and Steven Lukes (eds.), *Multicultural Questions* (Oxford, Oxford University Press, 1999), p. 2.

emergent states of affairs of this kind must be occurring frequently, then subsiding or growing into fully fledged political battles.

All this looks, to some degree, like a storm in a teacup. It is probably true that the same protective and pro-active measures for the black communities could have been instituted by the council without the need for 'divisiveness' or for anything that looked like black 'exceptionalism'. Elderly tenants felt the sting of this putative exceptionalism intensely. But was this, as appears from these materials, the dramatisation, acted out in a public arena, of a conflict between universalistic liberal principles of justice on the one hand and a communitarian claim being made on the other? The allusions to 'quotas' – never a real issue in the UK – and appeals to a conception of justice that does not include individual exceptions and special cases as communitarian concepts of justice do,[19] suggest at least parts of the ideological apparatus underlying the white TA activists' perceptions. However, this case differs from some of the larger disputes over multiculturalism evoked by the recourse to these arguments. The dispute did not involve any historical or other claim for special treatment to correct past wrongs, neither was it about any singular cultural practice. What was sought by BEMTA was a ratification of its claim that special attention needed to be given to the safety of black tenants because there had been high levels of racial harassment and two racist murders in the Eltham area. This was not a claim about inadequate policing, it was a request for an expression of humanitarian concern and community vigilance over racial violence. The request can be regarded as a parallel to the expectation of equal treatment and protection under the law – with no special pleading involved. In that respect it was just as the Area Director argued in his long ameliorative speech to the Forum meeting.

If this is true, the dispute was ultimately about the reality of racism more than any other matter – as Donna had insisted. This case also illuminates the fact that at least some claims by anti-racists can be made from well within the terms of the liberal position over justice. They sit comfortably with the forms of multiculturalism that are based on human rights and with those that argue for a multiculturalism where 'minority rights co-exist with human rights' and where 'minority rights are limited by principles of individual liberty, democracy, and social justice'.[20]

What is evident in the case of BEMTA, however, is a local struggle fought out with the fragments and armoury of previous ideological

---

[19] Charles Taylor, *Multiculturalism and 'The Politics of Recognition'* (Princeton, Princeton University Press, 1992); Amy Gutman (ed.), *Multiculturalism: Examining the Politics of Recognition* (Princeton, N. J., Princeton University Press, 1994).

[20] Kymlicka, *Multicultural Citizenship*, p. 6.

battles. BEMTA was seen by the Forum members as representing an unreasonable demand by a black minority group with support from the local state. They are positioned by the most respectable of liberal claims, yet, as at certain points in the Forum meetings was starkly apparent, these over-laid some deep reservoirs of hostility and naked racism. The *dramatis personae* of this ensemble performance by the TAs were not, however, each of a similar kind. They shared in the construction of the tableau but had several quite different motivations and perceptions. Nevertheless, the composite effect was one of 'recognition' declined. It appears, therefore, that even where a claim by a black group is made on purely liberal grounds, these can be misrepresented and characterised as – and indeed *felt* to be – objectionable for 'all reasonable people'.

6   'Race' and 'culture' in education: from neighbourhood schools to the multicultural highway

In an article in *The Times* in 1996 Chris Woodhead, the Chief Inspector of English schools, warned about what he saw as the most important challenge to education in the UK: the persistent failure of white working-class boys to succeed in the school system. They were, he said, leaving school with the lowest results of any group. They suffered from a culture of failure and anti-school attitudes and left facing unemployment as a result. Their education, he argued, presented a major challenge to the educational establishment.[1]

Woodhead's concerns received some attention from other sections of the press[2] and from academics.[3] His views were challenged by some feminist researchers who believed they saw in them an attack on female teachers and girl pupils for 'denying boys a fair chance'. They were also challenged by some educationalists who saw his observations as racist in prioritising white boys over African-Caribbean boys who were long recognised as failing in the system.[4]

Because of inconsistencies in local education authority monitoring classifications, figures were disputed. Nevertheless, the issue continued to be of concern and some London boroughs in time came to identify

---

[1] Chris Woodhead, 'Boys Who Learn to Be Losers', *Times*, 6 Mar. 1996, p. 18.

[2] 'Great White Dopes: Working-Class White Boys are the Big Failures in Britain's Schools', *Sun*, 7 Mar. 1996, p. 2.

[3] Madeline Arnot, John Gray, Mary James, Jean Rudduck with Gerard Duveen, *Recent Research on Gender and Educational Performance* (London, The Stationery Office, 1998).

[4] David Gillborn and Caroline Gipps, *Recent Research on the Achievements of Ethnic Minority Pupils* (Report for the Office for Standards in English, London, HMSO); David Gillborn and Deborah Youdell, *Rationing Education: Policy, Practice, Reform and Equity* (Buckingham, Open University Press, 2000), pp. 34–41; David Gillborn and Heidi Safia Mirza, *Educational Inequality: Mapping Race, Class and Gender: A Synthesis of Research Evidence* (London, Office for Standards in Education, 2000); Debborah Epstein, Jannette Elwood, Valerie Hey and Janet Maw (eds.), *Failing Boys? Issues in Gender and Achievement* (Buckingham, Open University Press, 1998); Patricia Murphy and Jannette Elwood, 'Gendered Experiences, Choices and Achievement – Exploring the Links', *International Journal of Inclusive Education*, 2,2 (1998), pp. 95–118.

more exactly the phenomenon in their own school populations.[5] This also presented them with some political difficulties in devising appropriate interventions where attempts were made to earmark resources against the lobbying of some minority groups. While even those minority groups, such as the Bangladeshis, that had once trailed behind all others, showed clear improvement after the late 1990s and certain ethnic groups such as the Chinese and Indians consistently outstrip white pupils from middle-class professional and managerial homes, the performance of white working-class boys in the capital has remained unchanged. They continue to be as poor and in some cases poorer than African-Caribbean boys.[6]

The political sensitivity of targeting these white pupils at the local level was also apparent in Greenwich when, in 1997, at the launch of a European Community-funded project to address racism amongst marginalised white youth, the proposals were attacked by local community activists. The project was accused of being a waste of resources which should have been spent on black youth, much to the distress of the youth workers who were tentatively beginning to pilot ways to tackle the problem of adolescent racism on the estates in new ways.[7] Indeed, almost any kind of attention to this social group has been persistently contentious despite its being identified with a range of social problems.

In Greenwich the problems of racism amongst white adolescents had a long history stretching back to the 1970s when racist organisations, including the National Front and the British Movement, were very active in the area, when large skinhead gangs were numerous and when cases of racial harassment were also common.[8] The three racist murders in the early 1990s marked the low point in a trough of adolescent racist violence. The response of the local authority was to take a range of measures through its various departments. Within its Directorate of Education, the monitoring of racist incidents between pupils was increased, training in anti-racist work with young people was stepped up and attention was paid to emphasising positively the multicultural make-up of the borough. While this endeavour was successful with many young people, a negative reaction to anti-racism and multicultural policies in schools was marked amongst white pupils across the estates

[5] See, for example, Kate Myers, *Underachievement of White Working Class Pupils in Camden Schools: A Report of the PACE Project* (London, Camden Council, 2004).
[6] Gillborn and Youdell, *Rationing Education*, pp. 38–9.
[7] European Cities Anti-Racist Project, launch, Greenwich Council, Town Hall, 1997.
[8] See Roger Hewitt, *White Talk Black Talk: Inter-Racial Friendship and Communication amongst Adolescents* (Cambridge, Cambridge University Press, 1986), pp. 30–7; Hewitt, *Routes of Racism*, p. 5.

and beyond. This was often expressed in terms that were reminiscent of reactions to race equalities policies elsewhere. It was 'backlash phenomena' of a kind, yet it was unsupported by any groundswell of adult interest. Parents took no part in it and neither was it articulated in any public arena – only across the relays of adolescent communication by young whites who had inherited the downside of 'restructuring' without the prospect of any more positive future. The strong areas of the economy lay in service industries and IT where educational qualifications beyond their imaginings were required. Apprenticeships in traditional trades had dwindled to nothing.[9]

The framework in which educational change occurred in response to equalities issues was substantially different to earlier periods in the history of 'white backlash'. The immediately preceding period in the UK had been much concerned with the very public battle over multicultural education that had taken place mainly in Labour-controlled urban boroughs and been aired in the national press on an unprecedented scale. In the period preceding that bilingual education had been an important issue, as, for a while, had the question of 'bussing' – although neither of these assumed the importance they had had in the USA. Bussing, practised fleetingly and on a minute scale in the UK, would have been far more a matter for minority ethnic protest than white as it involved the dispersal of south Asian pupils so that no white school would be 'oversubscribed'. White children were never subjected to it.

The demographics of colour and ethnicity were also very different in the UK and the USA with something around only 3 per cent of the UK population in the 1970s being from black minorities as against some 12 per cent in the USA. Nevertheless, in coming to understand the range of issues and the changes that have been evident in backlash phenomena over the post-equalities period, comparisons are instructive.

I

Race, equality and multicultural education

In the USA, of all race equalities activity, across the period from 1954 until the mid-1990s, it was educational change which generated the strongest reactions. The primary struggle from *Brown vs The Board of*

[9] Linda McDowell, 'Transitions to Work: Masculine Identities, Youth Inequality and Labour Market Change', *Gender, Place and Culture*, 9, 1 (2002), pp. 39–59; Robert MacDonald, 'Youth Transitions and Social exclusion: Some Issues for Youth Research in the UK', *Journal of Youth Studies*, 1 (1998), pp. 163–76; Andy Furlong and F. Cartmel, *Young People and Social Change: Individualisation and Risk in Late Modernity* (Milton Keynes, Open University Press, 1997).

Education to the crisis over bussing in the 1960s and 1970s was about equality and the attempt to correct the long-established process of racial disadvantage occurring through residential segregation and the unequal distribution of educational resources. The struggle for equality and justice was a struggle against institutional racism. The idea of 'multicultural education' was only just being developed across the border in Canada and the notion of the 'recognition of difference' would have seemed a callous eccentricity in the face of black educational exclusion as it stood in the USA in the 1950s and early 1960s.

By the early 1970s, however, increasingly school curricula in some states were including some form of black studies and reflecting diversity more widely – a movement towards a kind of multiculturalism but not yet in name. The 'ethnic revival' of the 1960s and 1970s also gave a new prominence to ethnicities in the USA[10] and at the same time the attention in educational race politics focussed on admissions and programmes in tertiary education. By the late 1980s and early 1990s the idea of multiculturalism had increased in volume dramatically, taking on a far broader meaning than in any other national setting, including sexual and gendered identities alongside religious, ethnic and 'racial' ones. A struggle over the content of the curriculum in schools and universities became prominent and 'multicultural education' came to embrace far more issues than institutional racism. This much was reflected in journalist Richard Bernstein's book *Dictatorship of Virtue: How the Battle over Multiculturalism is Reshaping our Schools, our Country, and our Lives*. It had much to say about topics such as the decision to remove a putatively celebrated course in European history at a Massachusetts high school on the grounds of Eurocentrism in the curriculum, but also about the monitoring of sexist language and gender bias in the texts used in colleges and universities.[11]

This widely read book, along with Danish D'Souza's *Illiberal Education: The Politics of Race and Sex on Campus* (1991), carried forward an attack on multiculturalism that had already got under way with Alan Bloom's *The Closing of the American Mind* (1987) which argued the case that anti-racism and multiculturalism actually generated racism. Similar arguments were made in E. D. Hirsh's also influential *Cultural Literacy* (1987).[12] These were significant salvos in the 'Culture

---

[10] Kymlicka, *Multicultural Citizenship*, pp. 61–5.

[11] Richard Bernstein, *Dictatorship of Virtue: How the Battle over Multiculturalism Is Reshaping our Schools, our Country, and our Lives* (New York, Vintage Books, 1994), pp. 137–46, 235–91.

[12] Danish D'Souza *Illiberal Education: The Politics of Race and Sex on Campus* (New York, Free Press, 1991); Alan Bloom, *The Closing of the American Mind* (New York, Simon and

Wars' that raged, not without some politically motivated fuelling from right-wing think-tanks such as the American Enterprise Institute, which funded D'Souza's work – as did the John M. Olin Foundation which also supported Alan Bloom.[13] They were also an important component in the second wave of backlash that was established at the level of national politics during the Reagan/Bush period.[14]

The contrast of this later cultural and political backlash with the forms that backlash had assumed in the late 1960s and early 1970s – and with the forms of backlash evident in the early 1990s in the UK – are instructive when we examine the struggles over bussing. Never called the 'Bussing Wars' but operating on a scale and with an intensity that would not have gone unnoticed by anyone, these were almost foundational in the image of 'white backlash' in the USA.

Desegregation, bussing and the white backlash in the USA

The early phases of school desegregation outside the South faced head-on the major obstacle of racial residential patterns and in so doing also threw into relief the contours of class and racism on which they were grounded.[15] The early to mid-1970s proved to be the eye of the storm with regard to *popular* reactions against civil rights legislation. Among these, education spawned an almost definitive series of 'backlash' responses. At that time the failure to desegregate comprehensively had been recognised; the issue had been broadened beyond the South to include the North and West, and school districts were now required by federal law to draw up and implement plans to integrate. Local official policies that created or maintained segregated schools were deemed to constitute *de jure* not merely *de facto* segregation, and thus to violate federal anti-segregation law. The issue of neighbourhood schools and racial intake became a national matter, one in which the remedy of bussing students of different races within districts to achieve integration rapidly became central. Thus it was possible for Gary Orfield to write: 'Busing was the last important issue to emerge from the civil rights

Schuster, 1987); E. D. Hirsch Jr, *Cultural Literacy: What Every American Needs to Know* (Boston, Houghton Mifflin, 1987).
[13] Gitlin, *The Twilight of Common Dreams*, p. 182.
[14] For an aggressively argued account of the backlash from within US universities and outside, see, Steinberg, *Turning Back*.
[15] Gary Orfield, Susan E. Eaton and the Harvard Project on School Desegregation, *Dismantling Desegregation: The Quiet Reversal of Brown v. Board of Education* (New York, The New Press, 1996), pp. 291–330.

movement of the 1960s and the only one to directly affect the lives of large numbers of whites outside the South.[16]

Once judges began to examine school district practices in the North and West they found widespread violations of many kinds. These included discriminatory drawing of attendance zones, discriminatory location of new schools and school boards' failure to relieve overcrowding at white schools by transferring students to available places in nearby minority schools. These and other practices were evident in many cities in the USA outside of the South including Cleveland, San Francisco, Indianapolis and Boston.[17] Despite similarities between cases, how bussing worked or failed to work in different areas depended much on the specific local politics, demography and history of race issues. These local features affected the nature and extent of any backlash.

Of all the examples of popular white resistance to the national imposition of civil rights measures outside the South, that of bussing within the Boston school system was undoubtedly amongst the most widely known, if not the most typical.[18] The segregational practices of the Boston school committee had provoked early protests from the National Association for the Advancement of Colored People (NAACP) which had been consistently rebuffed. The 1950s and 1960s had seen massive suburbanisation, re-enforced by the city's largest influx of blacks, the loss of several thousand jobs in the city and a gain of 66,000 new jobs on the high tech complex off Route 128 – where blacks were unlikely to find work or housing – later dubbed 'Boston's Road to Segregation'.[19] With economic pressure on Boston's white working class, particularly the Irish working class, the scene was set for deepseated resentments to be played out in the nationally most prominent conflicts over bussing in the USA.

The ugly scenes and violence seen on televisions across the world became the known face of bussing, ultimately contributing to widespread opposition by politicians. Senator Ted Kennedy, who did

---

[16] Gary Orfield, *Must We Bus? Segregated Schools and National Policy* (Washington DC, The Brookings Institution, 1978), p. 1.

[17] Ibid., Table 1–1 'Discrimination Found by Federal Courts in Northern School Desegregation Cases, 1956–76', pp. 20–2; Robert L. Crain, *The Politics of School Desegregation: Comparative Case Studies of Community Structure and Policy-Making* (Chicago, Aldine Publishing Company, 1968).

[18] See J. Michael Ross and William M. Berg, '*I Respectfully Disagree with the Judge's Order*': *The Boston School Desegregation Controversy* (Washington, University Press of America, 1981); Emmett H. Buell Jr, with Richard A. Brisbin Jr, *School Desegregation and Defended Neighborhoods: The Boston Controversy* (Lexington, Mass., Lexington Books, 1982); Formisano, *Boston against Busing*.

[19] Formisano, *Boston against Busing*, pp. 12–13

not oppose the bussing orders, came to epitomise the potential fate of politicians falling foul of the white backlash when he was harried from City Hall Plaza by a crowd of several thousand protesters. The feeling, especially amongst the Irish Catholics, was that he 'of all people' had 'betrayed' them. Nixon on the other hand was quick to condemn the 'enforced desegregation' represented by bussing orders and Wallace, too, long vocal on this issue, put his voice behind popular feeling. This synchronisation of nationally prominent local backlashes and their public endorsement by canny politicians became a common feature of reactions to bussing as to equalities policies in general.

Class was a major factor in Boston's crisis, as judge W. Arthur Garrity Jr's bussing orders seemed to impact most forcefully on white and black working-class neighbourhoods like South Boston and Charlestown, Dorchester and Roxbury. At the same time, while it undoubtedly included racists, the revolt also included many working-class moderates and middle-class liberals who opposed bussing on moral and political grounds. Furthermore, it came to embrace wider middle-class interests as issues emerged about how much of the metropolitan area was to be included to achieve desegregation.[20] Nationally this articulation of middle-class concerns also came to combine in popular political consciousness with another current and strongly middle-class concern of the period – the issue of competition for higher education access. Indeed the Bakke case, relating to quotas for minority students in the University of California–Davis medical school, was becoming prominent and fiercely disputed during exactly the same period that bussing was achieving its profile as a potentially middle-class concern – the latter temporarily relieved by *Milliken vs Bradley 1974* when suburban areas were ruled out of the reckoning.[21]

This was not what gave the Boston struggles their singular ferocity, however. The consistent refusal of the school committee to accept criticism, its decision to ride with the tide of popular feeling against bussing, together with the high degree of organised resistance by parents' groups – by ROAR ('Restore Our Alienated Rights') in particular, dominated by 'anti-busing's Mother Superior', Louise Day Hicks – combined to create a major confrontation.[22] As Ronald P. Formisano pointed out: 'Like many other citizens' movements of the 1970s, antibusing expressed rampant citizen alienation from impersonal government, drawing on an ingrained, deeply felt sense of injustice,

[20] Ibid., p. 16.
[21] Orfield et al., *Dismantling Desegregation*, pp. 12–13.
[22] S. J. L. Taylor, *Desegregation in Boston and Buffalo: The Influence of Local Leaders* (Albany, N.Y., State University of New York Press, 1998).

unfairness, and deprivation of rights.'[23] Furthermore, this structure of relationships between the white Irish, black working-class and middle-class liberals was to some degree built on an ancient frame which ran back

deep into Boston's history, to the mid-nineteenth century when peculiar group dynamics among Yankee Protestants, lower-class Irish Catholic immigrants, and a small black population exacerbated an already hostile relationship between the two low-status groups. While most Protestants mingled with neither group, Yankee reformers treated the blacks with a paternalistic benevolence, however distant, and regarded the Catholic Irish with fear, disdain, or contempt. The two pariah groups shared competition for jobs at the bottom as well as the symbolic status as the 'niggers' of Anglo-Protestant society, which was enough for the Irish to adopt an unforgiving attitude towards the African Americans.[24]

This, in the context of the national exemption of suburbs from school segregation plans, in the end 'made any plan applied only to Boston highly biased in terms of class'.[25]

The melange of groups and interests involved in this revolt generated a number of features that were to be seen in other 'backlash' settings. In particular the style of protest borrowed heavily from the civil rights tradition and, at the same time, the theme of the protesters struggling to get a 'voice' also reared its head. Formisano provides a detailed portrait of the perception amongst the anti-bussers of their powerlessness and their absence of 'voice'. He argues:

The antibusers' complaints that they lacked 'voice' tapped into attitudes as powerful as any other in motivating protest and generating widespread discontent. Having no voice meant that they were essentially powerless; not being heard was the condition of those who were being unjustly imposed on by a too-powerful government and what they saw as the arbitrary whims of an appointed federal judge.[26]

As the anti-bussers came to organise themselves their natural imagery was that of 1960s protest, inverted and re-cycled. It blended those who were not given to expressing themselves through racism with those who unambiguously were, and produced hybrids like the photograph of the South Boston anti-bussing protester with his long hair, peace symbol and racist effigy of a black figure.[27] Formisano argues that in particular the organised active expressions of anti-bussing should be seen as examples of the 'reactionary populism' evident frequently in American history,[28] which, if it 'continues to be misunderstood as it has been, particularly by

---

[23] Formisano, *Boston against Busing*, p. 3.
[24] Ibid., p. 225.   [25] Ibid.   [26] Ibid., pp. 190–1.
[27] Ibid., p. 144.   [28] Ibid., p. 3.

liberals and progressives, then conservative politicians – whose trickle-down economic policies consistently favor corporations and the wealthy – will continue to reap votes among the very "little people" whose social well-being is made so precarious by those same policies'.[29]

Despite the prominence of Boston's bussing conflicts, nationally the picture with respect to desegregation was, according to Gary Orfield, extremely varied and modulated by local historical conditions. Certain patterns of political relationships and alignments could be seen to re-occur – conflicting pressures within school boards, strong feelings about the coherence of neighbourhoods, protesters attracting political backing to fight orders – but how these played out varied considerably. In some instances desegregation was achieved with little fuss, in others the outcomes – even following a backlash – achieved a form of compromise that established racial integration where there had been none.[30] The case of Richmond school district, California, was of this kind.[31]

Richmond in the mid-1960s was a factory workers' town close to San Fransisco Bay, with a 35 per cent black population. In 1965 its school district was extended to include a group of local towns, all predomin-antly white. The school board had a long pre-history of being well disposed towards racial equality. In its first year the board of the Richmond Unified School District was presented with a detailed report by the local Congress of Racial Equality (CORE) chapter that was critical of the extent of elementary segregation. Unusually this liberally minded board had 'tacitly initiated the confrontation and was favourably disposed to CORE's position'.[32] The board formally acknowledged the need to achieve a racial balance in the schools and appointed a 'citizens advisory committee' that was predominantly liberal in outlook to produce a report with recommendations. From the board's point of view the committee's strategic function was to legitimise the process of desegregation as democratically achieved amongst a somewhat uncer-tain local citizenry. The board would then have some form of mandate to begin the process of racially reforming the school district. Those who had run for office on the school board at that time were 'a different breed' than earlier candidates – more cosmopolitan, less 'local'. Their concerns over racial equity were, it has been argued, 'derived from a

[29] Ibid., pp. 236–7.
[30] Orfield, *Must We Bus? passim.*
[31] The most detailed accounts are to be found in Lillian Rubin, *Busing and Backlash: White against White in a California School District* (Berkeley, University of California Press, 1972); David L. Kirp, *Just Schools: The Idea of Racial Equality in American Education* (Berkeley, University of California Press, 1982), pp. 117–47.
[32] Rubin, *Busing and Backlash*, pp. 84–9; Kirp, *Just Schools*, p. 123.

national frame of reference stressing equal opportunity and the elimination of racial barriers'.[33]

By May 1966 white residents had come to understand for the first time that the school board may be considering re-assigning students to achieve racial balance. A 'Citizens Committee for Neighborhood Schools' (CCNS) was rapidly formed and an 11,000 signature petition opposing re-assignment and 'forced busing' presented to the board and rejected.[34] In response, black groups, including CORE, anxious that their efforts would be forced off the agenda, demanded immediate desegregation and threatened to organise boycotts at two predominantly black junior high schools.

The board sought to reassure the black organisations and community through a number of significant measures. It believed that it was possible to bring black and white together despite their differences. However, when the report of the 'citizens advisory committee' came in March 1967 its recommendations did not include elementary desegregation as expected but proposed instead a complex set of alternative measures which only antagonised the different groups. Thus the school board's attempt to secure community legitimation for its race equality strategy failed and was to rebound in a wider than wished-for politicisation of the issues. The CCNS managed to get two members on to the board in the 1967 election and the board's previous liberal consensus was lost. Further compromise attempts were made to establish the principle of desegregation – particularly through voluntary desegregation plans – but conflicting positions consistently predominated and new competing political groups emerged in a widespread backlash to the once ruling liberal group.[35] This backlash was largely developed from the unified vote of white working-class and lower-middle-class parents, particularly as expressed in an umbrella organisation, United School Parents (USP), the elected leaders of which were almost exclusively working-class whites. The more middle-class members were forced to take a backseat. As in Boston there was a strong strain of overt racism evident in the USP: 'The overt racism that was articulate and rampant often offended middle-class sensibilities, and many left the organisation. Many others who stayed were always a little apologetic.'[36]

The 1969 school board election became a watershed and a rout for the liberal board with a massive turnout of voters organised, very vocal and successfully set on electing a conservative board that was

---

[33] Ibid., p. 124.   [34] Rubin, *Busing and Backlash*, p. 93.
[35] Kirp, *Just Schools*, p. 123.   [36] Rubin, *Busing and Backlash*, p. 135.

unambiguously anti-bussing.[37] The informal alliance of local liberal organisations was then forced to seek desegregation through the courts, instead of directly through the board. This proved a long-drawn-out and contradictory process, the upshot of which was, paradoxically, the implementation of a *voluntary* 'Richmond Integration Plan' – inevitably involving bussing – by a school board elected by the efforts of the popular anti-bussing movement. Time also proved the Plan to be far more than merely a formal acquiescence to a minimal desegregation process but an open enrolment that became incrementally productive of clear, if still imperfect, integration. Welcomed by conservatives as 'desegregation without enforcement' and brought about following a powerfully vocal and popular anti-bussing lobby, the strange dialectic of events had somehow produced a process of change that through most of the 1970s was observed to compare very favourably with other Northern cities in the levels of desegregation it achieved.[38]

The shift in school populations was produced almost entirely by black families opting for enrolment in predominantly white schools. It was characteristically adopted by families from the black middle class whose options, especially once subsidised bussing was cut from the local budget, were greater that those of black working-class families whose children continued to be concentrated in the worst city schools. Thus, while many of the familiar elements of anti-bussing agonistics were present in Richmond, and despite a politically and socially mixed backlash to initial attempts to bring about across-the-board integration, the process was neither reminiscent of the ugly scenes of Boston, nor did it resemble the prolonged stagnation of many other cities.

Bussing-related backlashes produced intriguing temporary alliances across class boundaries, yet they demonstrated forcefully the ubiquity of struggles growing out of the positioning of working-class communities by forces beyond their control. In Boston the contempt for the concerns of the whites in 'Southie' about their valued neighbourhood mingled with revulsion from the strain of aggressive racism that was also evident.[39] Unnecessarily punitive orders were placed on South Boston following the protest that with hindsight looked more vindictive than balanced. These were made possible both by the ugliness of the racism *and* the differing investments in emergent social orders. Formisano shows very clearly the distortions of perspective reaped when the white working class 'screams and acts out its frustrations in public', and notes how 'Neighbourhood militants and racists are catapulted into influence and to the forefront of

[37] Ibid., pp. 143–54.   [38] Kirp, *Just Schools*, pp. 127–8.
[39] Ross and Berg, '*I Respectfully Disagree with the Judge's Order*', pp. 18–19.

media attention, while an aura of shame begins to infect the atmosphere. This allows the rest of society, particularly middle-class liberals, to feel morally superior to the "racists" in South Boston.'[40]

Class also wound its way through the history of bussing in Richmond, to the benefit of middle-class blacks and whites, while perpetuating the gulf between the black working-class communities and the rest. The predominantly black elementary schools became more segregated than they were before open enrolment and, as David Kirp admits, 'Open enrolment helped to create two separate school systems in Richmond, one desegregated and one black. The former appears to be working reasonably well. The latter, in which most of Richmond's black students are enrolled, is in serious trouble.'[41] Despite this limitation, Kirp's sanguine view of the desegregation of Richmond's schools lies in the fact that he is concerned with how school systems can make as large a gain as possible in educational justice with the least amount of backlash and negative polarisation to impede its achievement. Furthermore, as desegregation became seen as one amongst several possible routes to educational equality and the focus on it alone began to recede, views on what was significant also broadened. Kirp's is an essentially political pragmatist's view that brings him to the conclusion that 'in terms of numerical desegregation and community reaction, Richmond has done better than many supposedly more enlightened places'.[42]

These examples from the early period of popular-based opposition to race equalities legislation demonstrate a few apparent similarities with features of equalities backlash activity in the multiculturalist post-1980s period. Some groups, such as South Boston's white working-class community, felt their concerns lacked recognition before an implacable judge and a vocal liberal elite. Their complaints about being without 'voice' in the absence of media acknowledgement or political representation were more accurately descriptions of the apparent powerlessness of their political allies at the local level, despite the profile some national politicians achieved by their exhibitions of support for the anti-bussers. This theme of discursive exclusion was developed in the wake of the highly visible and vocal civil rights movement, and the contrast itself was part of its resonance. By the 1990s discursive exclusion began to mean both more – in technological terms[43] – and less – in terms of urban

---

[40] Formisano, *Busing and Backlash*, p. 233.

[41] Kirp, *Just Schools*, p. 146.

[42] Ibid., p. 147.

[43] 6P, *Escaping Poverty: From Safety Nets to Networks of Opportunity* (London, Demos, 1997); Danny Kruger, 'Access Denied', in *Demos Collection, 12: The Wealth and Poverty of Networks: Tackling Social Exclusion* (London, Demos, 1997), pp. 20–1.

politics and neighbourhood activism. Neighbourhoods were no longer what they had been.

On the other hand, Richmond's white working-class anti-bussers could not complain. Their efforts had achieved conservative control of the previously liberal school board and their organisations had provided them with a platform for their feelings and opinions. At least in the moment of conflict they had defeated the middle-class liberal managers of the Richmond Unified School District. Their victory was primarily of symbolic importance – even part of class struggle, 'white against white' as Lillian Rubin's book *Busing and Backlash* has it. The fact that all previously white schools became integrated in the years that followed was apparently not a matter of struggle, opposition or disappointment, merely part of a new reality that came to be taken as normal.

Each of these sets of events was occurring throughout the period in which Republican political strategists were coming to see and develop the potential of anti-race-equalities issues for harnessing the popular vote and turning the political tide decisively to the right. It was part of the dialogue that started with the difficulties and anxieties sparked in white working-class neighbourhoods as civil rights legislation and policies began to threaten to impact on them far more than on other of the beneficiaries of 'whiteness'. As that dialogue progressed, however, the actual voice of 'the little man' became less present *in person* and more obvious within the developing rhetoric of new right politicians. By the 1990s its real life sound was a political superfluity – its 'virtual' echo the 'reality'. This was partly because, as well as the decreasing significance of the manufacturing worker in the new economy, to a large extent the role of dismantling many of the gains of the civil rights movement had been taken on by federal government itself during the 1980s. It was also because the terrain had become crowded with a multiplicity of voices making claims concerned with cultural and political recognition through school and college syllabuses, among other means, as well as with the need for organisational accommodation to diversity. Multiculturalism was in this sense a new Pandora's box, coming to qualify and obscure the simpler profile of class and race contours evident in the earlier period.

While the 'little people' were no less conscious of social threat, and the prevalence of other voices in the cultural arena also came to compete with that of the white working and lower middle classes, the politics of backlash shifted into quite another gear. Macro political agendas actively manipulated issues that had once gained their political charge from the popular causes which now had become detached and transformed into symbolic tokens. Furthermore, despite the significant setbacks occurring to progress in racial equality – particularly as urban segregation continued to increase – a burgeoning discourse of multiculturalism created a new political target. Unlike the earlier phase of racial equalities development, multiculturalist discourse was somewhat disconnected from its constituencies of social interest. Nevertheless, throughout the 1980s it became predominantly embedded in educational institutions ensuring that its presence in US culture and politics would be more than fleeting. The era of the sound-bite backlash, the 'politics of recognition' and the 'culture wars' had arrived.

II

Education and multiculturalism in the UK

Whereas it was federal laws and government that were being locally resisted in the USA, in the UK it was the local state in the form of the education authorities that were the main source of the move towards change in keeping with the new diversity in the schools, while national governments remained cool. As late as 1979 this coolness was characterised by one American commentator on the British educational system as a deliberate 'inexplicitness' about race that permitted advances towards black and Asian equality to be made 'by stealth': 'At present, there exists no educational programs aimed directly at non-whites, no deliberate efforts to school non-whites and whites together, and little concern with the possibility of racial discrimination in education. At least as a matter of official educational policy, the British minimize the relevance of color.'[44] Even this sojourner in the UK, however, could sense the presence of the wave curling above his observations and the storm clouds gathering. A more vocal challenge to black under-performance in the school system, to racism in the classroom and the playground and to the absence of blacks and Asians in senior positions in education was turning into a roar even as he wrote.

The late 1970s was a period of rapid change with respect to race in the UK. The 1976 Race Relations Act specified for the first time that racial discrimination in education was unlawful and placed on local authorities an obligation to ensure that their schools take steps to redress it. This became of major significance at a time when the new urban left was

[44] David Kirp, *Doing Good by Doing Little: Race and Schooling in Britain* (Berkley and London, University of California Press, 1979), p. 2.

increasingly seeing local government as a primary domain of political activity. The Act also became a spur to intensified activity by racist political groups such as the National Front and the British Movement. This in turn prompted a strong response from anti-fascist and anti-racist organisations. In London awareness of the issues of racism in education was raised by the National Union of Teachers and additionally by ALTARF (All London Teachers against Racism and Fascism). Thus, although a critique of discrimination in education had already been brewing even before Bernard Coard's 1971 book, *How the West Indian Child Is Made Educationally Sub-Normal in the British School System*,[45] a number of elements conspired to make the late 1970s and early 1980s a period of unprecedented activity. This was evident in teacher training, in the development of classroom resources to service the demand for multiculturally aware materials and in the generation of local authority and school policies. The Inner London Education Authority (ILEA) also spent considerable energy in developing policies concerned with multiculturalism and anti-racism.

The ILEA was far from alone in its development of race-related guidelines and policies. However, it was appropriately comprehensive, given that, as it pointed out, London had become one of the most linguistically diverse cities in the world and 'more languages were spoken in London than New York'.[46] In 1983 the ILEA published a set of policy documents entitled *Race, Sex and Class* which set out to examine the question of achievement in education 'from the vantage point of working-class children, black children and girls'.[47] As the first of these documents proclaimed, the ILEA believed 'that the development of specific strategies to liberate the talents of those groups and classes of children is the next great challenge in public education'. This document lay out the research evidence concerning the impacts of class, gender and ethnicity. The second and third parts addressed multi-ethnic education and race. Alongside these there was an 'Anti-racist Statement' similar in form to the kind of statement each school and educational institution was encouraged to produce. This contained an outline of the concept of racism as understood by the Authority, a strong statement of its opposition to racism and an elaboration of what this implied for teachers, school and college managers and the Authority. It explicitly described colour-blind policies as potentially racist, and emphasised the

[45] Bernard Coard, *How the West Indian Child Is Made Educationally Sub-Normal in the British School System* (London, New Beacon Books, 1971).
[46] Inner London Education Authority, *Race, Sex and Class*, 1 (London, ILEA, 1983) p. 10.
[47] Ibid., p. 5.

invisibility of the full nature of racism to most – even all – white people. It provided detailed guidance on how institutions under its authority should implement these policies and constitutes one of the most significant policy documents produced in the UK with regard to race and education.

At the same time, it reflected a long-standing battle between anti-racists and the multiculturalists. The anti-racists were said to emphasise the structural nature of racism, analysing it within a predominantly Marxist framework. The multiculturalists were characterised as emphasising diversity and the need for mutual understanding, and putatively operated within a more 'liberal' paradigm.[48] In fact multiculturalists were themselves a diverse group and, on the ground, multicultural and anti-racist educational practices were commonly indistinguishable. Nevertheless, the ILEA made explicit its commitment and made clear how far it saw racism extending: 'It has been argued that . . . we are all in some way racist and must become consciously and rigorously anti-racist, examining ourselves in our individual behaviour as well as the institutional practices we work within. This is a stance supported by these guidelines.'[49] The implications of this for teacher training and for the provision of specialised racism awareness courses were also considerable. Furthermore, other possible consequences of this tough doctrine were not avoided. Document 2 contained the following paragraph: 'It must be acknowledged that this perspective may seem threatening and uncomfortable to many white people. This means that measures to promote racial equality need to be fully explained and thoroughly debated. It does not, however, mean that they should be avoided or de-emphasised for fear of backlash.'[50] In conjunction with warnings about the need to avoid 'colluding' with racism 'in interaction with pupils and students',[51] these guidelines gave the strongest message possible that the clear delivery of anti-racism was of primary importance and that vacillations and mitigations themselves constituted part of racism, albeit in hidden forms.

---

[48] Chris Mullard, *Racism in Society and Schools: History, Policy and Practice* (Centre for Multicultural Education, Institute of Education University of London, 1980); Chris Mullard, 'The Social Context and Meaning of Multicultural Education', *Educational Analysis*, 3,1 (1981), pp. 117–40; Barry Troyna (ed.), *Racial Inequality in Education* (London, Tavistock, 1987); Barry Troyna, 'The Career of an Antiracist Education School Policy: Some Observations on the Mismanagement of Change', in Anthony G. Green and Stephen J. Ball (eds.), *Progress and Inequality in Comprehensive Education* (London, Routledge, 1992), pp. 158–78; D. Gillborn, *Racism and Antiracism in Real Schools: Theory, Policy, Practice* (Buckingham, Open University Press, 1995).

[49] Inner London Education Authority, *Anti-Racist Statement* (London, ILEA, 1983), p. 4.

[50] Ibid., 2, p. 22 para c (ii).   [51] Ibid., p. 7.

The development of the ILEA guidelines and similar expressions by other local education authorities, however, undoubtedly *did* generate its backlash. This backlash did not at all resemble earlier American backlash activity. Indeed, what little popular level of activism was evident came already heavily mediated by other forces. It came in a number of forms and was to some extent energised by right-wing think-tanks including the Centre for Policy Studies and the Social Affairs Unit with publications like *The Kindness that Kills* edited by Digby Anderson, Antony Flew's *Education, Race and Revolution,* and *The Wayward Curriculum,* edited by Dennis O'Keefe.[52] Roger Scruton's weekly column in *The Times* during that period also focussed on anti-racism on a number of occasions and in particular attacked sociologist Chris Mullard whose ideas had contributed significantly to the anti-racist critique of multiculturalism.[53] Two important government-sponsored reports which sought to identify inequalities of outcome in different ethnic groups and to lay out an approach to diversity – the Rampton report (1982)[54] and the Swann report (1985)[55] also came under attack from a number of right-wing critics. In particular the contributors to *Anti-Racism: An Assault on Education and Value*[56] treated multicultural-ism and anti-racism as politically identical animals, although thereby they may have served to bring them a little closer together.

However, it was possibly the *causes célèbres* such as Ray Honeyford's 1983/4 rupture with the Asian parents of the multi-racial school in Bradford of which he was the head, following the publication of an article by him in the right-wing journal *Salisbury Review,*[57] and the dismissal of head teacher Maureen McGoldrick from her post in a Brent primary school, that led to the greatest public exposure to anti-racism and allowed it to burst upon the readership of the popular national press in a torrent of hostile and deriding copy.[58] The McGoldrick affair, over a query concerning the recruitment of a new teacher, sparked a massive polarisation of positions over the delivery of anti-racist education and

---

[52] Digby Anderson (ed.), *The Kindness that Kills* (London, Social Affairs Unit/SPCK, 1984); Flew, *Education, Race and Revolution*; Dennis O'Keefe (ed.), *The Wayward Curriculum* (London, Social Affairs Unit, 1986).

[53] See, for example, 'Who Are the Real Racists?', *Times*, 30 Oct. 1984, and 'The Paths Blocked by Anti-Racists', *Times*, 16 Apr. 1985.

[54] Department of Education and Science, *West Indian Children in our Schools* (London, Her Majesty's Stationery Office, 1982).

[55] Department of Education and Science, *Education For All* (London, Her Majesty's Stationery Office, 1985).

[56] Palmer (ed.), *Anti-Racism*.

[57] Ray Honeyford, 'Multi-Ethnic Intolerance', *Salisbury Review* (June, 1983).

[58] Lansley, Goss and Wolmar, *Councils in Conflict*, pp. 126–8.

propelled into prominence a number of inflammatory black activists in a climate already redolent with accusation and political posturing.[59]

Brent – a London borough with a black majority population of some 60 per cent – had a poor record of educational service delivery to its community. Black parents especially, but also white, were greatly concerned with this. However, a report by an inquiry team headed by Jocelyn Barrow, a BBC governor, had claimed that black parents in Brent had identified racism in the system and on the part of white teachers as being the cause of this failure. The evidence supporting this claim was slight indeed. One black parent alone out of only twenty-seven replies to an advertisement in the local black press suggested racism as the cause of the under-performance of Brent schools.[60] However, for over two years the brew of an educational authority attempting to implement a number of reasonable measures to improve educational performance and counter racism within the system, a teachers' union branch inflamed and aggressive over accusations of racism, and much political showboating, handed the reactionary press a gift. Furthermore, a change in the political balance of Brent Council had led to the appointment of John Marks – a right-wing critic of anti-racism and Social Affairs Unit author – to a Barrow inquiry team that included anti-racist theoretician Chris Mullard. Soon leaks and gossip found their way to the press, feeding the hungry media with further stories about the anti-racist excesses of Brent Council. The Maureen McGoldrick affair, small in itself, somehow lit a blaze of media-driven backlash that was deeply embarrassing to the Labour Party and damaging to any serious attempt to deal with the poor attainment of Brent pupils and with the achievement of racial equality.[61]

This 'bad press' was not only due to right-wing manipulation of the media. Anti-racist education of the kind espoused by the ILEA had many other critics, including some on the left.[62] Many teachers and educationalists were uncomfortable with its confrontational approach and its confessional practices at a time when accusations of racism in every aspect of local government were also rife. It was largely the clumsy

---

[59] Ibid.
[60] The author was a member of the research team supporting the work of the inquiry team during the mid-1980s.
[61] Lansley, Goss and Wolmar, *Councils in Conflict*, pp. 130–7.
[62] One of the contributors to Palmer (ed.), *Anti-Racism*, was Tom Hastie who declared himself a 'life-long socialist' and who provided a closely argued critique of certain anti-racist history resources. See Palmer (ed.), *Anti-Racism*, pp. 61–73. Other criticisms coming from the left included Phil Cohen, '"It's Racism What Dunnit": Hidden Narratives in Theories of Racism', in J. Donald and A. Rattansi (eds.) *'Race', Culture and Difference*, (London, Sage, 1992) pp. 62–103.

implementation of anti-racist policy rather than its content that caused concern. Furthermore, in time such policies came to be seen by many in the profession as inflexibly focussed on race in isolation, and leading to significant deficiencies in judgement. Criticisms of clumsily developed and implemented anti-racism were articulated very forcefully in the report of the inquiry into the murder of Ahmed Iqbal Ullah in the playground of Burnage High School, Manchester, in 1986. The report concluded its review of the impact of anti-racist education with the following words:

The fundamental error of . . . morally based anti-racist policies is that they assume that a complicated set of human relations, made up of many strands, including class, gender, age, size and race, can be slotted into a simple white versus black pigeon hole. It is the problem of white versus black that has to be dealt with. The other things are assumed and not dealt with. This simple model assumes that there is uniform access to power by all whites, and a uniform denial of access and power to all blacks. Clearly this is not the case.[63]

Education in Greenwich

The ILEA, together with the Greater London Council was scrapped by the Thatcher government in 1986 and the delivery of educational services was devolved to the individual boroughs. Following a period of adjustment, Greenwich Council established its own 'Directorate of Education' and took up the task of forging its policies and practices. These reflected many previous ILEA policies and the commitment to multiculturalism and anti-racism was part of that. It was not long, however, before the high levels of racial harassment in the borough and the racist murders gave a particular urgency to the problem of how to deal with racism through its school and youth service provision.

In the light of adolescent racist violence, the convergence of Conservative government policy and attacks by the Tory press on anti-racism/multiculturalism, disaffection amongst white youth on the estates took on a special significance with respect to 'backlash'. It also constituted another, locally inflected phase in the dance of multicultural/ equalities policy and its political 'others'. The Greenwich murders were perpetrated by adolescent males who would have gone through the local system and would have been on the receiving end of whatever form of anti-racist and multiculturalist education had been delivered in their schools. Schools were not all the same in this regard – whatever the

---

[63] I. Macdonald, *Murder in the Playground: The Burnage Report* (Longsight Press, London, 1989) p. 348.

policy of the local education authority as a whole. The failure of the system could, in theory, have been as much a result of schools *not* pursuing anti-racism with sufficient vigour as pursuing it too much or in deficient ways. From the empirical research locally conducted[64] it appeared that neighbourhood and social class were important variables and that while a majority of school pupils did not react negatively to the way schools implemented their policies, a large minority of young people in the south of the borough did. Indeed, the overwhelming majority of young people interviewed on the south and central Greenwich estates during the early 1990s expressed strong reactions to what was taken to be the favouring of black pupils and black culture. The anti-racist policies could thus be said to have 'worked' with regard to some groups and not with others.

Anti-racist strategies within educational services were rarely sociologically informed and socially targeted. Given variations at local level, an approach based on such knowledge would have been strategic. Its absence was evident in Greenwich no less than in other London boroughs and in two aspects – discipline and the celebration of cultural diversity – borough-wide strategies were recognised for what they were and deeply resented by the kinds of young people most in need of an informed, sensitive and non-doctrinaire approach.

In 1999, the Macpherson report on the murder of Stephen Lawrence recommended that schools keep a record of racist incidents. Such record-keeping had been formally part of ILEA policy since 1983 and like many other schools in London, Greenwich schools had been keeping such records at least since 1991 following the murder of Rolan Adams. Nevertheless, these records told a very incomplete story. There were issues about *what* was counted and of the ways in which racism was attributed. Some head teachers were less than aggressive in following this practice for fear of suffering in consequence of conveying a distorted picture of the levels of racism in their schools. Others were diligent and acutely aware of the implications of the murders for the quality of anti-racist education that had been delivered in the past. Schools and the local education authority walked a tightrope.

As with all areas of school discipline, the keeping of such records required that they were widely regarded as fair. However, amongst the estate youth of central and southern Greenwich in the mid-1990s the perception was that they were not. As one boy expressed it:

---

[64] Research was carried out in 1992 and 1994 involving observational work and the interviewing of pupils. The first project, funded by Greenwich Council, resulted in the following publication: Centre for Multicultural Education, *Sagaland*. The second resulted in Roger Hewitt, *Routes of Racism*.

They've got a racist book, and when like – say yer 'ave a fight wiv a black person, I reckon the school itself is racist, towards white people. You see they always take up a black kid's side and they don't want to know what your version of the story is. Like I had a couple of fights wiv black kids and stuff like that, and they never really took my point, like my story, and I just sort of got kicked out wiv that.

Whether regarded as fair or not, the keeping of the 'racial incidents book' was intended to demonstrate that schools took racism as a serious issue and to proclaim their commitment to dealing with it. However, complaints about how the rules were applied were numerous. Teachers themselves remained unaware of the extent of the negative reactions of white pupils and it was often not they who got to understand the wider context and impact of these tactics but youth workers and others beyond the school gates. As one youth worker explained:

Particularly through their school years, [they feel an unfairness] where there's been incidents when they've been in trouble or they've had a fight with a black kid or an Asian kid and straightaway it's deemed [by the school] as a racist attack. It becomes a much more serious incident because race is involved and from their point of view it's not always a race issue. It's just been a school or a playground fight. And they carry that with them and now the anger is . . . in a sense it's caused racism because they've carried that unfairness with them. They carry it and it's not gone away and it's festered, the unfairness has festered . . . It's what they come back to the whole time, 'but this happened to me'.

Punishments commonly provoke protests. But having a picture of the full range of a young person's circumstances made some youth professionals, who had to find ways of dealing with adolescent racism, conscious of how being accused of racism was received:

These young people can often miss whole chunks of themselves out. You know you don't get an awful lot of gentleness in them. Their life experiences have told them they [must] protect [themselves] when they walk in the club, [to show] they're not vulnerable. Their life experiences very often will come before they even get out on the estate, from families that have not shown the young person kindness and gentleness, not given them the degree of support that they've needed to develop. Those young people have learnt to build up a wall that says, 'You won't get near enough to be able to hurt me. You won't see my vulnerable side, so you won't be able to abuse that.' They're walking around with a tremendous amount of hurt. I sometimes wonder how they cope with it. I hear story after story that you're left feeling and understanding totally why they're so damaged. And if somebody hasn't got a sense of their own importance and their own worth, how in god's name are they expected to have any sense of yours. So if someone says to you. 'You're a racist, you've behaved in a certain way, you're dismissed', you're just confirming what they already know anyway . . . and you're just, if you want, making them even angrier. You're not teaching anybody anything.

Neglect and abuse of young people was only one part of the background to how multiculturalism and anti-racism were received. It also contributed to the formation of self-defensive masculinities and the aggression that melded with school failure to produce some of the ugliest forms of racism. Furthermore the dominant definition of racism evident across the range of training – 'prejudice plus power equals racism' – left professionals without a rudder where whiteness itself was deemed to bestow power. As one youth worker insisted:

When they talk glibly about white people having all the power, well the young people I work with haven't. They don't see they've got any power at all. I don't work with young people that have any power or their families have any power. But instead of people seeing equal opportunities as about building bridges between people, we concentrate on the divisions.

Within this training paradigm, the moral arguments over the social wrongs suffered by minorities were expected to be put directly to white working-class youth with the assumption that, simply by expressing the truth of minority disadvantage, they should be intellectually led to see their force. The same youth worker commented: 'You can't give someone equal opportunity at the expense of somebody else, you can't do that and expect the other people to say, "Oh that's OK. I've had my fair wack now."'

The 'wages of whiteness'?

Young people in Greenwich from these kinds of backgrounds failed to understand why ethnic minorities needed to be treated within a different framework of justice. They saw themselves as also constituting an aggrieved minority and there was considerable evidence that, indeed, they were. It was impossible for youth workers and teachers to convey why they paid particular attention to the grievances of black and Asian youth, in the face of the social marginalisation of these young people and the fragility of their own long-term prospects.

An example of this kind of contrast was the case of the white boy who had seen several Somali boys beating up a white girl in the school corridor. He went to protect her but was himself beaten by the boys. His head was banged on a radiator and he was taken to hospital with concussion. During the fight he had used racist language which was observed by another pupil and reported to the school. The boy was permanently excluded for fighting and using racist language. The Somali boys were not excluded. Recounting his side of the story a year later he was still very bitter. Interviews with adult professionals connected with the school closely matched the boy's version of these events. The boy's treatment by the school filled him with a feeling of injustice that he clearly found intolerable. It did not appear to result in any increase in negative feelings about Somalians, but it *did* leave him with the belief that the school's notion of justice and fairness was very different from his own and from most common notions.

Debates about the competing claims of groups and individuals have little relevance to the damage done to feelings of *shared justice* that are fundamental to any attempt to inculcate a multicultural and anti-racist ethos within schools. Schools seeking to create an holistic approach to anti-racism could not afford to operate with anything that looked like a two-tiered system. To some young people it did. It was a perception that went to the heart of the disaffection of many of the white young people interviewed. Breaches in shared justice, such as this one, rapidly became turned into yet another counter-narrative in the reservoir of counter-narratives to be told and re-told in response to the preachy forms of anti-racism received by young people in schools and through the youth services.

The principle of arriving at just outcomes by *not* being even-handed did not quite work with (a) young people who found the concept of 'even-handedness' more intuitively comprehensible than compensatory forms of justice, and (b) with young people who were also demonstrably disadvantaged and for whom their 'whiteness' did not have the payoff that it did for other groups of white people. The 'wages of whiteness' in David Roediger's phrase[65] have been very small for some. Indeed for some, the wage packet is entirely empty. It is psychologically worse than no pay: it is no pay wrapped up in the promise of pay. That, of course, would be equality if race were the only dimension – but it is not.

'Culture' lost and found

The second area of school policy that failed with the same minority of white youth throughout the 1990s related to the issue of cultural diversity. There was taken to be a discrepancy in the way schools treated symbols of white ethnicity and symbols of minority ethnicities. Multicultural policies were pursued to varying degrees of commitment by the schools within the borough but with regard to the underlying matter of cultural difference a complex issue emerged. The problem seemed to arise from the fact that each minority culture was often

---

[65] David R. Roediger, *The Wages of Whiteness: Race and the Making of the American Working Class* (London, Verso, 1991).

celebrated within the school system (1) as being unitary, rather than a mixture of different, changing and even contradictory aspects; and (2) that symbolisations of those 'unitary cultures' sometimes include national and other emblems and images. In contrast to the simplified versions of what 'being from a *different* culture' meant, white English pupils had no unitary concept of 'English culture' that was 'celebrated' because the internal variations and contradictions would have rendered that kind of reduction absurd. It was equally absurd that 'other' cultures were presented in these ways, but the representation of equality in diversity has often involved a stress on cultural 'roots' and lurid difference. It may have given educational multiculturalism a healthier start in the UK if the image of unified, traditional cultures had been avoided at the outset, and a more 'true to life' picture of the internally mixed, hybrid and changeable nature of all societies had been stressed.[66]

School 'celebration of diversity' approaches can seem to minority ethnic pupils like a pageant of some stereotypical ethnicity in which they do not quite feel themselves to participate, however welcome the references to familiar things. For some white English pupils, the celebration of cultural variety actually seemed to include all cultures that were not their own. It was not surprising that white children – especially young people from working-class homes – experienced themselves as having an invisible culture, of being even cultureless. In Eltham the impact of social class on cultural identity was particularly evident. On a hill overlooking the council estates stood Eltham Palace, a fine, old building where, in the fourteenth century, Geoffrey Chaucer, the 'father of English poetry', had once worked, where the Black Prince had stayed and where Henry VII and Henry the VIII and his children also lived. A local school once a year took pupils to Westminster Abbey to see the plaque to the Black Prince and Eltham Palace was the stimulus for frequent projects of one kind or another. It is one of those places that might be thought of as a local emblem of some significant strand of Englishness. For those who looked elsewhere for their Englishness there was also – though not so immediately present as Eltham Palace – a great deal else that might have been turned to in the area. There was the strong history of working-class politics and collective organisation, and even the Peasants' Revolt, one important site of which was only half a

---

[66] R. Hewitt, 'Language, Youth and the Destabilization of Ethnicity', in C. Palmgren, K. Lovegren and G. Bolin (eds.), *Ethnicity in Youth Culture* (Stockholm, University of Stockholm, USU, 1992); Gerhardt Baumann, *Contesting Culture: Discourses of Identity in Multi-Ethnic London* (Cambridge, Cambridge University Press, 1996); S. Hall, 'New Ethnicities', in J. Donald and A. Rattansi (eds.), *'Race' Culture and Difference* (London, Sage Publications/Open University, 1992).

mile to the north. There was also a rich local naval and military history and current presence. Yet, in discussions about the representation of different cultures in school, most of the white English children who took part were at a loss to suggest anything that might be called *their* culture. The only cultural item that they could suggest was 'pie and mash' – a traditional cafeteria food of the London working class since the 1920s – perhaps in imitation of how 'other cultures' were represented to them.

Despite this vacuum they did, nevertheless, mimic the *symbolisation* of cultures in national blazonry of various kinds and this frequently got them in trouble. When they would turn to the symbols and emblems of 'their' cultural identity, they found in the case of the Union flag that it was already a contested battle ground and appropriated by racist political groups. It was John Tyndall, leader of the BNP, who endorsed the Union Jack to make it 'to the niggers what the swastika is to the Jews'.[67] In the context of school anti-racism, naïvete about the political mixed messages of the Union Jack had unexpected consequences. The following extract from an interview with a group of boys demonstrates how this tangle of problems can lead straight into the arms of racist politics:

BOY 1. [In school] you can't wear a belt wiv the Union Jack on, nothin'.
BOY 2. Like some kid in our class, he's got his Union Jack belt, same as that, a big buckle. It's got the Union Jack and it's got a 'British Bulldog' on it. And all the teachers were saying, 'I want that off.'
BOY 3. Yeah, and all the niggers wear, like, Jamaican coats.
BOY 2. Like all the niggers are allowed to tuck up their thingies, come up to 'ere.
BOY 1. They wear 'Black With Attitude' caps, anyfing like that.
BOY 2. All the teachers are scared of the blacks.
BOY 3. This black kid, he's got a fucking Jamaican coat. On the hood it's got the colours, a little flag on the back, the shape of the country on it and 'Jamaica' underneath. He ain't got to take that off.
BOY 1. If we wonna support our country it's up to us. If we wanna show that we're proud to be British, just like he's wearing that Jamaican coat.
INTERVIEWER: But isn't it true that wearing a Union Jack means that you're into the BNP?
BOY 2. Not really.
BOY 3. But we could wear anyfing else, like wear an English football top.
INTERVIEWER: But the teachers presumably think that the Union Jack is often worn by racists.
BOY 2. What, can't we support our own flag now?
BOY 1. Yeah, but its our flag, but they're probably trying to ban it, or put black into it. Like they've banned the 'blackboard' aint they? It's 'chalk board' now. Golliwogs, took the golliwogs off the jam jar. Can't say 'baa baa black sheep', that's 'racist' now.

[67] *At War with Society: A Searchlight Mole inside the BNP* (London, Searchlight, 1993).

This discussion effectively links school multiculturalist policies to issues of identity and national identification and back again to the 'unfairness to whites' discourse. This starts with their own actual experiences of disciplinary issues in school and with the contrast they feel between how ethnic minority insignia and their own chosen emblems of identity are treated. Where this discussion ends, however, is in a realm determined not by local but *national* commentary. The instances cited by the last speaker in the extract above were derived directly from popular press diatribes against the anti-racist policies that appeared several years earlier in the 1980s. In these press stories local authorities that introduced anti-racist policies were attacked for their 'political correctness'. This notion of anti-racism as a violation of common sense and everyday reasoning clearly articulated well with the discursive elements displayed here. These same ideas were taken up by the BNP and other racist political organisations and became part of the discourse of everyday racism. This speaker's reference to the Union Jack being banned or having the colour black added to it is directly derived from the National Front song 'There Ain't No Black in the Union Jack'. This discussion binds together school experience, anti-leftist propaganda from the Tory press and extreme right-wing scare tactics into a single thrust of racist articulation.

At the same time there is a coherent viewpoint being concocted within this talk which is not grounded exclusively on naked racism. There clearly is a strong racist line running through it, but it is working *on* something, and that something is, in part, the felt absence of any 'culture' with which these young people can identify. It is exactly this absence that drove young people into their symbolic identification with racist political groups. As one boy said on another occasion: 'If we didn't 'ave the BNP, like, we'd probably 'ave a black government. If we didn't 'ave them we wouldn't 'ave nuffing. We wouldn't have a sort of government, we wouldn't 'ave no-one sticking up for the whites. We wouldn't 'ave none of that, and then that would be it. They'd probably take over.' These kinds of feelings are not dissimilar to the talk of some American southern loyalists around the significance of the Confederate flag. They share a common nightmare of an alliance between blacks and the powerful white groups who would relinquish government to them. One protester, demonstrating against the abandonment of the flying of the Confederate battle flag above South Carolina's statehouse, told writer Tony Horwitz: 'This fight's about today, about the ethnic cleansing of Southern whites – same thing that's happening in Bosnia. There's black history month, there's a black Miss America pageant, there's even a black yellow pages in South Carolina. Can you imagine a yellow pages for whites? No way. Anything for whites is PIC politically incorrect'.[68]

Flags often do extra symbolic work when 'ways of life' are thought to be under threat. Like the Rebel flag, the Union Jack brought together a number of themes and seemed to aid these teenagers in their attempt to draw in a super-ordinate power to a crumbling sense of belonging and cultural coherence. Most education-based backlashes internationally have not involved this dimension. As one youth worker commented about young whites searching for such symbols:

Isn't it sad that when we look at the British flag, the Union Jack, what do we think? We see it as a National Front emblem. We don't see it as the representation of our country, and why? How did that happen? And suddenly if somebody wanted to wear a Union Jack tee shirt we'd be fairly embarrassed and advising young people against that.

And, seeing young people's attraction to the flag as tragically diverted from its authentic destination, she sympathised with their misrecognition.

Horwitz described some of the starker differences within his Southern heritage celebrators. Some, like the Sons of Confederate Veterans he had met, dwelt on it in terms of the valour and sacrifice of their ancestors. Others saw their heritage as segregation and white supremacy. 'Was it possible', Horwitz wondered, 'to honor one heritage without upholding the other?'[69] There was potential for a similar question to be asked of these white teenagers' turn to the Union Jack. Was their commitment to this symbol separable from the racism in which it, like they themselves, was now entangled. Were their protestations of 'Can't we support our own flag now?' as disingenuous as they appeared or was there here some more innocent national feeling that many adult British people, black and white, would share though it would lead them nowhere?

These themes of justice/injustice, and belonging/not belonging displayed in the talk of young people in Greenwich during a period of intense local authority concern over racist violence did not find expression in any adult activity, such as parental support for their grievances. Beyond an expected level of occasional parental complaint about disciplinary decisions, the only audible sound of a backlash to school measures was in the mouths of very marginalised white youth. It was an active ingredient in local adolescent relations and attitudes and, among some sections of white youth, was partly what gave the young

[68] Horwitz, *Confederates in the Attic*, p. 79.
[69] Ibid. p. 80.

men accused of the Lawrence murder a certain heroic status for a while, not for their possible involvement in the murder but for being out of the same mould as many of the local youths – of going to the same schools and hanging out on the same estates and for being publicly reviled for their racism. This was a bond of the accused. As was once argued of the American 'white ethnic' Catholics who 'felt the accusing, jabbing finger of Protestant moralists': 'There are few quicker ways to stoke smouldering resentment and to awaken an unendurable inner hatred than to look down upon others from some moral height.'[70] Anti-racism primarily succeeded in making these young people feel exactly this way.

The problem in Greenwich in the early 1990s was with the *kind* of anti-racism and multiculturalism that was being delivered in the schools and youth services. Furthermore, with all three of the racist murders in Greenwich having been committed by young white men who had gone through the local school system, and with very high levels of racial harassment in the borough generally, there was no room for complacency. However much the 'right messages' had been sent out, the 'wrong ears' were receiving them and little attention had been given to devising new ways of designing anti-racist educational strategies that worked with the young people who needed them most. The search for 'racial justice' for black and ethnic minorities in the borough clearly needed to include the development of such strategies. Their absence allowed the impact of the changed economy and the marooning of working-class young people to result – just as it had in earlier decades – in a racism which offered itself as the answer to all ills.

Coda

Clearly the forms of racism for which educational remedies were sought in the 1960s and 1970s differed substantially from those of the 1990s. The early struggles in the USA with the educational consequences of decades of racialised housing and the low priority given to the education of black children showed up these *institutional* forms of racism for what they were. What has been described above of the condition of white English youth in the 1990s was part of a wider blight affecting all young people, black and white, caught on the wrong side of the widening gulf between the poor and the rest set in motion during the Reagan/Thatcher years. The same blight was apparent amongst American youth during the same period. William Finnegan's harrowing profile of youth poverty in his book *Cold New World: Growing up in a Harder Country* describes

[70] Novak, *The Rise of the Unmeltable Ethnics*, p. 13.

young people in several states ensnared by drugs, petty crime, racism and violence during the early 1990s. Whatever the disparities between the communities involved in California's early bussing issues described above, they were of a different order and orderliness to those evident in that state by the 1990s. As Finnegan reports, between 1970 and 1996 the poverty rate for children and adolescents in California more than doubled to 27 per cent. Between 1980 and 1995 the state's incarceration rate *quadrupled* and its youth incarceration rate was the highest in the country.[71] Just as disaffection amongst young people on London's housing estates increased as the benefits of the new techno-service economy became the norm for many, so a similar, though even less ameliorated, scene was being acted out in the USA.

Well before solutions to these problems could be identified, let alone implemented, the numbers of people, young and old, were swelled by new migrants from an increasing number of different countries. In both the UK and the USA the scope of what 'multicultural society' encompassed transcended all earlier definitions. The capacity for generating new hostilities, as well as alliances, pushed the meanings of 'racism' beyond the bounds of even metaphor. By the early twenty-first century the histories of how young people came to find themselves on this multicultural highway seem lost or meaningless. It remains to be seen how the older racisms fade or endure in the face of mass migration and the official responses to it, when even the seeking of 'recognition' may seem like an appeal to comforting, by-gone securities.

---

[71] William Finnegan, *Cold New World: Growing up in a Harder Country* (New York, Modern Library, 1998), p. xvii. See also Mike A. Males, *The Scapegoat Generation: America's War on Adolescents* (Monroe, Common Courage Press, 1996).

7 Backlash, multicultural politics and the global turbine

I

Canada, Australia: state-sponsored multiculturalism and its others

While the issues arising in Greenwich described in the last three chapters may not have been *typical* of backlash phenomena in the 1990s, they do capture certain features that were and remain more widely significant within the politics of multiculturalism. Historically they reflected at least some of the fallout from the Reagan/Thatcher period within the context of transforming economies and social patterns. They also exemplified some of the *difficulties* involved in the adoption of an anti-racist multiculturalism and the relation of clumsy policy implementation to popular backlash. Furthermore, the expressive forms of backlash in Greenwich appeared to encode the deeper political dialogue of which they were a part. That dialogue also involved the development of the multicultural consensus and its discourses.

Across the range of multiculturalisms, two distinct material points of origin stand out: (1) the race equality reforms during the 1960s in the USA together with their expansion in the 1970s to additional groups; and (2) the state-sponsored multiculturalist responses to relationships between settled communities, new immigrants and 'first nations' in Canada and Australia. While the issue of racism and racial equality has always been an important component in the development of multiculturalist discourse in the USA – something that also came to be reflected in the UK version – that issue was not a point of origin for multiculturalism in Canada and only marginally so in Australia. Furthermore, in neither case has multicultural policy managed to enable aboriginal people to be unambiguously 'included'.

In Canada the issue of racism has commonly been treated as separate from multiculturalism. Canada's multiculturalism, like that of Australia, emerged from a 'whites only' immigration policy that was by the early 1960s already an anachronism. In the late nineteenth century Chinese immigrants were a small but significant presence. However, they became legally debarred from entry and excluded from citizenship by a series of laws passed between 1885 and 1923. These were aimed at preventing the growth of Asian settlement and became the basis for a *de facto* 'whites only' policy that lasted well into the post-World War II period. Thus, in addition to the British and French, what became the 'third force' in Canadian politics – white non-Anglophone and non-Francophone northern, eastern and southern Europeans – became the primary new settler communities of the twentieth century prior to the 1970s. It was, however, the issues of the Francophone community with regard to language rights and the Quebecois separatist movement that provided the most pressing motive for developing a political settlement concerned with cultural 'recognition' in addition to the historically recurrent need for labour.[1] Anti-racism with regard to Canada's 'first nation' and other non-white groups was a relatively insignificant issue. Thus, although measures to address the specific interests of the visible minorities were gradually introduced,[2] these matters have been generally treated as separate from the 'mosaic' vision of Canadian diversity.[3]

The post-World War II period, with the emergence of the new discourse of internationalism and human rights, also impacted on the racist character of Australian society and political arrangements. Furthermore, like Canada, Australia had an increasing need for immigrant labour. Its developing relationship with trade partners like Japan made its long-established 'White Australia' policy difficult to sustain. During the 1960s integration became official policy and, as a result of a number of pieces of legislation designed to loosen the law to permit non-European immigrants entry, by the end of the decade the 'White Australia' policy had been abandoned.[4]

In the early 1970s, under the influence of the Canadian example, the Gough Whitlam Australian Labour government moved away from assimilationism and began the development of an official, Australia-wide

---

[1] Peter Kivisto, *Multiculturalism in a Global Society* (Oxford, Blackwell, 2002), pp. 84–101.

[2] Nikolaos Liodakis and Vic Satzewich, 'From Solution to Problem: Multiculturalism and "Race Relations" as New Social Problems', in Les Samuelson and Wayne Antony (eds.), *Power and Resistance: Critical Thinking about Social Issues in Canada* (Halifax, Nova Scotia, Fernwood Publishing, 1998).

[3] Vic Satzewich (ed.), *Deconstructing a Nation: Immigration, Multiculturalism and Racism in '90s Canada* (Halifax, Nova Scotia, Fernwood Publishing, 1992); George J. Sefa Dei, 'Contesting the Future: Anti-Racism and Canadian Diversity', in Stephen Nancoo (ed.), *21st Century Canadian Diversity* (Ontario, Canadian Educators Press, 2000), pp. 295–319; Yasmeen Abu-Laban and Christina Gabriel, *Selling Diversity: Immigration, Multiculturalism, Employment Equity and Globalization* (Ontario, Broadview Press, 2002).

[4] Kivisto, *Multiculturalism in a Global Society*, p. 110.

multiculturalism concerned with both immigration and, to a lesser degree, with the Aboriginal community.[5] Subsequent developments of multicultural policy placed the notion of the ethnic group – culturally static and homogeneous – at its centre. Only later, under the influence of neo-liberal economics and a concern for integrating Australia with the Asian Pacific region, was the 'ethnic group' approach superseded by a more strategic and robust model announced in the *National Agenda for a Multicultural Australia* in 1989.[6] In this document multiculturalism was not defined in terms of cultural pluralism or minority rights, but as citizens' rights within a democratic state. This was an important move in securing its long-term success and in dampening the transition into identity politics evident in the USA.[7] What the *National Agenda* did not address, perhaps because it was a policy primarily generated from a concern with economic performance on the international stage, was the special status of the Aborigines and Torres Strait Islanders and the historical injustices and current racisms inflicted on them. In Australia as in Canada the nature of multiculturalism remained tied to national economic interests above all.

Backlash in Canada

The dialogue of multiculturalism with its political others was probably gentler within Canada, where the arguments *within* multiculturalism were most pressing, than in any other liberal democracy. Indeed, if anything, Canadian multiculturalism's most prominent critics have been from a left wing concerned with its shortcomings in relation to social justice, racism and the treatment of native Canadians.[8] From the right of the political spectrum reaction has been comparatively less vocal although undoubtedly evident.

The Canadian policy of state-sponsored multiculturalism began to lose ground within a year or two of the passing of its 1988 Multiculturalism Act. Soon after the Act came into force popular critiques like those of sociologist Reginald Bibby's *Mosaic Madness* (1990) appeared which saw Canada's commitment to multiculturalism as a virtue made out of necessity but as having encouraged the

---

[5] Ibid., pp. 109–10.
[6] Office of Multicultural Affairs, *National Agenda for a Multicultural Australia* (Office of Multicultural Affairs, 1989).
[7] Stephen Castles, *Ethnicity and Globalization* (London, Sage, 2000), p. 146.
[8] Vic Satzewich (ed.), *Racism and Social Inequality in Canada: Concepts, Controversies and Strategic Resistance* (Toronto, Thompson Educational, 1998); Peter Li (ed.), *Race and Ethnic Relations in Canada* (Toronto, Oxford University Press, 1999).

destructive individualisation of its ethnic fragments though extreme 'relativism'. Novelist Neil Bissoondath also mounted a prominent assault, arguing in his *Selling Illusions: The Cult of Multiculturalism in Canada* (1994) that ethnic cultures should be a private matter and not the object of national policy. However objectionable from the point of view of committed multiculturalists, these were both relatively measured and grounded on an everyday 'common sense' about the kinds of relationship that might obtain between the 'One and the Many'. Other attacks, such as William Gairdner's *The Trouble with Canada* (1990), whose chapter on multiculturalism was headed 'The Silent Destruction of English Canada', were considerably less 'nuanced' than either of these. (Gairdner was a one time speaker at the Reform Party meetings until his expressed hostility to south-east Asians became an embarrassment to the party.[9]) Each struck a nerve of sorts in a part of the popular Canadian political imagination. They also had their peers on the international stage – particularly in the USA in the early 1990s. Arthur Schlesinger Jr's *Disuniting of America* and Robert Hughes' *Culture of Complaint* are only the most obvious examples. These Canadian authors were, indeed, part of the early 1990s international wave of post Reagan/ Bush backlash. Such voices as these began to qualify popular commitment to the multiculturalists' emphasis on cultural particularities as against the holistic Canadian picture.

Despite some research pointing to strong public support for multiculturalism in the early 1990s, an overview of all the polls and other evidence showed a clear overall decline between 1989 and 1995.[10] This period was critical in the course of Canadian multiculturalism in showing some signs of the backlash evident in other countries – particularly through the impact of neo-liberal economic theory. A commission appointed by Brian Mulrony's Conservative government in 1990–1 to gain the views of Canadians recommended that federal funding for multicultural activities of a cultural kind should be 'eliminated'.[11] As a result of pressures such as these, during the 1990s there was a diminishing commitment by national governments to multiculturalism, including a substantial drop in the national budget for

[9] David Laycock, *The New Right and Democracy in Canada: Understanding Reform and the Canadian Alliance* (Ontario, Oxford University Press, 2003), p. 24.
[10] Louis Musto, 'Public Opinion on Multiculturalism and Canadian Identity', in Andrew Cardozo and Louis Musto (eds.), *The Battle over Multiculturalism* (Ottawa, PSI, 1997), cited in Joseph Mensah, *Black Canadians* (Halifax, Nova Scotia, Fernwood Publishing, 2002), pp. 208–9.
[11] Canada, *Citizens' Forum on Canada's Future* (Ottawa, Minister of Supply and Services, Canada, 1991), p. 129.

multiculturalism.[12] The Department of Multiculturalism and Citizenship was dismantled by the Kim Campbell Conservative government in 1993 and some of its functions dispersed. It was also during this period that, in the arena of public debate and in the context of the views of Bibby and Bisoondath, Pierre Trudeau's original supposition that national unity and multiculturalism were mutually supportive became strenuously questioned in the face of proliferating ethnic sectional interests and political jostling by minority group leaders. The equation was thus rhetorically turned on its head. 'National unity' came to be regarded by many as threatened rather than nurtured by developing the strength of each fragment in the Canadian 'mosaic'. Both views took for granted the notion that it is a shared *culture* that effects unity amongst a people. Their differences were with regard to scale and inclusiveness.

The influence of the Reform Party during the 1990s on the erosion of government support for multiculturalism was an aspect of its intention to bring a stronger, anti-interventionist and more ideological right-wing element into Canadian mainstream politics. Reform had been established in 1987 on the back of widespread discontent with Trudeau's Liberal Party and with the Conservative government of Mulrony that had disappointed many Canadians. Initially it drew together many and diverse political elements, although the prevailing trend was towards neo-liberal economics and traditional moral conservatism. There were also unapologetic extremists aboard whose presence frequently came to wrong-foot the party when it was attempting to make its impact on the national stage.[13] Quite unlike Australia's small populist One Nation Party, which was not ideologically opposed to state interventionism in social and economic affairs and was built primarily on popular feelings against immigration and multiculturalism, the Reform Party was vocal about a wide range of issues. It also drew on a pre-existing far-right presence, particularly in western Canada where it had its base. During the 1970s and 1980s a number of organisations had appeared espousing neo-conservative ideas based around moral conservatism and economic liberalism. These included Renaissance Canada – the Canadian counterpart to the USA's Moral Majority movement – and the Canadian Association for Free Enterprise. There were also movements and small-press publications concerned with the imposition of bilingualism and fears of encroaching 'French' power. The right-wing think-tank The Fraser Institute, offshoot of Antony Fisher's Institute of Economic

---

[12] Abu-Laban and Gabriel, *Selling Diversity*, pp. 112–15.
[13] Trevor Harrison, *Of Passionate Intensity: Right-Wing Populism and the Reform Party of Canada* (Toronto, University of Toronto Press, 1995).

Affairs in the UK,[14] was founded in British Columbia in 1974 and came to include an impressive array of visiting experts including Milton Friedman and Sir Alan Waters, Margaret Thatcher's economic advisor.[15] Thus there was already an ideological stream that saw itself as under-represented by the Progressive Conservative Party. The failure of the Mulrony government to gain popular respect provided an opportunity for the Reform Party to present itself as an alternative on significant issues such as the budget deficit.

In 2003 it became incorporated into the Conservative Party but during the 1990s Reform had enjoyed significant political success with some impressive national poll results and frequent policy endorsements from the national press.[16] Its relationship to multiculturalism during this period is particularly salient to the profile of international trends. It was, despite its leader's care to distance Reform from the far right racist movement, the logical party to follow for those strongly opposed to immigration and multiculturalism. Its focus, however, was on the broad national picture and its policies were never directly or crudely anti-minority. Indeed, it made attempts in two elections to field ethnic minority candidates and, although the accusation of racism was made from time to time, it was successful in retaining its mainstream legitimacy.[17]

In 1991, early in its history, it had asserted its own policy to end funding for the federal multicultural programme and to abolish the Department of Multiculturalism. Reform's attacks on multiculturalism were mainly through a generalized opposition to the welfare state that also included getting rid of federally assisted social housing programmes, unemployment insurance and health-care schemes. In this they were close to the Republicans in the USA, and there was a well-established and mutually supportive link between Preston Manning, Reform's leader, and the Republican senate leader Newt Gingrich. Like the Republicans, Reform's voters included those who were most against affirmative action programmes of all kinds, but, similarly, for the most part the party steered away from racialised language, although Reform activists and policy advisors showed consistent insensitivity and hostility to the interests of native Canadians.[18] Thus arguments that their policies were *effectively racist* are not difficult to make.[19] However, as David Laycock argues:

[14] See Chapter 2.
[15] Harrison, *Of Passionate Intensity*, pp. 47–54.
[16] Laycock, *The New Right*, p. 133.
[17] Harrison, *Of Passionate Intensity*, pp. 139–77; Laycock, *The New Right*, p. 144.
[18] Laycock, *The New Right*, pp. 140–6.
[19] Della Kirkham, 'The Reform Party of Canada: A Discourse of Race, Ethnicity and Equality', in Satzewich (ed.), *Racism and Social Inequality*.

The Reform party never directly appealed to racism in the ugly and blatant way that virtually every new right-populist party in Europe has done. In light of the views on immigration held by Progress party supporters in Denmark and Sweden, the Reform party appears to have been more moderate than conventional conservative parties in Scandinavia, and thus far more moderate than Progress supporters. In fact, available evidence strongly suggests that Reform party voters and activists were significantly more tolerant of both visible-minority immigration and multiculturalism than supporters of Norway and Denmark's long-dominant social-democratic parties.[20]

Despite the fact that Canada receives more immigrants per head of population than any other country,[21] its 'backlash' to multiculturalism would seem to have been relatively muted and largely contained within the bounds of government policy and public debate, *even during the 1990s*. The Reform Party's electoral base was always primarily white, middle-class and suburban, which made its supporters' motivations different from those of right-populist 'backlash' parties in many other countries.[22] Canada's unique history and relationship to multicultural-ism also seems to have maintained the legitimacy of multiculturalism across many transformations and internal political re-alignments including – and perhaps to some extent because of – its central issue of Quebec's autonomy. Despite the neo-liberal attacks on intervention-ism, the continuing commitment of business interests to multiculturalist rhetoric has also provided it with considerable resilience. Thus the kind of language advanced by John Cleghorn, President of the Royal Bank of Canada, perfectly exemplifies Canadian multiculturalism's protean durability:

Multiculturalism . . . is one of the greatest competitive advantages we could have. It is the internal globalization of Canada. And it will be key to our succeeding in the global economy. Without diversity of thought, without workers feeling valued for their individuality and uniqueness, firms can spend millions on quality efforts to little or no avail.[23]

In the long run the questions raised from the left with regard to social justice are likely to prove more persistent thorns in the side of Canada's state-sponsored multiculturalism than those from the right.[24]

[20] Laycock, *The New Right*, pp. 144–5.
[21] Kivisto, *Multiculturalism*, p. 97.
[22] Laycock, *The New Right*, pp. 144–5.
[23] Canada, Department of Canadian Heritage, *Annual Report on the Operation of the Canadian Multiculturalism Act, 1993–1994*, Ottawa, Ministry of Supply and Services Canada, 1995, p. 7. Cited in Abu-Laban and Gabriel, *Selling Diversity*, p. 105.
[24] Frances Henry, Carol Tator, Winston Mattis and Tim Rees, *The Colour of Democracy: Racism in Canadian Society* (Toronto, Harcourt, 1995); Satzewich (ed.), *Racism and Social Inequality*; Li (ed.), *Race and Ethnic Relations*.

Australia's backlash

In Australia the shadows cast from US and UK post-equalities era politics took on familiar, if somewhat re-configured, forms. During the 1960s Aboriginal activists and allies, struggling against segregation in the outback, had imitated the freedom rides of US civil rights activists in the South, and the example of black American protest and the radical concepts that were prevailing at the time were not lost on community activists. From the ending of the White Australia policy in 1970, the Australian Labour Party took a close interest in civil rights in the US and Canadian multiculturalism. It had taken a number of their concepts into government policy in its approaches to minority ethnic recognition, as well as compensatory policies for Aboriginals.[25] By the early 1980s cross-party consensus over immigration and multiculturalism was beginning to show signs of occasional ungluing. However, a general consensus did exist that was achieved partly through the convergence of a strong pro-immigration lobby from real-estate, construction and other business interests concerned with labour supplies and the liberal-left support for the same objective but with a humanitarian/internationalist motivation. The broad political consensus over immigration was not strongly supported by the Australian electorate in all quarters, however. Indeed, reservations with regard to immigration policy expressed by Liberal leader John Howard in the late 1980s, particularly over Asian immigration, were clearly in accord with the electorate despite the objections expressed in the press by his political opponents.

Howard has been characterised as practising a form of political manipulation at that time similar to that of Reagan and Bush in seeking to drive a wedge between the Labour Party and its traditional followers through the issue of immigration and multiculturalism. Just as industrial workers and other traditional Democrat voters had been wooed by Reagan's appeal to a homogeneous society of decent and like-minded citizens so, it has been argued, Howard attempted to appeal to the white farmers and small business people, and economically marginalised blue-collar workers by talk of the 'gathering resentment of the Australian people' and by choosing as the coalition's slogan for the 1996 national election: 'For All of Us'.[26] It was also not the Liberal Party that was primarily responsible for promoting the economic strategies that threatened the traditionally nationalist small communities of Australia,

---

[25] Mark Lopez, *The Origins of Multiculturalism in Australian Politics, 1945–1975* (Melbourne, Melbourne University Press, 2000) pp. 69–71.

[26] Bill Cope and Mary Kalantzis, *A Place in the Sun: Re-creating the Australian Way of Life* (Sydney, Harper Collins, 2000), pp. 244–5.

but the Australian Labour Party. In particular it was the Hawke government of the early 1980s that bowed to the international pressure from the neo-liberal economists of that time. The Economic Planning Advisory Council produced many reports and assessments of the economy that were strongly reflective of the ascendant neo-liberalism and the policies Margaret Thatcher was pursuing in the UK. It was these same free-market ideas that threatened the provision of public services and contributed to the erosion of the manufacturing base on which many jobs depended.[27] Unemployment continued high for the next decade and gave added resonance to Pauline Hanson's attack on the 'multiculturalist elite' who appeared to have so little time or sympathy with the 'parochial' Australians – non-beneficiaries of the global economy *and* of internationalism's multicultural values.[28] Clearly multiculturalism could have a variety of ideological allies and enemies on the international stage and meant different things in different contexts. Nevertheless, it was – in both the USA and Australia but significantly *not* in Canada – linked by its political enemies to 'political correctness' and associated with high-handed disregard – even contempt – for 'ordinary people'.

It was this economic and political environment that provided the launch-pad for Pauline Hanson's maiden speech in the Australian House of Representatives. This was classic old-style populism with its attacks on the government and its 'kowtowing to financial markets, international organisations, world bankers, investment companies and big business people' and on economic experts: 'I may be only a "fish and chip shop lady" but some of these economists need to get their heads out of the text books and get a job in the real world. I would not even let one of them handle my grocery shopping.'[29] At the same time, like Powell, Wallace and others before her, Hanson set out to be a lightning rod for popular sentiments over immigration:

I and most Australians want our immigration policy radically reviewed and that of multiculturalism abolished. I believe we are in danger of being swamped by Asians. Between 1994 and 1995, 40% of all migrants coming into this country were of Asian origin. They have their own culture and religion, form ghettos and do not assimilate.[30]

[27] Tod Moore, 'Economic Rationalism and Economic Nationalism', in Grant (ed.), *Pauline Hanson*, pp. 50–62. See also Tim Battin, *Abandoning Keynes: Australia's Capital Mistake* (Sydney, Macmillan, 1997).
[28] Betts, *The Great Divide*.
[29] Australian House of Representatives, *Official (Weekly) Hansard*, 10 Sept. 1996, pp. 3860–3.
[30] Ibid.

She also borrowed the notion of 'reverse discrimination' from the Reagan lexicon:

We now have a situation where a type of reverse racism is applied to mainstream Australians by those who promote political correctness and those who control the various taxpayer funded industries that flourish in our society servicing Aboriginals, multiculturalists and a host of other minority groups.[31]

By whatever means the One Nation Party developed its political rhetoric and conceived of its primary audience, some of its publications betrayed an intriguing anachronistic residue: 'Fragmentation, produced by *new class* policies such as immigration, multiculturalism, Asianisation and Aboriginalism (romantic primitivism) ultimately divided us and weakened us.' And:

The so-called Aboriginal debate, initiated by Pauline Hanson, is not merely about the problem of Aborigines . . . [T]heir concerns are not high on the agenda of the *new class elite*. When it suits their ends these poor people are used . . . It is a credit to Pauline Hanson's intuitive genius that she has recognised this and addressed the issue in the public policy debate. Ordinary Australians do have a common enemy, but it is not Aborigines, Asians or people of any particular colour, race or creed. Our common oppressors are a class of raceless, placeless cosmopolitan elites who are exercising almost absolute power over us [italics added].[32]

These references to a 'new class' occurring in the late 1990s formed an important part of the political rationale of the One Nation Party and its appeal to 'ordinary Australians'. They derived from the less strident but essentially identical account of Australian class relations presented in social scientist Katherine Betts' 1988 book *Ideology and Immigration*.[33] Betts is a founding editor of the Australian journal *People and Place* and has devoted much time to analysing immigration issues in relation to public opinion and political trends.[34] She has also made the influence of left-liberal intellectuals a central plank in her argument that multicul- turalist policies and immigration have continued to prevail despite the fact that, as she put it, 'disinterested experts refute most of the arguments for immigration and are equivocal on nearly all of the others'.[35] She argues that members of the 'new class' display a contempt for the views on immigration of large numbers of Australians –

[31] Ibid.
[32] One Nation party (10/21/97) http://www.gwb.com.au/onenation/truth/conclus.html.
[33] Katherine Betts, *Ideology and Immigration: Australia, 1976–1987* (Melbourne, Mel- bourne University Press,1988).
[34] Katherine Betts, 'Immigration and Public Opinion in Australia', *People and Place*, 4, 3 (1996), pp. 9–20.
[35] Betts, *The Great Divide*, p. 71.

particularly as expressed in opinion polls, surveys and voting patterns – and that their political impact on Australian politics has been disproportionate to the merits of their argument and their size. She emphasises the cosmopolitanism of the 'new class' intellectuals, which she sets in contrast to the less-educated 'parochials'.

In *The Great Divide: Immigration Politics in Australia* (1999) – a revised and updated version of her earlier book – she included a chapter called 'The Revolt of the Parochials' in which she described the 'new class censorship of criticism of immigration in Australia'.[36] The source of this censorship, she argues, lies in the fact that 'most members of the new class will not want to criticise immigration-fuelled population growth because they have come to associate such criticism with racism and parochialism'. By the 1990s, she argues, an economic recession had set in, a climate had emerged in which some politicians were less cowed by 'new class' multicultural political correctness and some professional organisations were becoming very sceptical about the wisdom of skilled immigration.[37]

When Pauline Hanson made her maiden speech for the Liberal Party in September 1996 and then some eight months later formed the Pauline Hanson One Nation Party, it seemed to signal a new turn in the lobby against immigration and Aboriginal rights. Betts reports that she soon mobilised a distinct following: 'Crowds formed wherever she appeared and working-class men were particularly taken by her.'[38] She was seen as a 'down-to-earth Australian working woman, obviously sincere, and struggling to offer her supporters a positive image of their country and themselves'.[39] In the 1998 state election in Queensland, the One Nation Party took 22.7 per cent of the vote and eleven seats. This was the high water mark of its electoral popularity. Betts' account of the Hanson period strives to suggest that Hanson was the voice that 'new class' multiculturalists would not allow to speak.[40]

However accurate this profile was – and even Betts makes clear that Hanson was not the only source of opposition to left-liberal ideas on immigration and multiculturalism – the structure seems extremely familiar as an international phenomenon by the late 1990s, although One Nation's following was also reminiscent of earlier periods. Like some groups that formed part of the backlash to equalities policies in the USA during the 1970s, Hanson's supporters came predominantly from areas where blue-collar industrial workers lived and in some rural areas where livelihoods were under threat. Betts account of this again seems to reflect the earlier American situation:

---

[36] Ibid., p. 301.   [37] Ibid.   [38] Ibid., p. 318.
[39] Ibid.   [40] Ibid., pp. 322–3.

Men and women who have lost ground during the extensive economic changes of the last twenty years felt that the mainstream parties had ignored their plight and they were strongly attracted to a program which offered a return to economic regulation and protection. But the cultural message emanating from city-based cultural elites (including some politicians) magnified their sense of grievance by trivialising their situation and by appearing to despise their sense of longing for a national community and an identity worthy of respect.[41]

Although Betts is careful to place her analysis within the context of globalisation processes which left many working-class communities without a job *and* a voice, and she locates the 'new class' within the larger trends towards what others called the *knowledge economy*, her main target is a moral one. In this regard she shares something with – and clearly borrows from – the American neo-conservative writers described in Chapter 1 above who honed the jibe of 'new class idealism' at exactly this group in the USA during the 1970s. Furthermore, she seems no less sympathetic to the communities whose attitudes were the butt of liberal scorn for their limited concerns and racist formulations than, say, the early Michael Novak did, although the neo-conservatives would not have got on with her approval of regulation. Nevertheless, these American neo-conservative writers were undoubtedly an important source for her work. Through her, their ideas found their way to the group of advisors around Pauline Hanson some twenty years after their first volleys were fired.

There is a forlorn feeling about much of Betts' writing and, most recently, transparent disappointment when she finds popular support for official immigration policy being sustained in opinion poll data.[42] Her frustration appears to share much with all those who have watched with incredulity as multiculturalist discourse gained in currency and acceptance as the decades wore on.

Despite the minor but significant backlash evident in the One Nation story, multiculturalism has continued to be an important plank in Australia's economic and social policy. Its 1989 *Agenda* was replaced in 2000 with *A New Agenda for Multicultural Australia* which included a 'statement on racial tolerance' and specifically 'reaffirmed' its 'commitment to the process of reconciliation with Aboriginal and Torres Strait Islander people, in the context of redressing their profound social and economic disadvantage'. Nevertheless, like Canada, beyond the obvious benefits to any country dependent on immigration and continued global

---

[41] Ibid., p. 321.
[42] Betts, 'Immigration and Public Opinion and Opinion about Opinion', *People and Place*, 8, 3 (2000), pp. 60–7.

and regional competitiveness, any contradiction of multiculturalist promises and practice could lead to complex challenges in the future.[43]

For both Canada and Australia levels of migration, asylum seekers, illegal immigrants, all – like the issue of racism – will come into abrasive contact with the practice of state-sponsored multiculturalism and will do so by highlighting the contradictions within its discourse of rights, citizenship, equality and culture. Even in countries like Australia and Canada tensions between the kinds of multiculturalism that oil the wheels of global economics and the scale and nature of global migration may bring about a 'withering away' of multiculturalist discourse. However, the economic logic behind the rapid development of state-sponsored multiculturalism in these two countries after the late 1960s is inescapable. The last quarter of the twentieth century was its 'golden hour'. How appropriate its discourses will be to the political realities of the twenty-first century remains to be seen, but both countries weathered the 1990s storms of backlash only a little dented. In being the only two countries that have adopted multiculturalism as national policy, the relative peacefulness of their politics in this regard, though possibly a temporary matter, is not reflected elsewhere. In the UK and in the USA as well as in a number of European countries the 'multicultural question' shows no sign of losing its topicality. For all liberal democracies, however, changes in the nature and scale of international migration are already allowing the implicit contours of multiculturalism to become exposed, raising new questions about residence, citizenship and belonging. Without a stability of 'groups' the classical issues in multiculturalism concerning individual and collective justice may themselves begin to look like a faraway homeland.

II

Individual and collective justice

Outside of Canada and Australia multiculturalism has always been a more contentious issue. There, especially in the USA and the UK and perhaps because of the stronger concern over anti-racism, thrust and backlash has been an intrinsic part of its fabric. The predominant issue regarding multiculturalism in the UK has historically been education, although before the turn of the twenty-first century religious faiths had already become more the focus of related political debate, first as a result

---

[43] David Fickling, 'Inquiries Begin into Boy's Death and Sydney Riot', *Guardian*, 17 Feb. 2004, p. 12; Gillian Cowlishaw, *Blackfellas Whitefellas and the Hidden Injuries of Race* (Oxford, Blackwell, 2004).

of the Rushdie fatwa. Later this was amplified following community conflicts in northern English towns.

It has been argued that there is what amounts to a soft version of multiculturalism which emphasises an openness to diversity, its representation and inclusiveness and a hard version that seeks to stress and re-enforce cultural differences and incommensurability. As was argued in Chapter 1, on the international stage the former has become widely acceptable. As Christian Joppke and Steven Lukes put it in 1999: 'A safe way to misunderstand multiculturalism is to take its claims at face value. For multiculturalism is not the oppositional movement its protagonists generally proclaim it to be. Rather, multicultural claims for recognising ethnic, religious, or sexual difference have been widely accommodated and institutionalized in the *fin-de-millennium* liberal states.'[44]

In Nathan Glazer's famous phrase: 'we are all multiculturalists now'.[45] At the same time a liberal egalitarian critique also sees the multiculturalism based in exclusive, essentialist communitarianism as an obstacle to the achievement of equity. This kind of multiculturalism is grounded, some argue, on a fundamental contradiction between an orientation to human values based primarily on the equal treatment of individuals and one based on 'encompassing groups' – collectivities, communities – with distinct cultural attributes. Because in a national context such an 'encompassing' also implies at least one 'other' – and often many – the potential for human conflict and inequality (given the human record) is increased.[46] The critique has been made both from this pragmatist position and on the basis that this form of multiculturalism is, by definition as well as practice, incompatible with the objective of equality of opportunity in general and access to education in particular.[47]

Examples of this incompatibility have included the legal judgement that Amish parents in the USA be permitted to exempt their children from a full secondary education, and similar legal exemption in the UK freeing gypsy parents to allow their children shorter academic term times than their peers. In such cases cultural groups exercise power over the well-being of their young which the state normally deems best served by a different set of educational practices.[48] Similarly, contradictions

[44] Joppke and Lukes (eds.), *Multicultural Questions*, p. 1.
[45] Glazer, *We Are All Multiculturalists Now*.
[46] Steven Lukes, *Liberals and Cannibals: The Implications of Diversity* (London, Verso, 2003), pp. 166–7; Kelly, 'Introduction: Between Culture and Equality', in Kelly (ed.), *Multiculturalism Reconsidered*, pp. 1–15.
[47] Barry, *Culture and Equality*, pp. 194–249.
[48] Ibid., pp. 207–8, 238–40.

between human rights and the claims of cultural practice have been substantially highlighted by feminist writers. The 'cultural defense' in legal cases involving immigrant defendants in the USA represent one aspect of this. Thus cases such as that of the Chinese American woman beaten to death by a husband who accounted for his actions as according with the Chinese custom of removing the shame brought on him by an unfaithful wife and his acquittal from murder charges are not unfamiliar.[49]

As Seyla Benhabib points out in *The Claims of Culture: Equality and Diversity in the Global Era*, the use of the cultural defence strategy in such cases

subverts some of the basic elements of the anti-discrimination clause of U.S. law in two ways: first, to the extent that the cultural defense strategy is used to excuse some perpetrators from criminal prosecution or to commute others' sentences it results in the disparate treatment of individuals from foreign cultures; second, the acceptance by the courts of different cultural norms, some of which are inherently discriminatory in that they devalue women and children and condone their treatment as morally and politically less valued beings, undermines aspects of the multiculturalist agenda itself.[50]

Additionally there are the more widely discussed issues of women's subordination within certain cultures and the practices through which that subordination is effected.[51]

The political positionings over these issues are complicated by the fact that the difference between a *notion of justice* grounded on the individual, autonomous self and one grounded in an understanding of the *social* nature of the individual becomes conflated with *identity commitments* to community cultures versus commitments to a self beyond culture. The commitment to different interpretative methodologies (methodological individualism, methodological communitarianism) also becomes tangled up with each of these issues. Communitarians profess to have demonstrated that the facts of multicultural societies – in which access to social goods is distorted by discrepancies of power – have revealed the inadequacy of liberal notions of justice which seek only a level playing field for the interaction of individuals. On this basis multiculturalism's commitment to group identities and rights is proposed as the only route to social justice as well as being a reflection of the increasing real-world

---

[49] Doriane Lambelet Coleman, 'Individualising Justice through Multiculturalism: The Liberals' Dilemma', *Columbia Law Review*, 96, 5 (1996), pp. 1093–167.

[50] Seyla Benhabib, *The Claims of Culture: Equality and Diversity in the Global Era* (Princeton, N.J., Princeton University Press, 2002), pp. 87–8.

[51] Ibid., pp. 82–104; S. Moller Okin, *Is Multiculturalism Bad for Women?* (Princeton, N.J., Princeton University Press, 1999).

salience of group membership.[52] On the other hand egalitarian liberals point to the clear injustices that occur when, for example, group norms and internal rules debar members from accessing rights and goods of the wider society.[53] These issues and their relationship to social coherence and the 'unravelling' of national unity increasingly find their way into public discourse and popular debate.[54]

As was briefly touched on in Chapter 6, in the UK during the early 1980s there was a somewhat different critique of multiculturalism with regard to its relationship to equality and justice. This critique was developed by those who were not concerned with the problem of the autonomy of cultural groups within the wider polity but, like Stephen Steinberg in the USA,[55] with the possibility that the affirmation of cultural pluralism as a fact to be celebrated obscured the more fundamental issues of racial equality and of racisms embedded in the educational system which worked against the achievement of equal opportunities and outcomes for black school and college students. Sociologist Chris Mullard writing in 1981 criticised multiculturalism for its emphasis on ethnic groups, going so far as to call it 'the cultural representation of the ideological form of racism' and for 'institutionalising ethnic/cultural differences'. 'In so doing', Mullard argued, 'ethnicist policies and practices also tend to obfuscate the common experience that might exist between black and certain white class and gender groups in society.'[56] In the same year two other critiques of multicultural education also appeared. In a widely cited paper for the Centre for Contemporary Cultural Studies at Birmingham University, Hazel Carby's *Multicultural Fictions* argued that

It is not the opinions of racial and ethnic minorities that are voiced through multiculturalism. Nor are official documents or educational theories about multicultural curricula addressed to them directly. Rather, racial and ethnic minorities are the object of discussion, predefined as constituting 'the problem'. The audience is the White middle class group of educationalists that have to contain/deal with the 'problem'.[57]

---

[52] Young, *Justice and the Politics of Difference*; Nancy Fraser, *Justice Interruptus* (New York, Routledge, 1997).

[53] See especially, Barry, *Culture and Equality*, and Kelly, 'Introduction', in Kelly (ed.), *Multiculturalism Reconsidered*.

[54] See, for example, David Goodhart, 'Too Diverse?', *Prospect*, www.prospect-magazine. co.uk (Feb. 2004).

[55] Stephen Steinberg, *The Ethnic Myth: Race, Ethnicity and Class in America* (Boston, Beacon Press, 1981).

[56] Chris Mullard, 'The Social Context and Meaning of Multicultural Education', *Educational Analysis*, 3, 1 (1981), pp. 117–40.

[57] Hazel Carby, *Multicultural Fictions* (stencilled paper, race series SP no. 58, Birmingham, Centre for Contemporary Cultural Studies, Birmingham University).

In *The Education of the Black Child in Britain: The Myth of Multicultural Education* Maureen Stone attacked multicultural education with the perspective of black parents clearly in mind. She argued:

By focussing on self-esteem, it manages to ignore the vast body of evidence showing that working-class and black families have much less access to power, to resources of every kind, than middle-class children. 'Self-concept' becomes a way of evading the real, and uncomfortable, issue of class and privilege in our society.[58]

Multicultural education – including what was called at that time 'multi-racial education' – was, she wrote, conceptually unsound:

I want to argue [that] its theoretical and practical implications have not been worked out and that it represents a developing feature of urban education aimed at watering down the curriculum and 'cooling out' black city children while at the same time creating for teachers, both radical and liberal, the illusion that they are doing something special for a particularly disadvantaged group.[59]

It is interesting that both Mullard and Stone specifically mention the predicament of white working-class and black groups as closely related. This kind of association became later not only lost but, worse still, any concern with the issue was taken to be a symptom of racism.

Curiously, the drift of many of these arguments is very close to some of the arguments put more recently in Brian Barry's fairly scathing attack on leading theorists of multiculturalism in his *Culture and Equality* (2001). Indeed, in its assertion of the contradiction between egalitarianism and culturalism, Barry's text could be read as a parallel to – even incorporation of – the earlier anti-racist attack[60] taken up into the domain of political philosophy. Both are concerned with defending a notion of justice that is not constricted by cultural claims.

The early criticisms outlined above came to impact on the prevailing model of multiculturalism in the UK during the 1980s, giving it a much greater emphasis on anti-racism and issues of racial equality. Culturalism was played down and the 'ethnicism' involved in the multiculturalist agenda regarded by many involved in urban education as part of a white 'divide and rule' attempt to build defensive barriers to significant social change. As a sign of the times, in 1985, following a conference address by Chris Mullard, the National Association for Multi-Racial Education (NAME) changed its name – without loss of acronym – to 'National Anti-Racist Movement in Education'. These largely black radical voices

[58] Maureen Stone, *The Education of the Black Child in Britain: The Myth of Multicultural Education* (Glasgow, Fontana, 1981), p. 8.
[59] Ibid., p. 100.
[60] See, for example, Barry, *Culture and Equality*, pp. 11–12.

of critique were soon joined by the right-wing attacks on multicultural-ism discussed in earlier chapters that came to characterise the mid- to late 1980s.[61]

The contemporary predicament

It is interesting to see somewhat more sophisticated versions of similar positions towards culturalism being taken up again in the early twenty-first century. Thus Himani Bannerji mounts a powerful attack on fellow Canadian Charles Taylor's influential essay 'The Politics of Recognition' in her book *The Dark Side of the Nation*, on grounds that clearly resonate with several of the anti-racist critiques of multiculturalism described above. In a detailed chapter she examines a number of issues relating to Taylor's positioning in relation to his audience and the assumptions underlying it. She argues that although Taylor's essay has been widely read and admired, it has not been sufficiently explored or critiqued but framed within a limited theoretical parameter of communitarianism versus liberalism which, she believes, should be opened up 'allowing for other positions of collectivity'.[62] She sees his theoretical endeavour as offering a modification to the tenets of liberalism in order to save it. His writings may be seen, she argues, as 'the erection of a communitarian fortification around the current core of liberal democracy and the liberal state'.[63]

As outlined in his *Multiculturalism and the Politics of Recognition* and *Reconciling Solitudes*,[64] Taylor's critique of state-sponsored multicul-turalism such as Canada's and Australia's rests in part on his objection that in combining a recognition of cultural *differences* between constitu-ent communities, together with arguments of political *equality*, the multiculturalist state is appealing to universalist arguments to support the recognition of difference. It argues, however, that the basis of equality lies not in the cultural particularity of groups but in the difference-denuded, rights-bearing individual. At the same time Taylor

---

[61] This account accords with Tariq Modood's characterisation of the 1980s within his argument that South Asian cultures were subsumed within an anti-racism that privi-ledged black diasporic African identities. See Tariq Modood, '"Difference", Cultural Racism and Anti-Racism', in Pnina Werbner and Tariq Modood (eds.), *Debating Cul-tural Hybridity: Multi-Cultural Identities and the Politics of Anti-Racism* (London, Zed Books, 1997), pp. 154–72.

[62] Himani Bannerji, *The Dark Side of the Nation: Essays in Multiculturalism, Nationalism and Gender* (Toronto, Canadian Scholar's Press, 2000), p. 127.

[63] Ibid., p. 128.

[64] Charles Taylor, *Reconciling Solitudes: Essays on Canadian Federalism and Nationalism*, ed. Guy Laforest (Montreal, McGill-Queen's University Press, 1995); Charles Taylor, 'The Politics of Recognition'.

is paradoxically reluctant to relinquish the possibility of the equality of cultures altogether and presses the argument that although cultures may not be actually equal in any particular regard, in the interest of working towards the possibility of an intercultural Gadamerian 'fusion of horizons', there needs to be a universalisable 'presumption' of equality. Taylor argues: 'If withholding the presumption [of equal respect] is tantamount to a denial of equality, and if important consequences flow from people's identity from the absence of recognition, then a case can be made for insisting on the universalisation of the presumption as a logical extension of the politics of dignity.'[65]

Bannerji asserts that his position on equality and culture, despite this willed re-introduction of culture, allows Taylor the opening for separating politics from culture *and* of configuring his discussion of the relevant worth of cultures in terms that implicitly maintain the pre-eminence of Western civilisation's elite culture – allowing or disallowing equality to be acknowledged.

Bannerji is not alone in seeing Taylor's maintenance of the separation of equality and culture and the argument for a 'presumption of equal value' as both contradictory and philosophically opportunistic. From a different stance Brian Barry also attacks Taylor for 'having his cake and eating it too', arguing that 'he still tries to whistle a tune about the equal value of cultures while at the same time continuing to sing the old song about incommensurability'.[66] Bannerji's case against Taylor, however, is more focussed, detailed and unrelenting than Barry's. The crux of her argument lies in exposing the ultimate vacuity of the concept of recognition devoid of political content. She argues that Taylor's

apolitical perception is articulated by him from the very beginning as he disassociates culture from politics, which allows him to convert class struggle or rights struggles into pleas for recognition of one's cultural identity. If 'they' themselves deny his interpretation Taylor for one is not taken in by what he considers to be spurious political talk. 'They' are merely unable to know what 'they' really want, thus the politics of social justice needs to be displaced by the politics of charitable recognition.[67]

And later: 'It is not a plea for recognition that "they" put forward, but rather a struggle to end exploitation and injustice.'[68]

The reason why this particular territory is such a battleground is, of course, because, during the 1990s, claims about the relationship between rights and cultural identity became the basis for an identity

---

[65] Taylor, 'The Politics of Recognition', p. 68.
[66] Barry, *Culture and Equality*, p. 265.
[67] Bannerji, *Dark Side*, p. 143.   [68] Ibid., p. 147.

politics riven with issues that simultaneously undermined any basis for cross-community solidarity, collective action, shared politics and mutuality. Commonly in the *fin de siècle* multiculturalism especially evident in the USA but also infecting the politics of difference globally, the narrowest of identity co-ordinates were permitted in a gross convergence producing a competitive individualism of group rights. This was not a matter of liberalism *versus* communitarianism – the hybrid was already produced. It was a closed-up self-interest often played out between the very groups that could have most benefited from more dialogue, fewer barriers and more communicative good will. It also infected group relations and claims in such a way as to invite a torrent of criticism from multiculturalism's political opponents and from some of its natural allies.

III

Theory meets politics

Bannerji's acknowledgement of the work of Iris Marion Young[69] suggests that it is not multiculturalism itself that she is arguing against, only de-politicised versions of it. In fact she makes plain at the outset that 'Pitfalls of political consciousness associated with multiculturalism should not prevent us from realizing that its meaning is context specific. Meaning and application of multiculturalism vary depending on who initiates it, on what theoretical and practical grounds, and why.'[70]

As criticisms of major struts in multicultural theory pile up on all sides, it becomes clear that both egalitarian liberals and radical anti-racists can regard multiculturalism in itself as being surplus to the needs of their conceptions of social justice. There have also long been a number of feminist critiques of multiculturalism that point to the contradictions that can arise between respecting cultural traditions and protecting women's rights.[71] Contradictions between the aims of social justice and those of multiculturalism have been vigorously argued by commentators, many, such as these feminists, from the left of the political spectrum.[72] At the same time, the political march of

[69] Ibid., p. 146.   [70] Ibid., p. 125.

[71] Okin, *Is Multiculturalism Bad for Women?*; M. Nussbaum, *Sex and Social Justice* (New York, Oxford University Press, 1999); Nira Yuval-Davis, 'Ethnicity, Gender Relations and Multiculturalism', in Werbner and Modood (eds.), *Debating Cultural Hybridity*, pp. 193–208; Jeannie Martin, 'Multiculturalism and Feminism', in G. Bottomley, M. de Lepervanche and J. Martin (eds.), *Intersexions* (Sydney, Allen and Unwin, 1991), pp. 110–31.

[72] See for example, David Goldberg (ed.), *Multiculturalism: A Critical Reader* (Oxford, Blackwell, 1994); Peter McLaren, *Revolutionary Multiculturalism: Pedagogies of Dissent for the New Millenium* (Boulder, Colo., Westview Press, 1999).

multiculturalism across the world stage has been a very inconsistent respecter of philosophical arguments from any side. As was apparent in Greenwich, on any local political battleground what becomes characterised as 'multiculturalism' depends more on the immediate political history of an event than on the value of any underlying argument.

Neither the conflicts within the educational field nor those related to local democracy evident in Greenwich during the 1990s actually derived exclusively from multiculturalism, despite appearing to. They were both adequately sustained by other, earlier sources of social policy. The cultural diversity evident and 'celebrated' in Greenwich schools was also not a problem of multiculturalism *per se*, even for those white English children who seemed to be blinded to their own cultural resources by it. The principles articulated in the letter of Greenwich education authority's multicultural policy were those of equal access, across-the-board cultural affirmation and the application of standards of fairness in the content of anti-racist policy. Where the problems arose was in the *application* of those principles in an already political field. The objections to the fairness with which anti-racism was applied in schools – the ways in which racial incidents were recorded and the differential weight given to accusations and accounts – were little to do with the differences between liberal and communitarian notions of equality or justice or with any claim for special treatment. The pageant of these classic debates over multiculturalism were produced more as epiphenomena brought into existence by the charged field of political relations and discursive transformations taking place at the local and national levels. Even without the obvious inadequacies of local educational delivery and the obvious faults of policies at other times and places, there was a considerable warping of communication evident such that, clean, untrammelled meanings over 'culture' and 'racism' could not be exchanged. Habermasian distortion-free communication seemed even more remote than usual.

Similarly with the issues of local democracy brought out by the conflict over the creation of a black and ethnic minority tenants' association. Ultimately, the conflict played out as the promotion of a 'special interest group' by a local authority that was imposing its racialisation of democratic process against the will of a victim white community. The term 'quotas' applied by some of the TA activists arrived out of the blue from American neo-conservatism. These enacted readings of the situation were, however, not intrinsic to what BEMTA were attempting to achieve. What they were derived from was no fault of logic or mismatch between differing conceptions of justice. Indeed, there was nothing that departed from the broadly accepted UK mainstream principles of egalitarianism. They came, rather, out of actual political relations and the history of those relations locally, nationally and even internationally over the previous twenty years.

Such arguments as those appearing in Greenwich can be regarded as the regular fare of democratic politics. At the height of this 1990s backlash Henry Louis Gates argued that American multiculturalism had come to be distorted by its forced association with an identity politics that had sought to use it as a stalking horse and as a result of which 'the real sources of contemporary cohesion' had been persistently obscured. It was the tangle of these two that had brought multiculturalism to 'something of an impasse'.[73] Nevertheless, he argued, the very vigour of the arguments about multiculturalism was suggestive of a family row. 'Do we not talk', he wrote, 'of "hammering out" an issue?'[74] This too, he argued, is the normal stuff of democracy in action.

Yet the 'family argument' retains its underlying benignity so long as the family stays together and/or its members do not abuse each other. Not all popular commentators were so sanguine at that time. Todd Gitlin, for example, argued powerfully from the left that family interests, or what he calls a 'commons', need to underwrite all claims on our attentions and resources:

To recognise diversity, more than diversity is needed. The commons is needed. To affirm the rights of minorities, majorities must be formed. Democracy is more than a license to celebrate (and exaggerate) differences. It cannot afford to live in the past – anyone's past. It is a political system of mutual reliance and common moral obligations. Mutuality needs tending. If multiculturalism is not tempered by a stake in the commons, then centrifugal energy overwhelms any commitment to a larger good. This is where multiculturalism as a faith has proved a trap even – or especially – for people in the name of whom the partisans of identity purport to speak. Affirming the virtues of the margins, identity politics has left the centres of power uncontested.[75]

Even Stuart Hall seeking to go 'beyond existing political vocabularies',[76] seems to be offering a structuralist version of this argument when he says that the framework within which 'serious conflicts of outlook, belief and interest can be negotiated' cannot be that of 'Eurocentric assimilationism' but that nevertheless: 'The specific and particular "difference" of a group or community cannot be asserted absolutely, without regard to

---

[73] Henry Louis Gates, 'The Weaning of America', New Yorker, 19 Apr., 1993, p. 116.

[74] Ibid.

[75] Gitlin, The Twilight of Common Dreams, p. 236.

[76] Stuart Hall, 'Conclusion: The Multi-Cultural Question', in Barnor Hesse (ed.), Un/settled Multiculturalisms: Diasporas, Entanglements, Transruptions (London, Zed Books, 2000, pp. 209–41.

the wider context provided by all those "others" in relation to whom "particularity" acquires a relative value.'

Hall attempts to keep this discussion as 'philosophical' as it can be made – although the argument sounds unmistakably more like classical structural linguistics – and makes no concrete suggestions concerning the *material means by which* the 'wider contexts' of 'others' might be 'negotiated'. Finally, we are presented with the ancient paradox of cultural relativism and moral universalism (though heavily disguised) first offered by Herder. Thus, 'we must look for how both the greater recognition of difference and greater equality and justice for all can become part of a common "horizon"'.[77] All of the arguments indeed seem as reasonable as they always have. To how many they would constitute a 'new political logic' is hard to say.

The number of issues that test the scope and adequacy of multiculturalism increased almost daily during the first years of the twenty-first century. Arguments from the left seem to be increasingly that multiculturalism is either harmful or unnecessary but that it somehow cannot be let go of. If Gates was right that there exists a multiculturalism uncontaminated by identity agendas and grounded on a belief in commonalities existing beyond cultures but structured through relations of power, it may be that the 'ism' can beneficially be lost – at least in some parts of the globe. The differing histories of national encounters with multiculturalism make it impossible that one future will 'fit all'. There is no shortage of lessons from the past to light the way and, within these, backlash responses have to be fully understood in all their contradictory political complexity.

Much of the political history of the USA in the last quarter of the twentieth century was accompanied by the increasing sophistication of approaches to the management of potentially damaging backlashes over almost any area of political, policy or social interest. Self-reflexive, high-speed, media-driven and digitalised micro-backlashes have now become almost the humus of American public and political life, making old-fashioned counter-narrative look like an underwater mime. It is difficult to predict what such a medium of public discourse will result in for issues of social justice, although multiculturalism as an 'ism' appears to have run its course there. In the UK there are also signs that while multicultural society has achieved normative status, as a movement its days may be numbered. When the head of the Commission for Racial Equality announces, as he did in March 2004, that the UK needs to put aside the emphasis on cultural particularisms and embrace a vision of

[77] Ibid., p. 237.

national culture, it would seem that a change of political language is on the way. Confidence that the far right extremist groups of British politics are incapable of making any significant impression on the British electorate – unlike, it is said, the right-wing populist parties of mainland Europe – may be prompting this departure from equalities tradition.[78] It may also be that, post-9/11 and the Iraq war, some involved with racial equalities do not wish to see the cargo of anti-racism go down with the ship of communitarianism.

There is little for Europe in general to be complacent about. The facts of contemporary multicultural societies, though they have been clear to many for some time, are still unaccepted by large swathes of Europe's population. In Italy, Germany, France, Belgium, The Netherlands and across Scandinavia far right parties, some of them populist, maintain a fluctuating but significant position in national politics. High levels of international migration for both economic and political reasons may slow but are unlikely to cease. Indeed, the great turbine of migratory movement across the globe may, perhaps, only just now be getting into its stride. Innumerable local 'backlashes' – not necessarily reflected in anti-immigrant political parties and groups – are potential, even likely. The lessons of the past are less to do with these as social phenomena in themselves – they grow out of everyday perceptions of social threats both mistaken and real – but more with how politicians relate to them. Governments quite commonly respond with immediate tactics designed to defuse criticism and disarm their political opponents. In the UK a form of strategic illiberalism has been employed by New Labour – particularly under David Blunket as Home Secretary – precisely governed by a concern with not being wrong-footed again by the issue of immigration, while making a wing-and-a-prayer calculus of the policy's negative impact on 'community relations' – i.e. backlash. These approaches are inevitably hostages to fortune. Under these conditions multiculturalism's nagging voice may need to be kept alive a little longer – and in the same 'strategic' spirit.

Backlash itself, however, is unlikely to vanish. Indeed, in the current order of global migration the political framing of migration has become fundamental to its public construction. As Stephen Castles has pointed out, 'international migration is an integral part of relationships between societies' and 'if there is a crisis [over migration]. . . it is an ideological

---

[78] For an analysis of the differences between the BNP and populist parties of the far right in the rest of Europe see Hainsworth (ed.), *The Politics of the Extreme Right*; Herbert Kitschelt, *The Radical Right in Western Europe: A Comparative Analysis* (Ann Arbor, University of Michigan Press, 1995), pp. 241–56; Hans-George Betz, *Radical Right-Wing Populism in Western Europe* (Basingstoke, Macmillan, 1994).

and political one'.[79] In this regard the treatment of the issue of political asylum and refugee communities by the UK press – which frequently amounts to an incitement to backlash – is not a peripheral matter. Indeed, it is barely recognised in the UK just how aberrant in international perspective is the extremism of the UK press and how inadequate the Press Complaints Commission has been in responding to objections to the high levels of distortion and untruth. The Council of Europe's European Commission against Racism and Intolerance, in its *Second Report* on the United Kingdom, stated that: 'Particular concern is expressed at the consistent inflammatory attacks on asylum seekers and migrants coming to the United Kingdom which have appeared in local but also some national mainstream newspapers',[80] while Amnesty International's *Annual Report* for 2001 asserted that 'very negative coverage pandered to racial prejudice and created a hostile environment for many asylum seekers'. Thus, while New Labour's strategies for avoiding being caught on the wrong side of public opinion – local governance, partnerships and 'public involvement' in policy processes – have been earnestly applied to an ecumenical range of issues, immigration has been narrowed down to a call and response between politicians' pronouncements and sections of the news media determinedly restricting the terms of 'the debate' to racist caricature.[81]

If the pursuit of common cultures is a red herring driven by a crude and static notion of culture, then the pursuit of a common framework of interaction and justice becomes all the more important in any diverse society. The dialogue between politicians and the press is in essence brought to life only by the spectre of backlash, with each lowering or raising the temperature in accordance with its reading of the 'public'. Both bear a responsibility for broadening the ground of democratic process.

---

[79] Castles, 'The International Politics of Forced Migration'.
[80] Information Centre about Asylum and Refugees in the UK, *Media Image, Community Impact: Assessing the Impact of Media and Political Images of Refugees and Asylum Seekers on Community Relations in London*, report of a pilot study commissioned by the Mayor of London (London, ICAR, Kings College, University of London, Apr. 2004), p. 80.
[81] Paul Statham, *United Kingdom, Racism and Cultural Diversity in the Mass Media: An Overview of Research and Examples of Good Practice in the EU Member States, 1995–2000* (Vienna, European Monitoring Centre on Racism and Xenophobia, 2002) p. 409.

Select bibliography

Aarne, Antti and Thompson, Stith, *The Types of the Folktale: A Classification and Bibliography, Translated and Enlarged by Stith Thompson*, Folklore Fellows Communications (second revision), no. 184, Helsinki, 1961.

Abu-Laban, Yasmeen and Gabriel, Christina, *Selling Diversity: Immigration, Multiculturalism, Employment Equity and Globalization*, Ontario, Broadview Press, 2002.

Amaker, Norman C., *Civil Rights and the Reagan Administration*, Washington DC, Urban Institute Press, 1988.

Amaker, Norman C., 'Reagan and the Civil Rights Legacy', in Eric J. Schmertz, Natalie Datlof and Alexej Ugninsky (eds.), *Ronald Reagan's America*, vol. I, Westport, Conn., Greenwood Press, 1997, pp. 163–74.

Ambrose, Stephen, *Nixon: The Triumph of a Politician 1962–1972*, London, Simon and Schuster, 1989.

Appelbaum, Eileen and Batt, Rosemary, *The New American Workplace: Transforming Work Systems in the United States*, Ithaca, Cornell University Press, 1994.

Arnold, Patricia, *A History of Britain's Parliamentary Constituencies: The Constituencies of the London Borough of Greenwich*, West Malling, Patricia Arnold, 1992.

Bakhtin, M. M., *The Dialogic Imagination: Four Essays*, ed. Michael Holq, Austin, Tex., University of Texas Press, 1981.

Speech Genres and Other Late Eassays, Austin, Tex., University of Texas Press, 1986.

Ball, Wendy and Solomos, John (eds.), *Race and Local Politics*, London, Macmillan, 1990.

Bannerji, Himani, *The Dark Side of the Nation: Essays in Multiculturalism, Nationalism and Gender*, Toronto, Canadian Scholar's Press, 2000.

Barry, Brian, *Culture and Equality: An Egalitarian Critique of Multiculturalism*, Cambridge, Polity Press, 2001.

Bauman, Richard, *Story, Performance and Event: Contextual Studies of Oral Narrative*, Cambridge, Cambridge University Press, 1986.

Bazelon, David, *Power in America: The Politics of the New Class*, New York, New American Library, 1967.

Bell, Daniel, *The Coming of Post-Industrial Society: A Venture in Social Forecasting*, New York, Basic Books, 1973.

Bell, Derrick, *Faces at the Bottom of the Well: The Permanence of Racism*, New York, Basic Books, 1992.

Benhabib, Seyla, *The Claims of Culture: Equality and Diversity in the Global Era*, Princeton, Princeton University Press, 2002.

Ben-Tovim, Gideon, Gabriel, John, Law, Ian and Stredder, Kathleen, *The Local Politics of Race*, Basingstoke, Macmillan, 1986.

Bernstein, Richard, *Dictatorship of Virtue: How the Battle over Multiculturalism Is Reshaping our Schools, our Country, and our Lives*, New York, Vintage Books, 1994.

Betts, Katherine, *The Great Divide: Immigration Politics in Australia*, Sydney, Duffy and Snellgrove, 1999.

Betz, Hans-George, *Radical Right-Wing Populism in Western Europe*, Basingstoke, Macmillan, 1994.

Bissoondath, Neil, *Selling Illusions: The Cult of Multiculturalism in Canada*, Toronto, Penguin Books, 1994.

Bjorklund, Tor, 'Radical Right-Wing Populism in Scandinavia: From Tax Revolt to Xenophobia', in P. Hainsworth (ed.), *The Politics of the Extreme Right: From Margins to the Mainstream*, London, Pinter, 2000, pp.193–223.

Bloom, Alan, *The Closing of the American Mind*, New York, Simon and Schuster, 1987.

Bloom, Jack, *Class, Race and the Civil Rights Movement*, Bloomington, Indiana University Press, 1987.

Bluestone, Barry and Harrison, Bennett, *The Deindustrialisation of America: Plant Closings, Community Abandonment and the Dismantling of Basic Industry*, New York, Basic Books, 1982.

Brubaker, William Rogers (ed.), *Immigration and the Politics of Citizenship in Europe and North America*, Lanham, Md., German Marshall Fund and University Press of America, 1989.

Bruce-Biggs, B., *The New Class?*, New Brunswick, N. J., Transaction Books, 1979.

Burford, Beverley and Watson, Julian (eds.), *Aspects of the Arsenal: The Royal Arsenal Woolwich*, London, Greenwich Borough Museum, 1997.

Butler, Judith, 'Endangered/Endangering: Schematic Racism and White Paranoia', in Robert Gooding-Williams (ed.), *Reading Rodney King: Reading Urban Uprising*, London, Routledge, 1993.

Excitable Speech: A Politics of the Performative, New York and London, Routledge, 1997.

'Performativity's Social Magic', in Richard Shusterman (ed.), *Bourdieu: A Critical Reader*, Oxford, Blackwell, 1999, pp. 113–28.

Campbell, B., *Goliath: Britain's Dangerous Places*, London, Methuen, 1993.

Carens, Joseph H., *Culture, Citizenship and Community: A Contextual Exploration of Justice as Evenhandedness*, Oxford, Oxford University Press, 2000.

Carmines, Edward and Stimson, James, *Issue Evolution: Race and the Transformation of American Politics*, Princeton, N. J., Princeton University Press, 1989.

Carter, Dan T., *From George Wallace to Newt Gingrich: Race in the Conservative Counter-Revolution*, Baton Rouge, Louisiana State University Press, 1996.

Castells, Manuel, *The Rise of the Network Society*, Oxford, Blackwell, 2000.

Castles, Stephen, *Ethnicity and Globalization*, London, Sage, 2000.

'The International Politics of Forced Migration', in Leo Panitch and Colin Leys (eds.), *Fighting Identities: Race, Religion and Ethno-Nationalism, The Socialist Register 2002*, London, Merlin Press, 2002, pp. 172–9.

Centre for Multicultural Education, *Sagaland: Youth Culture, Racism and Education, a Report on Research Carried out in Thamesmead*, London, Centre for Multicultural Education, Institute of Education, University of London, 1992.

Cockett, Richard, *Thinking the Unthinkable: Think-Tanks and the Economic Counter-Revolution 1931–1983*, London, Harper-Collins, 1994.

Cole, Robert and Erikson, Jan, *The Middle Americans: Proud and Uncertain*, Boston, Little Brown and Co., 1971.

Cortazzi, Martin, *Narrative Analysis*, London, Washington, Falmer Press, 1993.

Cowie, Jefferson and Heathcott, Joseph (eds.), *Beyond the Ruins: The Meaning of Deindustrialisation*, Ithaca, ILR Press, Cornell University Press, 2003.

Cowlishaw, Gillian, *Blackfellas Whitefellas and the Hidden Injuries of Race*, Oxford, Blackwell, 2004.

Crossick, Geoffrey, *An Artisan Elite in Victorian Society: Kentish London 1840–1880*, London, Croom Helm, 1978.

Curry, George E. (ed.), *The Affirmative Action Debates*, Reading, Mass., Addison-Wesley, 1996.

Daniel, W. W., *Whatever Happened to the Workers in Woolwich? A Survey of Redundancy in South East London*, London, PEP, 1972.

Davis, Steven J., Haltiwanger, John C. and Schuh, Scott, *Job Creation and Destruction*, Cambridge, Mass., MIT Press, 1997.

Delgado, Richard (ed.), *Critical Race Theory: The Cutting Edge*, Philadelphia, Temple University Press, 1995.

Department of Education and Science, *West Indian Children in our Schools*, London, Her Majesty's Stationery Office, 1982.

Education For All, London, Her Majesty's Stationery Office, 1985.

Dijk, Teun van, *Communicating Racism*, Newbury Park, Calif., Sage, 1987.

Elite Discourse and Racism, London, Sage, 1993.

Dorrien, Gary, *The Neoconservative Mind: Politics, Culture and the War of Ideology*, Philadelphia, Temple University Press, 1993.

Douglas, John Aubrey, 'Anatomy of Conflict: The Making and Unmaking of Affirmative Action at the University of California', in John David Skrentny (ed.), *Color Lines: Affirmative Action, Immigration and Civil Rights Options for America*, Chicago, University of Chicago Press, 2001, pp. 87–117.

Dreyfuss, Joel and Lawrence, Charles, *The Bakke Case: The Politics of Inequality*, New York, Harcourt Brace Jovanovich, 1979.

D'Souza, Danish, *Illiberal Education: The Politics of Race and Sex on Campus*, New York, Free Press, 1991.

Dugger, Ronnie, *On Reagan: The Man and his Presidency*, New York, McGraw-Hill, 1983.

Edsall, Thomas Byrne and Edsall, Mary D., *Chain Reaction: The Impact of Race, Rights and Taxes on American Politics*, New York, Norton, 1992.

Edwards, John, *When Race Counts: The Morality of Racial Preference in Britain and America*, London, Routledge, 1995.

Finnegan, William, *Cold New World: Growing Up in a Harder Country*, New York, Modern Library, 1998.

Flew, Antony, *Education, Race and Revolution*, London, Centre for Policy Studies, 1984.

Foot, Paul, *The Rise of Enoch Powell: An Examination of Enoch Powell's Attitude to Immigration and Race*, London, Cornmarket Press, 1969.

Formisano, R., *Boston against Busing: Race, Class and Ethnicity in the 1960s and 1970s*, Chapel Hill, University of North Carolina Press, 1991.

Foster, J., 'Class Struggle and the Industrial Revolution: Early Industrial Capitalism in Three English Towns', Ph.D. thesis, University of London, 1974.

Freeman, Gary P., 'Modes of Immigration Politics in Liberal Democratic States', *International Migration Review*, 29, 4 (1995), pp. 881–903.

Friedman, Murray, *Overcoming Middle Class Rage*, Philadelphia, Westminster Press, 1971.

Fryer, Peter, *Staying Power: The History of Black People in Britain*, London, Pluto Press, 1984.

Fysh, Peter and Wolfreys, Jim, *The Politics of Racism in France*, New York, Palgrave Macmillan, 2003.

Gillborn, David, *Racism and Antiracism in Real Schools: Theory, Policy, Practice*, Buckingham, Open University Press, 1995.

Gillborn, David and Mirza, Heidi Safia, *Educational Inequality: Mapping Race, Class and Gender: A Synthesis of Research Evidence*, London, Office for Standards in Education, 2000.

Gillborn, David and Youdell, Deborah, *Rationing Education: Policy, Practice, Reform and Equity*, Buckingham, Open University Press, 2000.

Gilroy, Paul, *There Ain't No Black in the Union Jack*, London, Hutchinson, 1987.

'The End of Anti-Racism', in Wendy Ball and John Solomos (eds.), *Race and Local Politics*, London, Macmillan, 1990, pp. 191–206.

Gitlin, Todd, *The Twilight of Common Dreams: Why America Is Wracked by Culture Wars*, New York, Henry Holt and Company, 1995.

Glazer, Nathan, *We Are All Multiculturalists Now*, Cambridge, Mass., Harvard University Press, 1997.

'Multiculturalism and American Exceptionalism', in Christian Joppke and Steven Lukes (eds.), *Multicultural Questions*, Oxford, Oxford University Press, 1999, pp. 183–98.

Goldberg, David (ed.), *Multiculturalism: A Critical Reader*, Oxford, Blackwell, 1994.

Gordon, Paul and Rosenberg, David, *Daily Racism: The Press and Black People in Britain*, London, The Runnymede Trust, 1989.

Grant, Bligh (ed.), *Pauline Hanson: One Nation and Australian Politics*, Armidale, Australia, University of New England Press, 1997.

Greenberg, Stanley, *Middle Class Dreams: The Politics and Power of the New American Majority*, New York, Times Books, 1996.

Guglielmo, Thomas A., *White on Arrival: Italians, Race, Colour and Power in Chicago 1890–1945*, New York, Oxford University Press, 2003.

Gutman, Amy (ed.), *Multiculturalism: Examining the Politics of Recognition*, Princeton, N. J., Princeton University Press, 1994.

Hainsworth, Paul (ed.), *The Politics of the Extreme Right: From Margins to Mainstream*, London, Pinter, 2000.

Hall, Stuart, 'New Ethnicities', in J. Donald and A. Rattansi (eds.), *'Race' Culture and Difference*, London, Sage Publications/Open University, 1992.

Hamilton, Richard, *Class and Politics in the United States*, New York, John Wiley and Sons, 1972.

Haraway, Donna, 'Situated Knowledge: The Science Question in Feminism and the Privilege of Partial Perspective', *Feminist Studies*, 14 (1988) 575–99.

Harrington, Michael, *Towards a Democratic Left: A Radical Program for a New Majority*, New York, Macmillan, 1968.

Harrison, Trevor, *Of Passionate Intensity: Right-Wing Populism and the Reform Party of Canada*, Toronto, University of Toronto Press, 1995.

Heffer, Simon, *Like the Roman: The Life of Enoch Powell*, Weidenfeld and Nicolson, 1998.

Hewitt, Roger, *White Talk Black Talk: Inter-Racial Friendship and Communication amongst Adolescents*, Cambridge, Cambridge University Press, 1986.

'Language, Youth and the Destabilization of Ethnicity', in C. Palmgren, K. Lovegren and G. Bolin (eds.), *Ethnicity in Youth Culture*, Stockholm, University of Stockholm, USU, 1992.

Routes of Racism: The Social Basis of Racist Action, Stoke-on-Trent, Trentham Books, 1996.

Higham, John (ed.), *Civil Rights and Social Wrongs: Black–White Relations since World War II*, University Park, Pennsylvania University Press, 1997.

Hirsch, Arnold, *Making the Second Ghetto: Race and Housing in Chicago, 1940–1960*, Cambridge, Cambridge University Press, 1983.

Hirsch, E. D. Jr, *Cultural Literacy: What Every American Needs to Know*, Boston, Houghton Mifflin, 1987.

Holland, K. and Parkin, G., *Reversing Racism: Lessons from America*, London, Social Affairs Unit, 1984.

Home Office, *The Stephen Lawrence Inquiry Report*, London, The Stationery Office, 1999.

Horwitz, Tony, *Confederates in the Attic: Dispatches from the Unfinished Civil War*, New York, Vintage Books, 1998.

Hughes, Robert, *The Culture of Complaint: The Fraying of America*, Oxford, Oxford University Press, 1993.

Inner London Education Authority, *Race, Sex and Class*, London, ILEA, 1983.

Jefferson, E. F. E., *The Woolwich Story 1890–1965*, London, The R. A. Printing Press Ltd, 1970.

Jenkins, R. and Solomos, J., *Racism and Equal Opportunity Policies in the 1980s*, Cambridge, Cambridge University Press, 1987.

Joppke, Christian and Lukes, Steven (eds.), *Multicultural Questions*, Oxford, Oxford University Press, 1999.

Katznelson, Ira, *Black Men White Cities: Race, Politics and Migration in the United States, 1900–30, and Britain 1948–68*, Chicago, University of Chicago Press, 1976.

Keller, Hansfried and Heubergern, Frank W. (eds.), *Hidden Technocrats: The New Class and New Capitalism*, New Brunswick, N. J., and London, 1992.

Kelly, Paul (ed.), *Multiculturalism Reconsidered*, Cambridge, Polity Press, 2002.

King, Martin Luther, Jr, *Where Do We Go from Here: Chaos or Community?*, New York, Harper Row, 1967.

Kinsella, Warren, *Web of Hate: Inside Canada's Far Right Network*, Toronto, Harper Collins, 1994.

Kirp, David L., *Doing Good by Doing Little: Race and Schooling in Britain*, Berkeley and London, University of California Press, 1979.

    Just Schools: The Idea of Racial Equality in American Education, Berkeley, University of California Press, 1982.

Kitschelt, Herbert, *The Radical Right in Western Europe: A Comparative Analysis*, Ann Arbor, University of Michigan Press, 1995.

Kivisto, Peter, *Multiculturalism in a Global Society*, Oxford, Blackwell, 2002.

Kristol, Irving, *Two Cheers for Capitalism*, New York, Basic Books, 1978.

Kumar, Krishan, *From Post-Industrial to Post-Modern Society: New Theories of the Contemporary World*, Oxford, Blackwell, 1995.

Kymlicka, Will, *Multicultural Citizenship: A Liberal Theory of Minority Rights*, Oxford, Oxford University Press, 1995.

Labov, W. and Waletzky, J., 'Narrative Analysis: Oral Versions of Personal Experience', in J. Helm (ed.), *Essays on the Verbal and Visual Arts: Proceedings of the 1966 Annual Meeting of the American Ethnological Society*, Washington, University Press, 1967, pp. 12–44.

Lansley, Stewart, Goss, Sue and Wolmar, Christian, *Councils in Conflict: The Rise and Fall of the Municipal Left*, Basingstoke, Macmillan, 1989.

Laycock, David, *The New Right and Democracy in Canada: Understanding Reform and the Canadian Alliance*, Ontario, Oxford University Press, 2003.

Li, Peter (ed.), *Race and Ethnic Relations in Canada*, Toronto, Oxford University Press, 1999.

Lipset, Seymour Martin and Raab, Earl, *The Politics of Unreason: Right-Wing Extremism in America 1790–1977*, Chicago, University of Chicago Press, 1970.

Lopez, Mark, *The Origins of Multiculturalism in Australian Politics 1945–1975*, Carlton South, Vic., Melbourne University Press, 2000.

Lord, Albert, *The Singer of Tales*, Cambridge, Mass., Harvard University Press, 1958.

Lukes, Steven, *Liberals and Cannibals: The Implications of Diversity*, London, Verso, 2003.

Massey, Douglas and Denton, Nancy, *American Apartheid: Segregation and the Making of the Underclass*, Cambridge, Mass., Harvard University Press, 1993.

Matusow, Alan, *The Unravelling of America: A History of Liberalism in the 1960s*, New York, Harper Row, 1984.

Miles, Robert, *Racism*, London, Routledge, 1989.

Modood, Tariq, '"Difference", Cultural Racism and Anti-Racism', in Pnina Werbner and Tariq Modood (eds.), *Debating Cultural Hybridity: Multi-Cultural Identities and the Politics of Anti-Racism*, London, Zed Books, 1997, pp. 154–72.

Mullard, Chris, *Racism in Society and Schools: History, Policy and Practice*, Centre for Multicultural Education, Institute of Education University of London, 1980.

Murray, N., 'Anti-Racists and Other Demons: The Press and Ideology in Thatcher's Britain', *Race and Class*, 27, 3 (1986), pp. 1–19.

Nancoo, Stephen (ed.), *21st Century Canadian Diversity*, Ontario, Canadian Educators Press, 2000.

Novak, Michael, *The Rise of the Unmeltable Ethnics: Politics and Culture in the Seventies*, New York, Macmillan Publishing Co., Inc, 1972.

Okin, S. Moller, *Is Multiculturalism Bad for Women?*, Princeton, N. J., Princeton University Press, 1999.

Orfield, Gary, *Must We Bus? Segregated Schools and National Policy*, Washington DC, The Brookings Institution, 1978.

'Race and the Liberal Agenda: The Loss of the Integrationist Dream, 1965–1974', in Margaret Weir, Ann Shola Orloff and Theda Skocpol (eds.), *The Politics of Social Policy in the United States* (Princeton, N. J., Princeton University Press, 1988), pp. 313–55.

Orfield, Gary, Eaton, Susan E. and the Harvard Project on School Desegregation, *Dismantling Desegregation: The Quiet Reversal of Brown v. Board of Education*, New York, The New Press, 1996.

Osofsky, Gilbert, *Harlem: The Making of a Ghetto: Negro New York, 1890–1930*, 2nd edn, New York, Harper Torchbooks, 1971.

Palmer, Frank (ed.), *Anti-racism: An Assault on Education and Value*, London, Sherwood Press, 1986.

Palmer, John L. and Sawhill, Isabel V. (eds.), *The Reagan Record: An Assessment of America's Changing Domestic Priorities*, Cambridge, Mass., Ballinger Publishing Company, 1984.

Phillips, Kevin, *The Politics of Rich and Poor: Wealth and the American Electorate in the Reagan Aftermath*, New York, Random House, 1990.

Pierce, William, 'Industrial Relations in the Royal Arsenal', in Beverley Burford and Julian Watson (eds.), *Aspects of the Arsenal: The Royal Arsenal Woolwich*, London, Greenwich Borough Museum, 1997, pp. 111–25.

Powell, Enoch, *Freedom and Reality*, Harmondsworth, Penguin Books, 1969.

Propp, Vladimir, *Theory and History of Folklore*, Manchester, Manchester University Press, 1984.

Ramadin, Ron, *The Making of the Black Working Class in Britain*, Aldershot, Wildwood House Ltd, 1987.

Reeves, Frank, *Race and Borough Politics*, Aldershot, Averbury, 1989.

Reich, R., *The Work of Nations: Preparing Ourselves for Twenty-First Century Capitalism*, New York, Simon and Schuster, 1991.

Rieder, Jonathan, *Canarsie: The Jews and Italians of Brooklyn against Liberalism*, Cambridge, Mass., Harvard University Press, 1985.

'The Rise of the "Silent Majority"', in Steve Fraser and Gary Gerstle (eds.), *The Rise and Fall of the New Deal Order 1930–1980*, Princeton, N. J., Princeton University Press, 1989, pp. 243–68.

Rifkin, J., *The End of Work: The Decline of the Global Labour Force and the Dawn of the Post-Market Era*, New York, Putnam and Sons, 1996.

Roediger, David R., *The Wages of Whiteness: Race and the Making of the American Working Class*, London, Verso, 1991.

Rubin, Lillian, *Busing and Backlash: White against White in a California School District*, Berkeley, University of California Press, 1972.

Satzewich, Vic (ed.), *Racism and Social Inequality in Canada: Concepts, Controversies and Strategic Resistance*, Toronto, Thompson Educational, 1998.

Deconstructing a Nation: Immigration, Multiculturalism and Racism in 90's Canada, Halifax, Nova Scotia, Fernwood Publishing, 1992.

Schlesinger, Arthur, M., Jr, *The Disuniting of America*, New York, Norton, 1992.

Sennett, Richard, *The Corrosion of Character: The Personal Consequences of Work in the New Capitalism*, New York, Norton and Company, 1998.

Sennet, Richard and Cobb, Jonathan, *The Hidden Injuries of Class*, Cambridge, Cambridge University Press, 1972.

Shepherd, Robert, *Enoch Powell*, Hutchinson, London, 1996.

Skillen, Tony, 'Post-Marxist Modes of Production, or Discourse Fever', *Radical Philosophy*, 20 (1978), pp. 3–8.

Sleeper, Jim, *The Closest of Strangers: Liberalism and the Politics of Race in New York*, New York, W. W. Norton and Co., 1990.

Smith, Susan J., *The Politics of Race and Residence*, Cambridge, Polity Press, 1989.

'Residential Segregation and the Politics of Racialisation', in Malcolm Cross and Michael Keith (eds.), *Racism, the City and the State*, London, Routledge, 1993, pp. 128–43.

Solomos, John, 'The Local Politics of Racial Equality', in Malcolm Cross and Michael Keith (eds.), *Racism, the City and the State*, London, Routledge, 1993.

Solomos, John and Back, Les, *Racism and Society*, Basingstoke, Macmillan, 1996.

Sowell, Thomas, *Markets and Minorities*, Oxford, Basil Blackwell, 1981.

Ethnic America, New York, Basic Books, 1981.

Spencer, Ian, *British Immigration Policy since 1939: The Making of Multi-racial Britain*, London, Routledge, 1997.

Steinberg, Stephen, *The Ethnic Myth: Race, Ethnicity and Class in America*, Boston, Beacon Books, 1981.

Turning Back: The Retreat from Racial Justice in American Thought and Policy, Boston, Beacon Press, 1995.

Stocking, George W., Jr (ed.), *The Shaping of American Anthropology 1883–1911: A Franz Boas Reader*, New York, Basic Books, 1974.

Stoker, G., *The Politics of Local Government*, Basingstoke, Macmillan, 1988.

Sugrue, Thomas, 'Crabgrass-Roots Politics: Race, Rights and Reaction against Liberalism in the Urban North, 1940–1964', *Journal of American History*, 82 (1995), pp. 551–77.

The Origins of the Urban Crisis: Race and Inequality in Postwar Detroit, Princeton, N. J., Princeton University Press, 1996.

Taylor, Charles, 'The Politics of Recognition', in Amy Gutman (ed.), *Multiculturalism: Examining the Politics of Recognition*, Princeton, N. J., Princeton University Press, 1994, pp. 25–73.

Tonkin, Elizabeth, *Narrating our Pasts: The Social Construction of Oral History*, Cambridge, Cambridge University Press, 1992.

Trilling, Lionel, *Beyond Culture*, New York, Scribner's, 1955.

Trotter, Joe William, Jr, *The Great Migration in Historical Perspective: New Dimensions of Race, Class and Gender*, Bloomington and Indianapolis, Indiana University Press, 1991.

Troyna, Barry, 'The Career of an Antiracist Education School Policy: Some Observations on the Mismanagement of Change', in Anthony G. Green and Stephen J. Ball (eds.), *Progress and Inequality in Comprehensive Education*, London, Routledge, 1992, pp. 158–78.

Troyna, Barry (ed.), *Racial Inequality in Education*, London, Tavistock, 1987.

Tuttle, William M., Jr, *Race Riot: The Red Summer of 1919*, New York, Atheneum, 1970.

Tyler, Paul, 'The Origins of Labour Representation in Woolwich', *Labour History Review*, 59, 1 (1994), pp. 26–33.

Werbner, Pnina and Modood, Tariq (eds.), *Debating Cultural Hybridity: Multi-Cultural Identities and the Politics of Anti-Racism*, London, Zed Books, 1997.

Willett, Cynthia (ed.), *Theorizing Multiculturalism: A Guide to the Current Debate*, Oxford, Blackwell, 1998.

Williams, Walter, *The State against Blacks*, New York, McGraw-Hill, 1982.

Young, Iris Marion, *Justice and the Politics of Difference*, Princeton, N. J., Princeton University Press, 1990.

Index